Lost in Time

Lost in Time

Locating the Stranger in German Modernity

June J. Hwang

NORTHWESTERN UNIVERSITY PRESS
EVANSTON, ILLINOIS

Northwestern University Press
www.nupress.northwestern.edu

Printed in the United States of America

ISBN 978-0-8101-3325-9

The Library of Congress has cataloged the original, hardcover edition as follows:

Hwang, June J., author.
Lost in time : locating the stranger in German modernity / June J. Hwang.
pages cm
Originally presented as the author's thesis (doctoral)—University of California—Berkeley, 2007
Includes bibliographical references and index.
ISBN 978-0-8101-2982-5 (cloth : alk. paper)
1. German literature—19th century—History and criticism. 2. German literature—20th century—History and criticism. 3. Modernism (Literature)—Germany. 4. Strangers in literature. 5. Alienation (Social psychology) in literature. 6. Jews in literature. I. Title.
PT148.S77H93 2014
830.9353—dc23

2014011606

CONTENTS

ACKNOWLEDGMENTS

I am grateful to the many people who have contributed to this project along the way. Tony Kaes at U.C. Berkeley has played a significant role in shaping this project with his insights and advice from its inception to its current stage and continues to be a generous and valued mentor today. I also want to thank Bob Holub (now at Ohio State University), Chana Kronfeld, and Niklaus Largier for their thoughtful critique and questions while I was writing the dissertation. The lively and stimulating discussions with the members of the Berkeley Tübingen Wien Harvard working group (BTWH) were instrumental to my understanding of spaces of modernity. In particular, thanks to Siegi Mattl at the Institut für Zeitgeschichte (Universität Wien) for helping me navigate Vienna's libraries and archives, as well as for his challenging questions. Paul Reitter at Ohio State University patiently read multiple drafts of various parts of the manuscript and always had excellent suggestions on how to add nuance and clarity to my ideas. My colleagues at the University of Rochester, both in my home department of Modern Languages and Cultures and in other departments, have provided formal and informal opportunities to share my work and receive useful feedback. I would like to especially thank my chair, Sue Gustafson, for all of her help and advice. I have presented parts of this work at various national and regional conferences and workshops and have greatly benefited from the questions and comments from colleagues at these events.

A number of institutions, fellowships, and archives made my research possible, and this project would not exist without their support. The Berlin Program for Advanced German and European Studies, jointly administered by the Freie Universität Berlin and the German Studies Association with funds provided by the Freie Universität Berlin, provided a valuable space for intellectual exchange with other scholars and allowed me the time to research and explore my ideas in the early stages of this project, as did the UC Berkeley Dean's Normative Time Fellowship and Max Kade Summer Fellowship. I also received generous funding from the University of Rochester to do additional research in Vienna and Berlin. The Deutsche Kinemathek in Berlin, the Staatsbibliothek zu Berlin, and the Jewish Studies Program of the Universität Potsdam provided valuable resources and guidance, as did the Österreichische Nationalbibliothek and the Film Archiv Austria. At all these places I found people who were amazingly generous with their knowledge and their time. The conclusions, opinions, and other statements in this publication are of course mine and do not necessarily reflect those of these people or institutions.

I would also like to thank the editors at Northwestern University Press for their guidance and support and to thank the anonymous readers for their feedback and encouragement. Parts of this work have been published in earlier incarnations: "Not All Who Wander Are Lost: Alfred Döblin's *Reise in Polen* [*Journey to Poland,* 1925]" appeared in *Spatial Turns: Space, Place, and Mobility in German Literary and Visual Culture,* edited by Jaimey Fisher and Barbara Mennel (*Amsterdamer Beiträge zur neueren Germanistik,* Rodopi 2010) and "Alone in the City: Hugo Bettauer's *Er und Sie*" (Seminar 47.5, November 2011). My thanks to Rodopi and Seminar for permission to reprint.

To my friends and family: thank you for your support, understanding, and gentle (and at times necessarily not-so-gentle) nudging. This book is dedicated to Fred Tremallo, who showed me that the questions are the answers. I am sure I speak for all who knew you when I say that you are sorely missed.

ABBREVIATIONS

AD Alfred Döblin, *Reise in Polen.* Munich: Deutscher Taschenbuch Verlag, 1987.

ADE Alfred Döblin, *Journey to Poland.* Translated by Joachim Neugroschel and edited by Heinz Graber. New York: Paragon House Publishers, 1991.

BB Béla Balázs, "Bettauer—eine Wiener Erscheinung." *Die Bühne: Zeitung für Theater / Literatur / Film / Mode / Kunst / Gesellschaft / Sport,* March 26, 1925, 20–21.

ES Hugo Bettauer and Rudolf Olden, eds., *Er und Sie: Wochenschrift für Lebenskultur und Erotik.* Vienna, 1924.

JR Joseph Roth, *Juden auf Wanderschaft.* Edited by Eduard Trautner. Vol. 4, Berichte aus der Wirklichkeit. Berlin: Die Schmiede, 1927.

JRE Joseph Roth, *The Wandering Jews.* Translated by Michael Hofmann. New York: W. W. Norton & Company, 2001.

MB Martin Buber, *Die Geschichten des Rabbi Nachman.* Frankfurt am Main: Rütten und Loening, 1906.

MBE Martin Buber, *The Tales of Rabbi Nachman.* Translated by Maurice Friedman. New York: Horizon Press, 1956.

PG Helmuth Plessner, *Grenzen der Gemeinschaft: Eine Kritik des sozialen Radikalismus.* Frankfurt am Main: Suhrkamp Taschenbuch Wissenschaft, 2002.

PGE Helmuth Plessner, *The Limits of Community: A Critique of Social Radicalism.* Translated by Andrew Wallace. Amherst, New York: Humanity Books, 1999.

PS Helmuth Plessner, *Die Stufen des Organischen und der Mensch: Einleitung in die philosophische Anthropologie.* Edited by Günter Dux, Odo Marquard, and Elisabeth Ströcker. Vol. 4, *Gesammelte Schriften.* Frankfurt am Main: Suhrkamp Verlag, 1981.

SE Georg Simmel, *On Individuality and Social Forms.* Edited by Donald N. Levine. Chicago: University of Chicago Press, 1971.

SF Georg Simmel, "Exkurs über den Fremden." In *Soziologie: Untersuchungen über die Formen der Vergesellschaftung,* 764–71. Frankfurt am Main: Suhrkamp Taschenbuch Verlag, 1992.

SG Georg Simmel, "Die Großstädte und das Geistesleben." In *Georg Simmel: Aufsätze und Abhandlungen 1901–1908,* edited by Rüdiger Kramme, Angela Rammstedt, and Otthein Rammstedt, 116–31. Frankfurt am Main: Suhrkamp Verlag, 1995.

SJ Hugo Bettauer, *Die Stadt ohne Juden: Ein Roman von übermorgen.* Vienna: R. Löwit Verlag, 1924.

SK Siegfried Kracauer, "Der Detektiv-Roman: Ein philosophischer Trakt." In *Schriften I: Soziologie als Wissenschaft; Der Detektiv-Roman; Die Angestellten,* 103–204. Frankfurt am Main: Suhrkamp Verlag, 1971.

SS "Soziologie der Geselligkeit." In *Georg Simmel: Aufsätze und Abhandlungen 1909–1918,* edited by Rüdiger Kramme and Angela Rammstedt. Frankfurt am Main: Suhrkamp Verlag, 2001.

WB Walter Benjamin, *Ursprung des deutschen Trauerspiels.* Edited by Rolf Tiedemann. Frankfurt am Main: Suhrkamp Taschenbuch Verlag, 1978.

WBE Walter Benjamin, *The Origin of German Tragic Drama.* Translated by John Osborne. London: Verso, 1985.

Lost in Time

When possible, I have used published translations of the works cited. There were some instances where I felt that I needed to provide my own translation, or published translations were not readily available. Where not otherwise cited, the translation is my own.

Introduction

In the late nineteenth century and throughout the twentieth the figure of the stranger has served as an emblem of the modern urban condition.[1] He (for the figure is almost always male)[2] is a point of identification as he symbolizes an inability to connect with others; he is estranged and isolated by the anonymity and cold rationality of modern society. Yet at the same time, the stranger represents the strengths of an outsider position. He is mobile—he can come and go as he pleases because he is not tied to a particular place. This mobility, this ability to leave, has an impact on his relationships with others. He can see what they cannot because he is not bound by the same social norms and expectations. He comes from elsewhere and does not have to stay, and because of this the stranger has the distance necessary to be an objective observer and, when necessary, a fair arbiter. The stranger represents modernity as an alienating and anonymous experience, but he also represents it as an opportunity for freedom and privilege through mobility and a loosening of communal ties.

What is missing in this description of the stranger is a consideration of the historical and cultural contexts of the figure's universal nature. Discourses of modernity often use abstract concepts such as objectivity, mobility, and alienation to create a modernity that is a universal phenomenon, not tied to a specific time or place. And scholarship on these conceptualizations of a timeless and universal modernity has largely ignored the historical specificity of this ahistorical universalism. What gets lost are the historical and cultural idiosyncrasies of a particular modernity, and the resulting plurality of modernities. While fully acknowledging that these concepts of the ahistorical and universal are not merely projected onto writings about modernity, that the move toward abstraction and universalization is present in the texts themselves, I find that it is crucial to remember that a text that takes an ahistorical approach should not be read in an ahistorical manner.

This book historicizes discourses of timelessness in relation to the stranger and modernity in the works of central figures of German modernity such as Walter Benjamin, Georg Simmel, Siegfried Kracauer, and Helmuth Plessner, as well as those of Alfred Döblin, Joseph Roth, and

Hugo Bettauer. I argue that in the Weimar Republic the move toward ahistoricization itself has a historical context, one that can be understood by exploring the intersections of urban modernity, the stranger, and German Jewish identity.[3] The stranger in these discourses is neither universal nor historically specific, but rather a universal abstraction created within a historically specific moment. As such the stranger's position depends on a negotiation of these interactions and conflicts. These intersections shed light on conceptions of German Jewish identity that rely on a negation of the specific as a way to uproot the identity from a sociohistorical context. I claim that the move to erase the specificity of the stranger's position in part serves as a way to legitimize this position by linking it to a more generalized and non-Jewish image of the stranger. The stranger becomes an abstract representation of the modern condition, of a common experience shared by all. The historical specificity of the stranger is erased by creating a concept of modernity that encompasses everyone and is not tied to any one place or time. There was a time before modernity, but it is defined only by what is now lost.

By examining the intersections of German Jewish identity and the figure of the stranger within discourses of urban modernity in the Weimar period, we gain a better understanding of how a privileged minority position is formed and legitimized. Instead of a model of assimilation that views these texts as a capitulation to the dominant culture and a denial of Jewish identity, I argue that they are an integral part of the negotiations and interactions that create the pluralistic complex of Jewish identities during this time. These attempts to transcend the particular in favor of the universal reveal the entangled and complicit relationships between them, connections and interactions that are lost when the universal and abstract remain the focus.

My book contributes to a growing body of scholarship that examines discourses of assimilation in the German Jewish context as discourses of interaction and engagement. In works by scholars such as David Myers, Paul Mendes-Flohr, Jonathan Hess, Paul Reitter, Todd Presner, Steven Aschheim, and Willi Goetschel, assimilation ceases to be a concept of passive acceptance and disavowal of difference; instead it is a site of active negotiation that has an impact on both dominant and minority cultures. As a result, a more complex and dynamic discourse of German Jewish identity and assimilation emerges, one that sheds light on broader debates about modernity. The two most relevant interventions in relation to my own project are Jonathan Hess's *Germans, Jews and the Claims of Modernity* and David Myers's *Resisting History: Historicism and Its Discontents in German-Jewish Thought.*

In his *Germans, Jews and the Claims of Modernity* Jonathan Hess argues that Zygmunt Bauman's portrayal of Jews as "conscious pariahs" who were the first to recognize modernity's insistent uniformity and inability to tolerate difference makes an overly facile connection between the limits of assimilation and a critique of modernity. According to Hess, Bauman fails to make a distinction between a view of modernity as uniform and a uniform view of modernity, thus ignoring the contested nature of both modernity and assimilation.[4] By examining Jewish claims to modernity as debates within modernity rather than a postmodern critique, Hess offers a more nuanced understanding of the relationship between modernity and Jewish identity, a relationship in which Jews are active in shaping their own identity and contribute "both distinctly Jewish theories of modernity and distinctly modern theories of Judaism," and doing so "*both* for fellow Jews *and* for the dominant culture as a whole."[5] He explores notions of universal citizenship, Jewish emancipation, and the historicity of Judaism and Christianity in the late eighteenth and nineteenth centuries as interrelated and heavily debated concepts that played a significant role in diverse discourses of modernity.[6]

Like Hess, David Myers redefines Jewish assimilation to emphasize the "dynamic process of negotiation, mediation, and translation that defines interaction between groups."[7] *Resisting History: Historicism and Its Discontents in German-Jewish Thought* investigates the relationship between historicism and antihistoricism in German Jewish writings of the nineteenth and twentieth centuries as a way of moving away from an influence model in which the dominant group influences and the minority group either resists, thus preserving its authenticity, or succumbs and loses its own identity. Myers argues that just as antihistoricism engages with discourses of modernity and historicism rather than simply rejecting or negating them, Jewish history as a whole "operate[s] in the large gray area between assimilation and insularity."[8]

My project shares Hess's and Myers's interest in examining Jewish contributions to debates about modernity as acts of agency, even as I shift the focus from theological and political debates to debates about everyday urban life. And as with the texts that Myers and Hess explore, the common thread in the texts that I examine is a struggle to position oneself in relation to concepts of history. Sometimes the texts work against common ideas about history, sometimes with, and sometimes as an attempt to redefine or escape history altogether, but always with the understanding that one's conceptualization and understanding of history is central to one's understanding of the world and one's place in it. Thus I focus on the position of the stranger as it is his position—his interactions with his environment, with those around him, with history, and with time—rather than any fixed intrinsic qualities that defines the stranger. This position is the product of textual practice: the stranger's position is constantly being created through an engagement with contemporary discourses, rooting it in specific cultural and historical contexts. Whereas uprooting the stranger from a historical context turns the figure into a static phenomenon, focusing on the cultural and historical contexts allows for an exploration of the dynamic textual negotiations that create the stranger and the position he occupies.

It is impossible to look at this time period, particularly in the context of questions of German Jewish identity, without reading into the texts a sense of foreboding and loss, a lens created by our knowledge of what is to come. In both obvious and subtle ways, this knowledge has impacted our readings of these texts and these historical figures. It is easy to see the Weimar Republic as a glowing moment before the fall, the height of creativity and productivity fueled by the instability and political unrest that would soon bring everything to a crashing halt. We read and sometimes foreground the traces of antisemitic rhetoric in these texts as prophetic hints of future events. The position of the stranger in these texts straddles these views—he is both a potential victim and a potential privileged outsider. Examining the figure of the stranger in a historical context of a broader scope will not discount our knowledge of the Holocaust, but it will highlight aspects of these texts and their configurations of the stranger that are often ignored or disconnected from one another. Not all those who wrote about these topics are Jewish, but the participation of Jewish writers in the move toward abstraction and universalization in relation to urban experiences of modernity is significant. More specifically, in the intersections between German Jewish identity and modernity, abstraction serves as a method to legitimize the outsider position by making it a universal truth. Thus ahistoricity serves as a way of negotiating the historical realities of German Jewish identity. I will explore the relationship between discourses of German Jewish identity and urban modernity, while acknowledging that such an approach necessarily focuses on only a small part of the larger discourses.

By examining texts that span a wide range of genres, I demonstrate that these concerns about Jewish identity, modernity, and the ahistorical were part of the larger social and cultural geography of the time. The book is divided into three chapters. The first looks at theoretical approaches to the concept of the stranger and his environment in the writings of Georg Simmel, Walter Benjamin, Siegfried Kracauer, and Helmuth Plessner. The second examines the relationship between mobility, space, time, and

Jewish identity in the travel texts of Alfred Döblin and Joseph Roth. The third chapter examines the relationship between historically specific and timelessly universal in the case of Hugo Bettauer and his writings in order to show the prevalence of these discourses throughout Weimar culture as well as the limits of agency in defining oneself as a stranger.

Simmel, Benjamin, Kracauer, and Plessner link the figure of the stranger with modernity and the city. The four key concepts here are the historical, the ahistorical, the specific, and the universal. In these texts, the relationship between them is not a constant one. At times the historically specific is seen as a hindrance, something that needs to be overcome to be able to enjoy the privileges of being a stranger. Yet at other times the concept of timelessness is a used as a way to justify and legitimate a historical moment, to promote the view that modernity and the position of the stranger are part of a larger continuum rather than a break from what came before. And throughout, the universal is used to create the conditions necessary for the privileged stranger in a particular moment and time. The figures of the flâneur, the detective, and the stranger are created through these interactions and conflicts between the universal, the specific, the historical, and the ahistorical. On a metalevel, the same is true for the objective outsider position of Simmel, Kracauer, Benjamin, and Plessner within their own texts. All of these writers use ideas of the universal in order to formulate their viewpoints. The privileged position of the stranger depends on a universal identification with the figure as a symbol of the modern condition. The universalization of the stranger's position creates an experience of modernity in these texts that is the negotiation of subjective agency and an objective reality. As such, the stranger's position is not just one of estrangement and separation, but also one of interaction and privilege. The space the stranger occupies is rooted in the temporal reality of the everyday but also removed from it, thus creating an experience that is always more than an individual one, allowing the stranger to simultaneously be a lone, historically situated outsider and an emblem of a universal experience of a modernity that is also to some extent timeless.

In the second chapter, I move on to the travel writings of Alfred Döblin and Joseph Roth. By comparing the travelers in Döblin's *Reise in Polen* and Roth's *Juden auf Wanderschaft* to the stranger and other outsiders of the previous section, the importance of mobility to the stranger's position becomes clear. On the part of the traveler/narrator, physical movement is connected to more abstract aspects of the position and to the traveler's interactions with others. The narrator is a traveler who can come and go as he pleases and is always a stranger in his surroundings, much like

Simmel's stranger. Simmel describes the stranger as someone who can leave but chooses to stay. The traveler is defined by his ability to leave as well, but in this case he chooses to do so, again and again. Simmel's stranger is defined by his potential mobility, the traveler by his actual mobility.

Döblin and Roth complicate the model of the privileged urban stranger with a search for an "authentic" and distinctly unmodern form of Jewish identity. Döblin and Roth, who notably do not identify themselves as Jews in these texts, make the case that the "real" Jew is one that is not bound to a nation. The authenticity of the East European Jews stems from this lack of roots and the permanent state of wandering that this lack creates. When one's sense of home is not connected to a physical place, one can pick up and move on at a moment's notice. In conjunction with this concept of rootlessness is the idea that Jewish identity is removed from history and essentially timeless; this timelessness leaves the Jews untouched by the corrupting influences of modernity and modern ideas of nation. Another effect of this rootless identity is that it brings East European Jews together in a community; their outsider position allows them to maintain a connection to a religion that insists on the existence of the true, absolute, and eternal, a connection lost to West European Jews.

In the city, the stranger is alone and anonymous and to some extent represents the alienated inhabitants of the city. In their travel writings, Döblin and Roth occupy positions that resonate with the urban stranger. Whereas Döblin and Roth stand alone and removed from those around them, the outsider status of the East European Jews in these texts binds them together. They are the Wandering Jews, defined by their lack of roots. Döblin and Roth create a relationship between these two outsider positions, one urban and modern, the other timeless and primitive, to legitimize the latter using the authority of the former. At the same time, they also use notions of a timeless religious Jewish identity to critique and undermine secular Jewish modernity, more specifically assimilated West European Jewish culture. Roth and Döblin romanticize the conditions in which the East European Jews live, but in their writings they also represent a different kind of stranger. The contrast between the narrators and their surroundings emphasizes not only the unbridgeable distance between the two positions, but also the fact that Döblin and Roth occupy a position of choice and privilege, while the East European Jews they encounter do not have this luxury. They are not mobile in the way that travelers are. Their identity, at least in these texts, is tied to a forced mobility, and even if Roth and Döblin praise this culture, they do not plead for a "return" to this "natural state."

Both *Reise in Polen* and *Juden auf Wanderschaft* exhibit a nostalgia for a present that is already a past. Rather than point the way to a more authentic Jewish existence, these texts, Döblin's in particular, use the example of East European Jews to emphasize what West European Jews have lost. But their own positions of privilege depend on the same discourses of modernity that they criticize for the loss of authentic Jewish existence in Western Europe. As such, these discourses of Jewish identity are mapped onto debates about modernity and a loss of authenticity in a way that connects assimilation and secularization to urban modernity while simultaneously complicating this model.

These intersections and interactions take us back to the city and to questions of agency in the figure of the assimilated West European Jew. The third section focuses on Hugo Bettauer and his work. Bettauer is not a well-known writer, and much of his writing would not be widely regarded as intellectual. The topics he explored, however, all have to do with everyday life in the modern city, something that also concerned Simmel, Plessner, and the others. A look at his work will allow us to explore how these ideas appeared in texts that are meant for a more general public. Bettauer presents a reading of modernity that saw alienation and the inability to connect to others as a universal modern condition. The difference is that Bettauer was concerned with the individual less as an abstract entity, and more as the man or woman he encountered on the street. He used everyday language and drew on current events so as to reach as many people as he could. Bettauer thought it important that the "average" man or woman reading his work see him- or herself reflected in that work. Yet at the same time, throughout his novels and also in his journalistic writings, Bettauer utilizes the position of the stranger in order to provide this mirror, a stranger who is distanced from the others and possesses the ability to see more clearly than they can. In his works the stranger uses his position to reach the masses, but his authority is based on abilities that set him apart from them.

An Austrian journalist and novelist who worked in Germany, the United States, and Austria, Bettauer has been defined by his death at the hands of a dentist with National Socialist affiliations. In combination with the antisemitic rhetoric of the media attacks against him surrounding the *Er und Sie* controversy as well as the seemingly prophetic plot of one of his novels, *Die Stadt ohne Juden,* Bettauer is seen as a tragic victim of antisemitism and his death and novel as harbingers of the upcoming horrors of World War II. A closer look at his work and its reception, both in recent years and in the 1920s, shifts the focus to the role that agency plays in navigating the discourses of urban modernity and German Jewish identity. Bettauer's oeuvre and his role in Viennese culture did not focus on specifically Jewish topics, and this absence is itself significant. By looking at these texts, in particular Bettauer's short-lived periodical *Er und Sie: Wochenschrift für Lebenskultur und Erotik,* I will show how Bettauer positioned himself as a nonjudgmental advice giver, someone who could help others navigate the confusing and often lonely circumstances of urban life. As such Bettauer and his writings fit into another category of Jewish identity, that of an assimilated, secular, cosmopolitan Jew. This position relies on a universalization of modern alienation so as to make the outsider someone who can speak for others. When one looks at his writings, a picture emerges of a man who sees himself as an educator and facilitator, someone who helps others understand life in the city. Like Kracauer, Plessner, and the others, Bettauer occupies the position of a keen observer whose objectivity is connected to a distance from others—the position of a stranger—an outsider whose position is not rooted in the specifics of a Jewish identity. The advantages of such a position become clear when one looks at the controversies surrounding the periodical *Er und Sie*. There is a disconnect between the concerns of the journal—individuals seeking connections to others, freedom from the false morality of others, the ability to determine one's own life—and the antisemitic rhetoric of the attacks on Bettauer. This disconnect simultaneously shows what is at stake in creating a position of a stranger with nonspecific origins and the very real limitations of maintaining such a position. A reexamination of the novel and the film version of *Die Stadt ohne Juden* shows the tensions between a Jewish identity created by others and the one that an individual creates for himself, and in part explains the impulse to create a position that is decidedly non-Jewish in the face of such limitations.

Hugo Bettauer, his work, and its reception serve as an example of how cultural and historical context limit the ability of the outsider/stranger to determine his own position. The consequences of a particular kind of historical context being forced onto a text and a person demonstrate how being confined to a narrow historical context makes it impossible to perform the position of the stranger as one of privilege. Bettauer serves as a representative of the Jewish intellectual who identifies himself as a cosmopolitan urbanite, an outsider who maintains his position by not aligning himself too closely with any one particular category of identification, particularly any overtly Jewish identity. Yet as can be seen through a close reading of his work and by looking at the reception of this work, it becomes clear that such a position is only partially possible. The abstract nature of Simmel's stranger and the necessity thereof become clear when we see the failure of Bettauer's characters and Bettauer himself to be recognized as urban individuals rather than as Jews.

I believe that an exploration of the specificity of the relationship between urban modernity, German Jewish identity, and notions of the ahistorical in the Weimar Republic points the way to an approach that will help us better understand the concept of modernity today. Modernity is not a universal and ahistorical phenomenon, but these qualities are an integral part of the concept. Thus it is necessary to explore the historicity and uniqueness of a particular iteration of modernity through its definition and utilization of the universal and timeless. What is recovered is the concept of agency and, with it, the idea that modernity is a process. The position of the stranger, at the intersection of the universal and the specific, the historical and the ahistorical, is constantly being created in these texts. Focusing on modernity as a discursive practice allows us to see German Jews as individual agents, and their pursuit of a universal and timeless identity as integral to an understanding of German Jewish identity in this era.

Chapter 1

Situating the Stranger Within Modernity

In the writings of Walter Benjamin, Georg Simmel, Helmuth Plessner, and Siegfried Kracauer, the figure of the outsider—in the form of the flâneur, the stranger, the eccentric human, and the detective—plays a crucial role in questions of how one lives and interacts with others in the modern world. The figure is simultaneously one of unique privilege and a universal point of identification, both of the moment and outside it. As such, he represents the search for self-determination within discourses of modernity. The outsider's position is one of constant flux created by the negotiation between the historical and the ahistorical as the outsider seeks to create a position in which he is part of the world around him but also removed enough to act as an individual. Because these concepts of time affect our understanding of both the world and our place in it, they are inextricably bound to discourses of space and the sociology of human interactions.

The question of how modernity fits into the historical narrative is instrumental in defining not only the relationship between the historical and ahistorical, but also modernity's impact on everyday life. In these texts a positive view of modernity and modern life is dependent on the view that modernity is part of the historical continuum, a specific manifestation of timeless qualities that define humanity and human civilization. Thus modernity is legitimized through an insistence that it is not a radical break from what came before it. In other words, there are changes, but they do not touch our fundamental understanding of ourselves and the world around us. Thus modernity, like the outsider position, is a balancing act between the current moment and a more universal and timeless perspective, and this balancing act itself is simultaneously specific to this historical moment and connected to more absolute abstract concepts. Arguments against modernity also work within this paradigm. They share the belief that in order for a way of living and interacting with others to be valid, it must fit within the historical continuum. The difference is that these arguments against modernity do not agree that the current moment conforms to this description.

The struggle to define the role of artifice in everyday life is an example of the ways in which writings both for and against modernity work within common discourses about time and history. In order to create continuity between modernity and what came before it, Simmel and Plessner argue that artifice is an integral part of human existence rather than antithetical to the natural. By doing so, they posit that the artifice we observe in everyday life allows us to interact with one another in an authentic way, that there is no alternative in which we exist in an unmediated "natural" state where we are our "true" selves. We are distant from one another and use artifice to express ourselves and connect to others, but we are not alienated because our lives are just a particular manifestation of an existence that has always been true. Furthermore, the outsider, whose advantages stem from his distance to his surroundings and those around him, differs from the others only by the quality and degree of his distance, not the distance itself. The position of the outsider that Simmel and Plessner create is dependent on the notion that modernity is part of this greater continuity. In Kracauer's writings, this dependence is also manifest, but as a deeply ambivalent relationship with a privileged outsider position; the ambivalence stems from the impossibility of creating this position, which Kracauer occupies in his writings, without the discourses of modernity that he criticizes.

With each of the writers explored in this section, I will examine the interdependent relationship between their conceptualizations of a privileged outsider position and their representations of history, society, and urban modernity. All four make the link between the outsider position and modernity, and for each of them the stranger/outsider represents something important about modernity and the modern experience. It is important to remember that these texts do not record experiences of modernity—they create them. They create positions that navigate concepts of the ahistorical and the historical, defining time in a way that makes an outsider position a privileged and necessary one, and modernity a discourse in which the individual has agency. The connections between the stranger and modernity are about the experiences of the stranger and creating this experience for others. These experiences, this ability to place the reader in the position of the stranger, make it more challenging to situate the stranger within a historical context, as they are constantly in flux and often try to pull the reader out of his or her specific context and into a more abstract time and space of "modernity." In these works, modernity is a textual practice in which an emphasis on interpretation and on constant change allows for agency on the part of the reader and the writer and, through this experience, creates an identification with the outsider position. A closer examination of these textual experiences and their historical and cultural contexts will shed light on the importance of the stranger to our understanding of urban modernity in Germany and Austria of the interwar period.

Benjamin's Flâneur

Walter Benjamin's enduring popularity in cultural criticism can be explained in part by the seductive hope of transcendence that appears throughout his texts, a transcendence that hints at the possibility of an escape from our current reality into a world of absolute truths.[1] In the case of the flâneur, this possibility is linked to a type of movement that distinguishes the flâneur from the others, that marks the flâneur as a person of leisure who does not have to conform to the rhythms of the city; instead he creates his own. Benjamin's posthumously published *Arcades Project* encourages the reader to interact with the text in a nonlinear fashion, to flip through the pages, stopping here and there, in a form of reading as wandering. The text allows the reader to create his or her own path, to draw connections between different parts of the text through the order in which he or she reads them. The position that Benjamin's flâneur occupies is linked to this notion of nonlinear movement and agency.

The flâneur is a universal figure in a specific historical place and time. The flâneur is very much rooted in the environment of the city, yet the possibility of transcendence also connects him to more universal ideas of urban modernity. The universal and the specific interact to create the flâneur in two important contexts. The first is that of fin de siècle Paris. What makes it possible for the flâneur to exist in this particular place and in this particular moment is the intersection between nostalgia and renewal that exists there and then. The second is the discursive context that allows the figure to interact with his environment and distinguish himself from others; the flâneur's agency is rooted in an understanding of time that emphasizes a state of flux and constant deferment. In both of these contexts, Benjamin's concepts of the historical and the absolute or ahistorical interact with one another in an attempt to create a position that is a negotiation of the indirect relationship between the two, a relationship that requires an outsider position. Because of this position, the flâneur is both a historical phenomenon and an abstract symbol.

Benjamin sees late nineteenth-century Paris as the only place that the flâneur can exist. The architectural features of the city, such as the arcades, play an important role, but Paris's relationship to time is also crucial. The flâneur is strongly connected to a sense of loss, a nostalgia for a world that no longer exists, and Paris in this particular moment in time makes this loss palpable. Thus the sense of loss is rooted in a specific location and a time. And it is this historical context that allows the flâneur to move through the city as he does. According to Benjamin, Baudelaire's writings—which are the foundation for his conceptualization of the flâneur—are themselves an aestheticization of a particular physical and mental distance of privilege that is rooted in a specific historical moment and place.[2] And in Paris during this time, a distinct relationship between crowds, the city, and the flâneur arises. As Benjamin explains, the nineteenth century was a turning point in public opinion, moving from a criticism of crowds to a fascination with them and the cities that produce them. Benjamin emphasizes, however, that the flâneur is not a man of the masses:

> Der Mann der Menge ist kein Flaneur. In ihm hat der gelassene Habitus einem manischen Platz gemacht. Darum ist eher an ihm abzunehmen, was aus dem Flaneur werden mußte, wenn ihm die Umwelt, in die er gehört, genommen ward. Wurde sie ihm von London je gestellt, so gewiß nicht von dem, das bei Poe beschrieben ist. An ihm gemessen, wahrt Baudelaires Paris einige Züge aus guter alter Zeit . . . Es gab den Passanten, welcher sich in die Menge eineilt, doch gab es auch noch den Flaneur, der Spielraum braucht und sein Privatisieren nicht missen will.[3]

> The man of the crowd is no *flâneur.* In him, composure has given way to manic behavior. Hence he exemplifies, rather, what had to become of the *flâneur* once he was deprived of the milieu to which he belonged. If London ever provided it for him, it was certainly not the setting described by Poe. In comparison, Baudelaire's Paris preserved some features that dated back to the happy old days . . . There was the pedestrian who would let himself be jostled by the crowd, but there was also the *flâneur* who demanded elbow room and was unwilling to forgo the life of a gentleman of leisure.[4]

The man of the crowd is just that—part of the crowd, with nothing to distinguish him from all the others in the crowd. His function is that of metonymy—he represents the experience of the many. And like the others in the crowd, his movement is always with a specific goal or purpose. In contrast, the flâneur is set apart from the others, both mentally and physically. He needs a certain amount of physical distance from the others so as to create a space in which practical efficiency is replaced by the luxury of aimless wandering. Unlike the man of the crowd, who lets the rhythms of the city and the others dictate his movements, the flâneur finds his own pace. The flâneur's aloofness and cool objectivity are products of this position of leisure and distance from others. He does, however, need the crowd, for without it he could not occupy a position of privilege; he needs the others in order to distinguish himself from them. This also means that the man of the crowd could be a flâneur, given the financial means and inclination; the position of the flâneur is produced by a confluence of events—the luxury of idleness and a city in which one can stroll aimlessly.

Benjamin's reading of Baudelaire emphasizes the flâneur's aloofness and lack of interaction. This reading of the flâneur is the one most often evoked in other explorations of the stranger and modernity. I would maintain, however, that key to understanding the stranger's role in modernity is that he interacts with others and his surroundings in a way that the rest cannot; he is in some ways more engaged rather than less. If he did not interact with others, the stranger would not be a stranger. Instead he would be an outcast—a hermit or a pariah. The unique interactions between the stranger and others, then, are what define him. Thus my focus is on the *position* of the stranger rather than the figure itself; this focus emphasizes the important role interactions and relationships with others play in constituting the stranger. This focus makes the historical context of the stranger more transparent, as it foregrounds his connection to a particular environment, to a particular set of discourses, and to others living in this context.

Paris not only represents a particular relationship to time; it also exists in Benjamin's writings as both a specific historical moment and place, and as a representative of a more abstract idea of "the city." In his conceptualization of both Paris and the flâneur, one can see a link between an abstract sense of time and an abstract sense of space; the less geographically and historically specific the spaces of the flâneur are, the more timeless and universal the figure becomes. The relationship between time and space is a crucial one in understanding the ahistorical aspects of the flâneur's position.[5] An example of this move toward the abstract and ahistorical can be seen in the following passage about Paris, Baudelaire, and the flâneur:

> Zum erstenmal wird bei Baudelaire Paris zum Gegenstand der lyrischen Dichtung. Diese Dichtung ist keine Heimatkunst, vielmehr ist der Blick des Allegorikers, der die Stadt trifft, der Blick

> des Entfremdeten. Es ist der Blick des Flaneurs, dessen Lebensform die kommende trostlose des Großstadtmenschen noch mit einem versöhnenden Schimmer umspielt. Der Flaneur steht noch auf der Schwelle, der Großstadt sowohl wie der Bürgerklasse. Keine von beiden hat ihn noch überwältigt. In keiner von beiden ist er zu Hause. Frühe Beiträge zur Physiognomik der Menge finden sich bei Engels und Poe. Die Menge ist der Schleier, durch den hindurch dem Flaneur die gewohnte Stadt als Phantasmagorie winkt. Beide bauen dann das Warenhaus auf, das die Flanerie selber dem Warenumsatz nutzbar macht. Das Warenhaus ist der letzte Streich des Flaneurs.[6]
>
> For the first time, with Baudelaire, Paris becomes the subject of lyric poetry. This poetry is no hymn to the homeland; rather, the gaze of the allegorist, as it falls on the city, is the gaze of the alienated man. It is the gaze of the flâneur, whose way of life still conceals behind a mitigating nimbus the coming desolation of the big-city dweller. The flâneur still stands on the threshold—of the metropolis as of the middle class. Neither has him in its power yet. In neither is he at home. He seeks refuge in the crowd. Early contributions to the physiognomics of the crowd are found in Engels and Poe. The crowd is the veil through which the familiar city beckons to the flâneur as phantasmagoria—now a landscape, now a room. Both become elements of the department store, which makes use of flânerie itself to sell goods. The department store is the last promenade for the flâneur.[7]

The historical and spatial specificity of a Paris with remnants of its nineteenth-century legacies has all but disappeared in the passage above; Engels and Poe are mentioned, but the two are mentioned only as belonging to the time before the current one; they are not situated within their cultural contexts. The reference to the commodification of flanerie as represented by the department store is also a relatively vague indicator of time, and not geographically specific. The crowd has been turned into a veil through which the flâneur sees Paris transformed into a "phantasmagoria"—a place outside our reality and time. The specificities of the one passage have become allegorical generalities in the second. Time is no longer a historical moment, but rather an abstract psychological state of liminality: the flâneur does not belong anywhere. Through lyrical poetry, Paris is transformed into an allegory of not quite belonging and of savoring that fleeting moment, an allegory that defines the modern condition.

Yet it is not a simple opposition between specific and general, historical and allegorical, in Benjamin's writings about Paris. Benjamin's use of allegory is still rooted in early twentieth-century conceptions of nineteenth-century Paris, and he has created a state that is both timeless and historical, both universal and specific, while at the same time questioning the concepts themselves. Allegory exists as a relationship between the present moment and a past moment, but in a space that is neither. As Samuel Weber points out in *Benjamin's -abilities,* Benjamin's use of the universal is grounded in the specific; it is about pushing the singular to its extreme, for it is an idea's uniqueness, not its generalities, that ties it to other ideas. Thus generalization is a paradoxical process in which things are brought together because of the individual unique aspects that link them to one another. As such, this process is one that is never completed; Weber describes it as "reinscribing established terms so that they part company with themselves."[8] This lack of completion, this constant deferment, leads to a complicated relationship with time. On the one hand, it is through the process of reading and interpretation that this reinscribing is possible, and these actions are bound to particular moments in time. In this context language is a historical phenomenon, since the terms are established by repetition and use. Yet there is also a sense that the goal is to escape this repetition: to "part company" means to find a way to separate the idea from its history. This task is never complete; language can capture traces of the "idea" but never the idea itself, which is rooted in language only as a symbol that is never represented in its pure form. As Weber points out, Benjamin speaks of "umschreiben" [circumscribe] rather than "beschreiben" [describe].[9] This belief in a pure form takes us back out of time; our attempts to reach it are temporal, but the symbolic resides in a time that is never now, yet always exists.

Benjamin's use of allegory is a way to connect to a particular context while allowing for the interpretative work necessary to hint at that which cannot be described directly. The importance of interpretation emphasizes engagement with these abstract concepts, and through this engagement, agency is possible, since it is only through interpretation that we gain this indirect access to a temporal space outside our own. These elisions of time pull us out of a specific space and time, just as the attempt to understand the concepts through interpretation of these allegories roots us in them. Benjamin's concepts of synchronicity and constellations force us to look at time as something that is not linear yet requires our presence and interpretation to exist for us. According to Weber, "the 'generality' of the text and of reading is not tied to the universality of the concept, but to the critical moment of *singularity* that marks the *disjunctive convergence* of the general and the particular, of the theoretical and the practical."[10] While I agree with Weber that this "disjunctive convergence" is at the heart of Benjamin's writings, I would also argue that it points to a blurring of these aspects, an erasing of the specific even as the writings insist on a tension between the specific and the universal, particularly through the insistence that truth, knowledge, or the pure idea exists outside our present and our past and is not attainable in our future.

This blurring of history and ahistoricity is a rhetorical move that is itself deeply embedded in notions of time and history that existed in the Weimar Republic. In Benjamin's writings one finds a broader exploration of this attempt to define the current moment through erasures of time that simultaneously distance one from the ahistorical and the universal in his struggle with the concept of representation. Benjamin begins *Ursprung des deutschen Trauerspiels* with an attack on philosophy and a problematization of representation:

> Es ist dem philosophischem Schrifttum eigen, mit jeder Wendung von neuem vor der Frage der Darstellung zu stehen. Zwar wird es in seiner abgeschlossenen Gestalt Lehre sein, solche Abgeschlossenheit ihm zu leihen aber liegt nicht in der Gewalt des bloßen Denkens. Philosophische Lehre beruht auf historischer Kodifikation. (WB, 9)

> It is characteristic of philosophical writing that it must continually confront the question of representation. In its finished form philosophy will, it is true, assume the quality of doctrine, but it does not lie within the power of mere thought to confer such a form. Philosophical doctrine is based on historical codification. (WBE, 27)

According to Benjamin, philosophy is too concerned with representation as a closed system, and these representations are false, since such a system is impossible to achieve through thought alone. The desire to represent truth and the desire for a closed system are mutually exclusive; Benjamin gives the example of mathematics, which has successful closed systems, but only because it does not attempt to represent truth. Implied is that history, through the process of repetition, leads to representations that appear to be whole and complete representations of truth, but history cannot be trusted as a source of truth and can at times be antithetical to it. When one attempts to represent something as abstract and absolute as an idea, which is, according to Benjamin, the goal of philosophy, that representation cannot be a closed system. Instead, like allegory, the representation of an idea circumscribes it, allowing access to the idea's truth, but never touching it.

A lack of intention and clear goal are fundamental to representation as an open system. For Benjamin a necessary precondition for this absence is a text without an internal authority. In other words, the abdication of authority allows the text to forgo a direct approach, to be freed from the notion of a closed system. He chooses the medium of the treatise as the ideal medium for philosophy because although it can be pedagogical in tone, it does not rely on its own authority to convey its lessons (WB, 10). Benjamin emphasizes the relationship between a lack of intention and the circumscribing nature of representation: "Darstellung ist der Inbegriff ihrer [referring to "die kanonische Form des Traktats"] Methode. Methode ist Umweg. Darstellung als Umweg—das ist denn der methodische Charakter des Traktats. Verzicht auf den unabgesetzten Lauf der Intention ist sein erstes Kennzeichen" (WB, 10). ["Its [referring to the "canonic form of the treatise"] method is essentially representation. Method is a digression. Representation as digression—such is the methodological nature of the treatise. The absence of an uninterrupted purposeful structure is its primary characteristic" (WBE, 28).] Representation detours; it never arrives at its destination. Lack of intention should not, however, be mistaken for lack of agency. In fact, the opposite holds true. Benjamin calls for a text that does not foreground subjectivity and individuality; there is a distance between personal desire and representation so that the reader can interact with and experience the text on his or her own terms. This distance is also crucial for the author's agency, as it allows the author to occupy an outsider position in his own text, to be (or at least give the appearance of being) less invested and influenced by the sociohistorical reality that is the text's context. Within this framework there is a distance from the present moment even as there is an insistence on being aware of it; the text contains the present moment but can only point to something beyond it by also being removed from it. The text allows both the author and the reader to also occupy this position of not-belonging and, in this position, creates the possibility for individual agency.

Although a representation of the truth cannot create a closed system, the truth itself is an unmediated, unified whole. Our inability to access this unity and represent it stems from the way we perceive and understand the world around us, and it also defines our relationship to truth. Benjamin takes a closer look at the relationship between truth, representation, and knowledge by distinguishing between ideas and knowledge:

> Wenn Darstellung als eigentliche Methode des philosophischen Traktates sich behaupten will, so muß sie Darstellung der Ideen sein. Die Wahrheit, vergegenwärtigt im Reigen der dargestellten Ideen,

> entgeht jeder wie immer gearteten Projektion in den Erkenntnisbereich. Erkenntnis ist ein Haben. Ihr Gegenstand selbst bestimmt sich dadurch, daß er im Bewußtsein—und sei es transzendental—innegehabt werden muß. Ihm bleibt der Besitzcharakter. (WB, 11)
>
> If representation is to stake its claim as the real methodology of the philosophical treatise, then it must be the representation of ideas. Truth, bodied forth in the dance of represented ideas, resists being projected, by whatever means, into the realm of knowledge. Knowledge is possession. Its very object is determined by the fact that it must be taken possession of—even if in a transcendental sense—in the consciousness. The quality of possession remains. (WBE, 29)

Erkenntnis (knowledge) has a finality, a static quality that allows what is perceived to be a finished object and thus something that can be possessed. The truth, according to Benjamin, cannot be represented in such a way because truth eludes such a direct representation. Truth can only be represented in the representation of ideas, which circumscribe the truth—layer upon layer of indirectness as methodology. This representation of truth as representation of ideas has a relationship with our consciousness not via *Erkenntnis,* but rather via existence itself, via *Sein:*

> Erkenntnis ist erfragbar, nicht aber die Wahrheit. Die Erkenntnis richtet sich auf das Einzelne, auf dessen Einheit aber nicht unmittelbar. Die Einheit der Erkenntnis—wenn anders sie bestünde—wäre vielmehr ein nur vermittelt, nämlich auf Grund der Einzelerkenntnisse und gewissermaßen durch deren Ausgleich, herstellbarer Zusammenhang, während im Wesen der Wahrheit die Einheit durchaus unvermittelt und direkte Bestimmung ist. Dieser Bestimmung als einer direkten ist es eigentümlich, nicht erfragt werden zu können . . . Als Einheit im Sein und nicht als Einheit im Begriff ist die Wahrheit außer aller Frage. (WB, 11–12)
>
> Knowledge is open to question, but truth is not. Knowledge is concerned with individual phenomena, but not directly with their unity. The unity of knowledge—if indeed it exists—would consist rather in a coherence which can be established only on the basis of individual insights and, to a certain extent, their modification of each other; whereas unity is present in truth as a direct and essential attribute, and as such it is not open to question . . . As a unity of essence rather than a conceptual unity, truth is beyond all question. (WBE, 30)

Knowledge has to do with learning through questioning or conceptualization and, as such, is a mediated process, whereas truth is unmediated. Interestingly, representations of ideas, by encompassing the truth without trying to represent it directly, respect the realm of the truth by not attempting to bring it into the realm of cognition and consciousness. Benjamin insists that the fundamental characteristics of truth are its unity and immediacy, but implicit in his exploration of truth's qualities is the argument that humans by their very nature cannot relate to truth on its own terms. That is to say, it is not modernity that creates this inability to understand and represent truth directly; rather, this inability is part of human existence, thus creating a continuity between the present moment and the past.

Not only is the representation of truth an indirect one through the representation of ideas; there is also an indirect relationship between empirical phenomena and ideas:

> Die Phänomene gehen aber nicht integral in ihrem rohen empirischen Bestande, dem der Schein sich beimischt, sondern in ihren Elementen allein, gerettet, in das Reich der Ideen ein. Ihrer falschen Einheit entäußern sie sich, um aufgeteilt an der echten der Wahrheit teilzuhaben. In dieser ihrer Aufteilung unterstehen die Phänomene den Begriffen. Die sind es, welche an den Dingen die Lösung in die Elemente vollziehen . . . Durch ihre Vermittlerrolle leihen die Begriffe den Phänomenen Anteil am Sein der Ideen. Und eben diese Vermittlerrolle macht sie tauglich zu der anderen, gleich ursprünglichen Aufgabe der Philosophie, zur Darstellung der Ideen. Indem die Rettung der Phänomene vermittels der Ideen sich vollzieht, vollzieht sich die Darstellung der Ideen im Mittel der Empirie. Denn nicht an sich selbst, sondern einzig und allein in einer Zuordnung dinglicher Elemente im Begriff stellen die Ideen sich dar. Und zwar tun sie es als deren Konfiguration. (WB, 15–16)
>
> Phenomena do not, however, enter into the realm of ideas whole, in their crude empirical state, adulterated by appearances, but only in their basic elements, redeemed. They are divested of their false unity so that, thus divided, they might partake of the genuine unity of truth. In this their division, phenomena are subordinate to concepts, for it is the latter which effect the resolution of objects into their constituent elements . . . Through their mediating role concepts enable phenomena to participate in the existence of ideas. It is this same mediating role which fits them for the other equally basic task of philosophy, the representation of ideas. As the salvation of

> phenomena by means of ideas takes place, so too does the representation of ideas through the medium of empirical reality. For ideas are not represented in themselves, but solely and exclusively in an arrangement of concrete elements in the concept: as the configuration of these elements. (WBE, 33–34)

In order for a phenomenon to participate in the *Sein* of an idea, it must first be broken down into its elements so as to rid it of a "false unity." In this state, the phenomena are subordinate to concepts, and in turn they mediate a relationship between the phenomena and the idea's existence, and as such the idea is represented through the tools of the empirical. Thus the empirical plays a role, but it does not have a direct relationship to the idea. Instead, together with conceptualization the empirical and the idea create a configuration in which the idea is expressed, but this succeeds only if the relationship between the empirical and the idea is an indirect one, just as the relationship between conceptualization and idea is also indirect. This configuration of indirect relationships is simultaneously rooted in a particular historical moment and outside it. The phenomena and the conceptualization of them are rooted temporally, but the idea and the truth escape a direct, unmediated relationship with that temporal context and, as such, to some extent exist outside it. Here, then, is an example of the complicated web of historical and ahistorical that permeates Benjamin's notions of representation.

Benjamin expands on this notion of truth and ideas as something outside the world of our experiences and thus outside our notions of time:

> Denn in Ideen sind die Phänomene nicht einverleibt. Sie sind in ihnen nicht enthalten. Vielmehr sind die Ideen deren objektive virtuelle Anordnung, sind deren objektive Interpretation . . . Die Ideen sind in der Welt der Phänomene nicht gegeben . . . Das Sein der Ideen kann als Gegenstand einer Anschauung überhaupt nicht gedacht werden, auch nicht der intellektuellen . . .Wahrheit tritt nie in eine Relation und insbesondere in keine intentionale. Der Gegenstand der Erkenntnis als ein in der Begriffsintention bestimmter ist nicht die Wahrheit. Die Wahrheit ist ein aus Ideen gebildetes intentionsloses Sein. Das ihr gemäße Verhalten ist demnach nicht ein Meinen im Erkennen, sondern ein in sie Eingehen und Verschwinden. Die Wahrheit ist der Tod der Intention. (WB, 16–18)

> For phenomena are not incorporated in ideas. They are not contained in them. Ideas are, rather, their objective, virtual arrangement, their

> objective interpretation . . . Ideas are not among the given elements of the world of phenomena . . . The being of ideas simply cannot be conceived of as the object of vision, even intellectual vision . . . Truth does not enter into relationships, particularly intentional ones. The object of knowledge, determined as it is by the intention inherent in the concept, is not the truth. Truth is an intentionless state of being, made up of ideas. The proper approach to it is not therefore one of intention and knowledge, but rather a total immersion and absorption in it. Truth is the death of intention. (WBE, 33–36)

Throughout this explanation of the relationship between phenomena, ideas, knowledge, and truth Benjamin emphasizes two things—truth is without intention, and ideas are not rooted in phenomena. Ideas cannot be the object of observation; the power is not with the observer but rather with the ideas themselves. The process begins not with the phenomena, as an empirical approach would, but with the ideas. Ideas, like truth itself, are rooted in a lack of intention. As such, truth cannot be reached through cognition; it eludes recognition's grasp at every turn because truth and ideas are not bound to time in the same way that experiences are.

The experiential should not attempt to reach this atemporal existence; Benjamin is against an inductive understanding of the world. In his exploration of the German mourning play, Benjamin attacks attempts to define tragedy through timeless commonalities. He insists on the need to consider the historical context in our definition of the genre and posits that ahistorical generalizations are by their very nature subjective and tell us more about the person writing or those around him than about the texts. The experiential world must remain firmly rooted in its temporal reality in order for a representation of the atemporal to be possible. The distance between the atemporal truth and our temporal existence and the lack of a direct connection between them make it difficult to balance the two aspects. Benjamin insists that the ephemeral phenomena of our daily existence do not lead us to the world of ideas and truth, and to try to understand truth through our conceptualizations of reality leads to deceptive representations. In order to prevent such false representations, we need to be aware of our current moment and not give in to a desire for a universal and all-encompassing history.

In *Das Passagen-Werk,* Benjamin compares the project to his work on the German mourning play and focuses on two similarities—the relationship between the present moment and the subject of his studies and the insistence that history is necessarily fragmented and incomplete. Pertaining to the first similarity, Benjamin writes: "Analog aber deutlicher als das

Barockbuch das 17te Jahrhundert durch die Gegenwart belichtet, muß es hier mit dem 19ten geschehen."[11] [The book on the Baroque exposed the seventeenth century to the light of the present day. Here, something analogous must be done for the nineteenth century, but with greater distinctness.][12] How we interpret a historical moment has everything to do with our own context, and we can only understand the past through its relationship with the present. As for the critique of a history that creates a sense of totality:

> Ein zentrales Problem des historischen Materialismus, das endlich gesehen werden sollte: Ob das marxistische Verständnis der Geschichte unbedingt mit ihrer Anschaulichkeit erkauft werden muß? Oder: auf welchem Wege es möglich ist, gesteigerte Anschaulichkeit mit der Durchführung der marxistischen Methode zu verbinden. Die erste Etappe dieses Weges wird sein, das Prinzip der Montage in die Geschichte zu übernehmen. Also die großen Konstruktionen aus kleinsten, scharf und schneidend konfektionierten Baugliedern zu errichten. Ja in der Analyse des kleinen Einzelmoments den Kristall des Totalgeschehens zu entdecken. Also mit dem historischen Vulgärnaturalismus zu brechen. Die Konstruktion der Geschichte als solche zu erfassen. In Kommentarstruktur.[13]
>
> A central problem of historical materialism that ought to be seen in the end: Must the Marxist understanding of history necessarily be acquired at the expense of the perceptibility of history? Or: in what way is it possible to conjoin a heightened graphicness to the realization of the Marxist method? The first stage in this undertaking will be to carry over the principle of montage into history. That is, to assemble large-scale constructions out of the smallest and most precisely cut components. Indeed, to discover in the analysis of the small individual moment the crystal of the total event. And, therefore, to break with vulgar historical naturalism. To grasp the construction of history as such. In the structure of commentary.[14]

Here Benjamin tries to reconcile a desire for clarity with Marxist methodology, and his solution is one that clearly shows its constructed and fragmented nature—montage.[15] The constructed aspect is important, as it emphasizes the role of interpretation and the refusal to conflate history with truth. Both texts focus on analysis and interpretation—it is not the construction itself that illuminates, but rather interactions with it. And they share a fraught relationship with a totality that cannot be represented as such but nevertheless exists. In this case, this totality is the "Totalgeschehen" [total event]. Yet here, in the crystal imagery, Benjamin leaves open the possibility that the piece can contain the whole. In both texts the relationship is one where this totality can only be represented in pieces, or more specifically in the interpretation of pieces. This emphasis on the construction of the montage provides a contrast to what Benjamin calls "vulgar historical naturalism," another way of talking about a representation that presents a falsely complete whole and emphasizes the man-made nature of history. At the same time, there is an erasing of the voice of the writer in this kind of montage and commentary; since the pieces refuse to create a whole, there is also, at least on the surface, a lack of an authoritative voice that provides an overview and a clear narrative. This erasing serves, however, to hide the authority of the text and the ways in which it steers the reader, rather than eliminating them entirely; a commentary does not intrude on the integrity of its subject but does, at the same time, shape how we see it.

This relationship between the present and the past works in both directions. This is Benjamin's concept of a constellation: in this position created by a particular understanding of a past that will never occur again, one is aware that this understanding of the past could only exist at this particular moment and that it thereby reveals the specificity of the present.[16] Benjamin draws connections between the present and the past and through these connections points toward timeless truths. The flâneur and Paris exist both as historical phenomena and as symbols, and if we are to look at the Benjaminian constellation that creates this relationship, we need to also examine the context in which Benjamin is exploring these topics through his writings. The concept of interpretation as constant deferment of a return to a purer relationship between an idea and its naming, of truth existing but outside our reach, of an allegorical approach to reality permeates not only Benjamin's writings about nineteenth-century Paris, but also his other writings. How Benjamin interprets Baudelaire or the origins of German tragic drama has to do with the contexts in which Baudelaire wrote and Germany in the baroque period respectively, but the themes he pulls from them have to do with a struggle to understand history and the role of the individual in the early twentieth century. By foregrounding these themes in a variety of contexts and time periods, Benjamin adds another layer of complexity to the concepts of time and historical context. On one level, this move could be seen as supporting Benjamin's notion that texts can only be read in specific moments in time or, to push this idea further, that they can only be read in certain ways in specific moments in time. Thus these readings root Benjamin's writings deep in the historical and cultural context in which they were produced. On another level, this move erases the importance of historical context in favor of the notion of a timeless truth; the threads that connect these various time periods to Benjamin's own hint at constants, even as the methodology insists on the texts' idiosyncrasies.

According to Benjamin, we are defined by our knowledge that a timeless absolute truth exists and by our inability to know it. This condition spurs Benjamin to consider the nature of representation and examine how methodology, rhetoric, and style affect our ability to represent through elision and circumscribing so as to keep these two aspects of knowledge in balance. He advocates a text that maintains a respectful distance from the unified totality of truth, because only through this distance is any representation possible. Similarly, in his writings about the flâneur, he emphasizes the necessity for distance—both psychological and spatial—so that the flâneur can move through the city on his own terms. By examining the earlier writings of Georg Simmel, we can see more clearly how these concerns relate to broader questions about modernity and urban life.[17]

Simmel's Stranger: A Study in the Positive Nature of Estrangement

One of Georg Simmel's lasting contributions, and an explanation for his importance in cultural studies today, is his refusal to create an overarching framework or structure into which a unifying narrative can be found.[18] Instead Simmel focused on fleeting phenomena and what they can tell us about our lives and the ways we interact with the people and environment around us. In his journals, Simmel acknowledges the somewhat amorphous nature of his legacy:

> Ich weiß, daß ich ohne geistige Erben sterben werde (und es ist gut so). Meine Hinterlassenschaft ist wie eine in barem Gelde, das an viele Erben verteilt wird, und jeder setzt sein Teil in irgendeinen Erwerb um, der *seiner* Natur entspricht: dem die Provenienz aus jener Hinterlassenschaft nicht anzusehen ist.[19]

> I know that I shall die without intellectual heirs, and that is as it should be. My legacy will be like cash, distributed to many heirs, each transforming his part into use according to *his* nature—a use which will no longer reveal its indebtedness to this heritage. (SE, xiii)

Simmel disavows his presence in his work, thereby allowing his reader to approach it as fragments that can be taken and used without consideration for the integrity of the whole. Yet the reason these pieces prove useful to others is that they have a relationship to more universal claims that push beyond the present moment, even as the focus on ephemera situates the writings in a particular time and place. Thus an understanding of Simmel's work necessitates a closer look at its relationship to time, in terms of both the work's content and its structure.

Simmel's approach allowed him to ask questions about modernity that had not been framed in such a way before him. H. J. Becher observes: "Simmel's alert, critical mind not only allowed the contemporary cultural currents to pass through it but also, simultaneously, as a sociologist and philosopher of culture, to question their content. In so doing, he 'elevated the social reality of the *present* into scientific consciousness.'"[20] And in the form of "scientific consciousness" Simmel's observations take on an objectivity that transforms the everyday into a timeless reality. Seen in this light, there are quite a few similarities between Simmel's approach and Benjamin's. Both foreground the fragmentary nature of representation, and in the work of both there is a complicated and at times paradoxical relationship between the historically specific and the timeless universal; in the case of Benjamin this timeless universal is truth, and in the case of Simmel it is science.[21]

Throughout his work, Simmel was ostensibly interested in fleeting phenomena, in the elusive fragments that constitute the experience of modernity. Modernity is rooted in a sociohistorical reality. What interests Simmel, however, is not this specificity but, rather, what an observation of it can tell us about how individuals interact with one another, about how societies are structured. Modernity is defined by its ephemeral quality, yet Simmel strives to distill objective truths about our lives from the ephemeral. Arthur Salz, a student of Simmel's, pointed out that "Simmel dealt with problems *sub specie aeternitatis* while feigning to deal with them *sub specie momenti.*"[22] Simmel's choice of writing style also plays a large role in the text's ability to navigate the relationship between an objective/timeless space and a specific sociohistorical one. As Simmel scholar David Frisby points out, Simmel's essays often lack footnotes or other source references.[23] This absence obscures the context and time in which Simmel is writing; his work gives the impression of existing on its own, without a connection to a specific moment or place or to other scholars. Furthermore, the very form of an essay, as opposed to the rigid scientific writing of other academics, sets Simmel apart as someone more interested in creativity than in structure and systems.[24] The essay form provides Simmel with an ahistorical framework in which to express universal truths that concern and stem from the current moment.

Simmel uses this connection between the ephemeral and a more timeless truth to explore a theme that can be seen throughout his writings—modernity is part of a continuum, and our everyday lives and concerns are the newest manifestation of universal truths about human nature. In what follows, I will first examine Simmel's conceptualization of the stranger and how through this figure Simmel explores the relationship between various discourses of time and space, as well as the impact of this relationship on human interactions in general. I will then look at the relationship between Simmel's stranger and his writings on city life in order to illuminate the role of the outsider position in Simmel's understanding of urban individuality. Finally, I will turn to Simmel's writings on *Gesellschaft* (society) and *Geselligkeit* (sociability), in which Simmel connects the ideas of the outsider, distance, and individuality to firmly place modernity and modern life into the historical continuum.

Central to understanding Simmel's concept of the stranger is an exploration of his observations about the relationship between individuals in spatial terms. In "Exkurs über den Fremden" (often referred to in English as "The Stranger") from his 1908 *Soziologie: Untersuchungen über die Vergesellschaftung* [Sociology: Investigations on the Forms of Sociation], Georg Simmel defines relationships in terms of proximity and distance. These spatial terms serve to map the relationship between individuals, particularly between the stranger and the group. These terms have both a physical and a symbolic side: "das Verhältnis zum Raum [ist] nur einerseits die Bedingung, andrerseits das Symbol der Verhältnisse zu Menschen" (SF, 764) ["spatial relations not only are determining conditions of relationships among men, but are also symbolic of those relationships"] (SE, 143). As Simmel demonstrates in his essay, the symbolic level of our relationship to space not only represents our relationship to others, but also creates it. Our conceptualizations of space, the ways we understand the space we occupy and move through, define our ability to interact with others and the form in which these interactions manifest themselves. Simmel weaves together symbolic and physical aspects of space to demonstrate that although it is our conceptualization of space rather than its physical reality that is at stake here, the relationship between the two—the sense that the symbolic space is connected to something concrete and outside of ourselves—is what gives the symbolic level its validity.

Simmel emphasizes that the stranger is an integral part of the group: "Der Fremde ist ein Element der Gruppe selbst, nicht anders als die Armen und die mannigfachen 'inneren Feinde'—ein Element, dessen immanente und Gliedstellung zugleich ein Außerhalb und Gegenüber einschließt" (SF, 765). ["The stranger is an element of the group itself, not unlike the poor and sundry 'inner enemies'—an element whose membership within the group involves both being outside it and confronting it" (SE, 144).] He contrasts his definition of the stranger with the Greek concept of the barbarian in order to emphasize his point. According to Simmel, the attitude the Greeks had toward barbarians shows a refusal to see any similarities between barbarians and humans, and the relationship is one of negation—the stranger as barbarian is all those things that the others are not (SF, 770). Simmel acknowledges that strangers are not always seen as welcome additions to the group by comparing the stranger to the poor and "inner enemies." Yet in the same sentence he insists that the stranger is part of the group, and as he demonstrates throughout the essay, the stranger has the potential to do much good for the group. This acknowledgment of prejudice against the stranger by comparing him to a figure of danger or neediness is counteracted throughout the essay; Simmel mentions it to show just how different the stranger is from these types of outsiders. Yet at the same time their existence points to the fragility of the position Simmel's stranger occupies, a topic we will address in more detail shortly.

According to Simmel, the relationship of the stranger to the group is that he is physically close but comes from far away, thus bringing the qualities of his faraway origins with him. Simmel writes of the stranger:

> Er ist innerhalb eines bestimmten räumlichen Umkreises—oder eines, dessen Grenzbestimmtheit der räumlichen analog ist—fixiert, aber seine Position in diesem ist dadurch wesentlich bestimmt, daß er nicht von vornherein in ihn gehört, daß er Qualitäten, die aus ihm nicht stammen und stammen können in ihn hineinträgt. (SF, 765)

> He is fixed within a certain spatial circle—or within a group whose boundaries are analogous to spatial boundaries—but his position within it is fundamentally affected by the fact that he does not belong in it initially and that he brings qualities into it that are not, and cannot be, indigenous to it. (SE, 143)

The combination of belonging and not belonging means that the group interacts with the stranger and these interactions define both the stranger and the group. The writing in the passage cited above reinforces this notion. The spatial point of reference is the group's physical and nonphysical boundaries; the special qualities the stranger possesses are defined by the fact that they are brought into an environment from which they could not originate. Everything in the passage is focused on the group and the stranger's role within it. The group and the stranger occupy the same physical space, but because the stranger comes from elsewhere, they do not occupy the same psychological space.

The stranger, because of his unique position of distance and nearness, enjoys an objectivity that is not possible for the others in the group. He is not bound by the prejudices and communal obligations of the rest of the group. The stranger's objectivity does not, however, imply a passive inactivity; instead his engagement with the community can prove advantageous for the others. The distance that he brings with him, in the form of foreign qualities and lack of local prejudices, allows him to serve in roles the others cannot fulfill. Simmel gives the example of Italian cities using judges from outside the city in question because the citizens were incapable of freeing themselves from familial and political ties (SF, 767).

Relationships are defined by the interplay of general/specific in terms of the similarities shared. These qualities determine the character of the distance and proximity that constitute a relationship. Simmel writes of the relationship of the stranger to the group:

> in dem Maße, in dem die Gleichheitsmomente allgemeines Wesen haben, wird der Wärme der Beziehung, die sie stiften, ein Element von Kühle, ein Gefühl von der Zufälligkeit grade *dieser* Beziehung beigesetzt . . . Der Fremde ist uns nah, insofern wir Gleichheiten nationaler oder sozialer, berufsmäßiger oder allgemein menschlicher Art zwischen ihm und uns fühlen; er ist uns fern, insofern diese Gleichheiten über ihn und uns hinausreichen und uns beide nur verbinden, weil sie überhaupt sehr Viele verbinden. (SF, 768–69)

> To the extent to which the similarities assume a universal nature, the warmth of the connection based on them will acquire an element of coolness, a sense of the contingent nature of precisely *this* relation . . . The stranger is close to us insofar as we feel between him and ourselves similarities of nationality or social position, of occupation or of general human nature. He is far from us insofar as these similarities extend beyond him and us, and connect us only because they connect a great many people. (SE, 147)

The more specific the similarities are, the closer two people are to each other. But when the similarities are general—for example, that both belong to humanity—the ties are much looser and distance is established. The second case is the relationship the stranger has to others in the group. The "coolness" that enters the relationship between the stranger and others because the similarities they share are general is by no means a regrettable circumstance; the privileged position of objectivity and increased agency the stranger enjoys is due to the distance produced by this coolness, by the lack of specific similarities. It is important to note that it is not the stranger himself who is defined by this coolness, but the relationship between the stranger and others. By placing the emphasis on the relationship rather than the figure, Simmel creates a discourse in which coolness and distance do not result in a miserable alienated individual and in which these qualities of estrangement are not seen as something unnatural or avoidable. Instead, they are just a part of every relationship, and the case of the stranger differs from that of others only in the degree of distance and coolness.

Simmel's description of erotic relationships serves to reinforce the notion that every relationship has elements of distance due to abstract similarities. This example makes it easier for others to identify with the position of the stranger by showing us that even the most intimate relationships have an element of distance and coolness. Simmel explains that in its first stages an erotic relationship refuses to recognize any generalities—this love is unique and no one has ever felt the way these two people feel. This feeling of complete uniqueness is, however, not sustainable:

> Eine Entfremdung pflegt—ob als Ursache, ob als Folge, ist schwer entscheidbar—in dem Augenblick einzusetzen, in dem der Beziehung ihr Einzigkeitsgefühl entschwindet . . .Vielleicht ist das in manchen Fällen die generellere, mindestens die unüberwindlichere Fremdheit, als die durch Differenzen und Unbegreiflichkeiten gegebene: daß zwar eine Gleichheit, Harmonie, Nähe besteht, aber mit dem Gefühle, daß diese eigentlich kein Alleinbesitz eben dieses Verhältnisses ist, sondern ein Allgemeineres, das potenziell zwischen uns und unbestimmt vielen Andern gilt und deshalb jenem allein realisierten Verhältnis keine innere und ausschließende Notwendigkeit zukommen läßt. (SF, 769–70)
>
> An estrangement is wont to set in (whether as cause or effect is hard to decide) at the moment when this feeling of uniqueness disappears from the relationship . . . Perhaps this is in many cases a more general, at least more insurmountable, strangeness than that due to differences and obscurities. It is strangeness caused by the fact that similarity, harmony, and closeness are accompanied by the

> feeling that they are actually not the exclusive property of this particular relation, but stem from a more general one—a relation that potentially includes us and an indeterminate number of others, and therefore prevents that relation which alone was experienced from having an inner and exclusive necessity. (SE, 147–48)

Simmel's use of the word "Entfremdung"—a word he does not use elsewhere in the essay—links the concept of estrangement to that of the stranger (*der Fremde*). This connection also exists in English—"stranger/estrangement." By using the word "estrangement" in a passage about the universal nature of the state, Simmel connects not only the stranger, but also the others in the group, to estrangement.

Simmel's theory of the stranger depends on the unity of the group, on the cohesion they have because of their specifically similar prejudices and backgrounds. In his discussion of erotic relationships, however, Simmel undermines the unity of the group by showing that no group is as harmonious as one might believe it to be. Yet at the same time, by showing that everyone is capable of feeling estranged, of feeling like a stranger, Simmel allows those who are not strangers to identify with the figure and his position. Simmel is also making an important statement about the nature of estrangement—it is not an unnatural state, nor is it one that is experienced only by those who do not belong. Instead it is a part of our everyday lives, regardless of who we are. And, as Simmel's stranger demonstrates, estrangement, or a distance between oneself and others, can be used to one's advantage. By claiming that estrangement is a universal experience but also that it exists in a unique form within the stranger, Simmel simultaneously allows the reader to identify with the stranger and makes it clear that not everyone is a stranger.

Simmel acknowledges that the tension created by a stranger in the community often leads to an emphasis on the characteristics that make a stranger different. This emphasis, however, can lead the community to place the stranger—whether he is a stranger by citizenship, race, or otherwise—into categories that deny the stranger his individuality:

> Als solches vielmehr ist er *zugleich* nah und fern, wie es in der Fundamentierung der Beziehung auf eine nur allgemein menschliche Gleichheit liegt. Zwischen jenen beiden Elementen aber erhebt sich eine besondere Spannung, indem das Bewußtsein, nur das überhaupt Allgemeine gemein zu haben, doch grade das, was nicht gemeinsam ist, zu besondrer Betonung bringt. Dies ist aber im Falle des Land-, Stadt-, Rassefremden etc. auch wieder nichts Individuelles,

> sondern eine fremde Herkunft, die vielen Fremden gemeinsam ist oder sein könnte. Darum werde die Fremden auch eigentlich nicht als Individuen, sondern als die Fremden eines bestimmten Typus überhaupt empfunden, das Moment der Ferne ist ihnen gegenüber nicht weniger generell als das der Nähe. Diese Form liegt z.B. einem so speziellen Fall wie der mittelalterlichen Judensteuer, wie sie in Frankfurt, aber auch sonst gefordert wurde, zu Grunde. Während die von den christlichen Bürgern gezahlte Beede nach dem jedesmaligen Stande des Vermögens wechselte, war die Steuer für jeden einzelnen Juden ein für allemal festgesetzt. Diese Fixiertheit beruhte darauf, daß der Jude seine soziale Position als *Jude* hatte, nicht als Träger bestimmter sachlicher Inhalte. (SF, 770)

> As such, the stranger is near and far *at the same time,* as in any relationship based on merely universal human similarities. Between these two factors of nearness and distance, however, a peculiar tension arises, since the consciousness of having only the absolutely general in common has exactly the effect of putting a special emphasis on that which is not common. For a stranger to the country, the city, the race, and so on, what is stressed is again nothing individual, but alien origin, a quality which he has, or could have, in common with many other strangers. For this reason strangers are not really perceived as individuals, but as strangers of a certain type. Their remoteness is no less general than their nearness. This form appears, for example, in so special a case as the tax levied on Jews in Frankfurt and elsewhere during the Middle Ages. Whereas the tax paid by Christian citizens varied according to their wealth at any given time, for every single Jew the tax was fixed once and for all. This amount was fixed because the Jew had his social position as a *Jew,* not as the bearer of certain objective contents. (SE, 148–49)

According to Simmel, one can be a true stranger only when one does not belong to any other category of identification. For Simmel the example of the Jewish tax during the Middle Ages shows the inherent injustice of treating someone as a "Jew" rather than as an individual. By categorizing a stranger as a member of a community of strangers, one makes assumptions about that person and his behavior, in part dictating his actions through their expectations. The stranger is robbed of his agency and freedom because he is locked into a category projected onto him.

In order for the stranger to be free, it is essential that the similarities to the others in the group are general and the differences specific. When the others in the group see the stranger's idiosyncratic differences, it means that they are close enough to the stranger to see him as an individual. When this is not the case, both similarities and differences are general and there is no basis to build a special relationship between the stranger and others. The stranger becomes a "type" and is lumped together with other strangers; he is judged and seen through preconceptions about a particular group of people and about the place from which they come. Simmel's text emphasizes this shift in the stranger's position with a shift from singular to plural in reference to the stranger. Throughout the text, the stranger is referred to as "der Fremde." This use of the singular highlights the stranger's position as an independent individual. In the last paragraph of the essay, in which the dangers of seeing the stranger as a member of a group are brought to our attention, the stranger's loss of individuality is enacted through the loss of the singular. No longer is the stranger "der Fremde." Instead he is now one of many strangers: "die Fremden." Interactions with others are essential to the stranger's position, but this position is one of privilege only if the stranger can act as an individual rather than as part of a group.

Throughout the essay Simmel attempts to erase any sense of the stranger belonging to anyone but himself; he may be a part of the group, but he is first and foremost an individual. As mentioned before, the stranger brings with him qualities that could not originate from the group, but their actual origins remain vague. The only mention of the stranger's origins in the essay is to warn of the dangers of categorizing the stranger according to a group of outsiders. In order for the stranger's differences from the others to be specific and agency to be possible, the stranger must not have qualities that establish him as a member of a specific group as an insider. Simmel decontextualizes and dehistoricizes the stranger and the position he occupies in order to make him an individual. Throughout the essay historical examples are used to support Simmel's claims. Since they are, however, taken from different countries and time periods without much contextualization, they serve to demonstrate the universal nature of Simmel's claims rather than root them in a specific sociohistorical context. The specific examples attest to the universal and timeless nature of the stranger—he has existed throughout the ages and will continue to do so in the future. The lack of geographical specificity is linked to the lack of temporal specificity to create a stranger who belongs to no particular time or place. He may be an integral part of the community in which he finds himself, but he can play this role only because his origins and affiliations remain abstract in nature.

The group also remains abstract both temporally and geographically. Implied is that people who live together do so for similar reasons and their interactions with one another are to some extent predictable. Throughout the text, Simmel mentions that specific similarities tie the members of the group to one another, but what exactly these specific similarities are is not important. This can be seen in the fact that Simmel does not elaborate on them, or on how one group's similarities differ from another's. In other words, the similarities that tie one group together may be different from the ones that tie another group together, but the quality of these similarities and the bonds they create between the members of the group are universal. He also does not specify whether said group is rural or urban. The ways in which he describes the groups does, however, touch on discourses of community and society, the former more associated with rural or small-town life, the latter with the city. Simmel does not use the word "community" to describe these groups, but he describes them in a way that fits within the discourses of community as they were understood at the time: the group is bound together by common history, social norms, and codes and can easily differentiate itself from other groups. Yet Simmel also uses discourses more commonly associated with urban societies in his definition of the stranger—potential mobility, a cosmopolitan homelessness, and a distance from others. In these discourses, everyone is a stranger because that is the urban condition; in a city the individual comes into contact with many people whom he does not know at all. While these discourses legitimize the stranger's position by making it universal, they simultaneously strip the position of its unique privileged stance. This tension between discourses of community and society creates the position of the modern stranger. The role that these at times conflicting discourses play in Simmel's conceptualization of the stranger and also of urban modernity becomes clearer in his writing about the city.

Everyone's a Stranger

Georg Simmel's famous essay "Die Großstädte und das Geistesleben" ["The Metropolis and Mental Life"] is neither a celebration nor a condemnation of city life, but rather an examination of the ways in which physical proximity and distance affect our personal lives, our interactions with others, and our conceptualizations of space and community. Simmel looks at the ways in which manifestations of the city's unique conceptualization of space correspond to personal aspects of an individual's life. His study of the *Großstadtmensch* resonates with his description of the stranger. Topics such as the necessity of distance in personal interactions and the central role of freedom of choice to one's existence as an individual appear in both essays. The parallels between the *Großstadtmensch* and the stranger highlight the use of urban discourses in creating the position of the stranger. In fact, Simmel's exploration of the individual within a city can be seen as a search to discover how everyone can be a stranger. The city gives the individual freedom previously only known to the stranger, but here, even more so than in his essay about the stranger, Simmel makes it clear that this freedom is complicated.

According to Simmel, the modern individual struggles to claim independence within society. On the one hand, there is the "Anspruch des Individuums" [claim of the individual], the desire to be free to choose one's actions and be independent of others. On the other, there are the "Übermächte der Gesellschaft" [dominance of society], the aspects of society that protect us and bring us together but also limit our ability to be sovereign individuals. In all of the social movements of the eighteenth and nineteenth centuries, there has been one constant: "der Widerstand des Subjekts, in einem gesellschaftlich-technischen Mechanismus nivelliert und verbraucht zu werden" (SG, 116) ["the resistance of the individual to being levelled, swallowed up in the social-technological mechanism" (SE, 324)]. Simmel paints this picture of history in order to show that city life is part of this tradition, but also to show us the idiosyncratic qualities of this particular struggle during this particular moment in history. The notion of continuity is an important one, as it serves to undermine the idea that city life is somehow unnatural and a disruption; just as Simmel uses historical examples to present the stranger and his position in a group as universal phenomena, here the universal struggle of the individual for agency is the lens through which Simmel explores the relationship between a city environment and its inhabitants. And this sense of continuity complicates the dichotomies that Simmel sets up between city life and country life by reminding the reader that although these are different environments whose qualities greatly affect how we live our lives, the search for individuality is a fundamental human quality rather than a product of modernity.

Simmel contrasts country life and city life in order to highlight the specific characteristics of the latter. He begins by stating that man depends on his ability to perceive differences; we are aware of our environment, differentiating one impression from the ones that came before and after it. In the city, the constant stream of different stimuli results in a "Steigerung des Nervenlebens" (SG, 116) ["intensification of emotional life" (SE, 325)]. Country life is marked by a slower, more regular rhythm, thus "Gemüt" and emotional bonds occur more often: "denn diese wurzeln in den unbewußteren Schichten der Seele und wachsen am ehesten an dem ruhigen Gleichmaß ununterbrochener Gewöhnungen" (SG, 117). ("These latter [referring to emotional bonds] are rooted in the unconscious levels of the mind and develop most readily in the steady equilibrium of unbroken customs" [SE, 325].) The central role that feelings play in country life is impossible in city life due to its tempo. Instead the city is about quickness and unpredictability, and as a result, the part of the individual that is most active in the urban individual is the "Ort des Verstandes (locus of reason)," which is "die durchsichtigen, bewußten, obersten Schichten unserer Seele, er ist die anpassungsfähigste unserer inneren Kräfte" ("the lucid, conscious upper strata of the mind and it is the most adaptable of our inner forces") (SG, 117, SE, 325). The emotions of country life come from the unconscious depths of the soul; the reason of city life stems from the conscious surface.

Simmel takes this reading of the city and reason and applies it to the monetary economy. He claims that commerce thrives in the city because it needs the city's tempo in order to become important. The importance reason has in the individual's life is mirrored in commerce by the ways in which the individual evaluates both people and things in a "purely matter-of-fact manner" (SG, 118). In other words, people view each other in terms of the services they can provide. There are echoes of Karl Marx in Simmel's observation that in the country production is for the customers, whereas in the city, production is for the market. The result is an alienation of the consumer from the product; the once direct relationship between the two is now mediated by money.

These surface phenomena have corresponding changes in the mind: "Der moderne Geist ist mehr und mehr ein rechnender geworden" (SG, 119). ["The modern mind has become more and more a calculating one" (SE, 327)]. The calculating qualities of money appear in the lives of individuals in the following qualities: "eine Präzision, eine Sicherheit in der Bestimmung von Gleichheiten und Ungleichheiten, eine Unzweideutigkeit in Verabredungen und Ausmachungen" (SG, 119) ["a precision and a degree of certainty in the definition of the equalities and inequalities and an unambiguousness in agreements and arrangements" (SE 328)]. A manifestation of these qualities is the ubiquitous pocket watch. In the city, with its extreme density and constant activity, the pocket watch represents the punctuality and accuracy required to prevent all interactions from dissolving into chaos. According to Simmel, it is not only characteristics such as privileging the quantifiable that result from living in the city. Every aspect of the individual's life is influenced by the city and its qualities; the environment excludes those instinctive and irrational impulses and traits that would define the individual from the inside. In other words, the urban individual's interior is primarily defined from reacting to the outside, rather than beginning in the inside and being projected outward (SG, 120). This reading of the urban individual does not lead, however, to a critique of urban life as less meaningful or less real than country life or preurban life in general. Instead, Simmel takes this surface existence and shows its advantages; he demonstrates that qualities like antipathy, a blasé attitude, and aloofness are what allow the urban individual more freedom than his country counterparts. Simmel emphasizes how these qualities differ from general apathy or indifference, characteristics often mentioned in critiques of the city and its inhabitants.

A blasé attitude is, according to Simmel, a common phenomenon in the city and is a result of "Nervenreize": overwhelmed by the constant stimuli, the urban individual can no longer react to each new change with the appropriate energy (SG, 121). Simmel again draws parallels between the money market and the individual; both are, the one on a larger scale and the other on a personal level, a blunting against differences. Instead of painting a picture of mindless and deadened individuals trudging through their lives, Simmel maintains that the blasé attitude is in fact an indication of intellect:

> [Blasiertheit] ist zunächst die Folge jener rasch wechselnden und in ihren Gegensätzen eng zusammengedrängten Nervenreize, aus denen uns auch die Steigerung der grosstädtischen Intellektualität hervorzugehen schien; weshalb denn auch dumme und von vornherein geistig unlebendige Menschen nicht gerade blasiert zu sein pflegen. (SG, 121)

> [A blasé outlook] is at first the consequence of those rapidly shifting stimulations of the nerves which are thrown together in all their contrasts and from which it seems to us the intensification of metropolitan intellectuality seems to be derived. On that account it is not likely that stupid persons who have been hitherto intellectually dead will be blasé. (SE, 329)

The first half of the sentence provides a fairly neutral explanation of the connections between a blasé attitude and urban intellect; the second half highlights the positive aspects of the two by describing those who do not share these qualities. "Dumme" and "geistig unlebendige" people are not blasé. Simmel also makes a distinction between "Abstumpfung" (blunting or dulling) and "stumpfsinnig" (dull). The blasé person's senses are not dull; he can perceive differences but deems them unimportant. By making a distinction between two words that share a common root, Simmel stresses the difference between someone incapable of taking in the world and the constant stream of stimuli in the city and someone who does have this ability but has a lessened reaction to them as a negotiation strategy.

Another quality of the urban individual is his aloofness or reserved nature. Similar to his explanation of the blasé attitude, Simmel's definition of aloofness subtly differentiates itself from that of the city's critics. According to Simmel, the most important element of a reserved nature is not indifference, but antipathy. The life of an urban individual is a "Verkehrsleben" [commercial life, but in German the word "Verkehr" also means traffic], a life of intersections and interactions that need to be carefully regulated by "sympathies, indifferences and aversions" (SG, 123). The amount of indifference in this combination is, however, less than one might expect. If the level of indifference were too high, it would prove difficult for the urban individual to negotiate the many daily choices he needs to make, since there would be few criteria for determining which option is more attractive. Thus antipathy prevents the individual from becoming overwhelmed by making some of the choices unattractive, and affection is necessary to make the choice among the remaining options easier. Antipathy has the additional role of creating distance and avoidance between individuals, without which it would be quite difficult to maintain the flow of interactions between individuals. The distance created by a reserved nature, fueled by antipathy, is also the source of the greater freedom that urban individuals experience in comparison to their rural counterparts.

The city is not only defined by an increase in population and a subsequent reduction of intense, close bonds between its inhabitants. City life also differs from rural life in a related change in general outlook. A tight-knit rural community depends on homogeneity and harmony, and the community is perceived as a closed-off whole. The focus is directed inward so that this structure can be maintained. The consciousness of the city, however, expands well beyond its physical boundaries, and this expansion has a profound impact on the meaning of individual life. When the physical border's importance disappears, activity becomes the defining factor: "Wie ein Mensch nicht zu Ende ist mit den Grenzen seines Körpers oder des Bezirkes, . . . so besteht auch eine Stadt erst aus der Gesamtheit der über ihre Unmittelbarkeit hinausreichenden Wirkungen" (SG, 127). ["A person does not end with limits of his physical body or with the area . . . In the same way the city exists only in the totality of the effects which transcend their immediate sphere" (SE, 335).] The urban individual does not need to subsume his individual desires for the community as his rural counterpart does; his life gains importance from the impact that his activity has on the world beyond the narrow physical boundaries of the city. Individual freedom is not only the ability to move around freely and the loss of certain constricting prejudices and viewpoints. Rather, Simmel emphasizes, it is also the ability to assert oneself as an individual:

> Daß wir den Gesetzen der eigenen Natur folgen—und dies ist doch Freiheit—wird uns und anderen erst dann ganz anschaulich und überzeugend, wenn die Äußerungen dieser Natur sich von denen anderer unterscheiden: erst unsere Unverwechselbarkeit mit anderen erweist, daß unsere Existenzart uns nicht von anderen aufgezwungen ist. (SG, 127)

> That we follow the laws of our inner nature—and this is what freedom is—becomes perceptible and convincing to us and to others only when the expressions of this nature distinguish themselves from others; it is our irreplaceability by others which shows that our mode of existence is not imposed upon us from the outside. (SE, 335)

This link drawn between a concept of one's own nature and freedom emphasizes the desire to be an individual as a universal human condition; Simmel claims that what we all have in common is that we are different from one another. As such, freedom is defined as the ability to be a true individual, which in turn is defined as being allowed to find out what makes an individual different from those around him or her. The parallels between the individual and the stranger are apparent—both are defined by their ability to live according to their own rules, their own nature, and not those that are imposed on them.

This ability to assert one's individuality is seen in the range of specialized jobs that appear in the city. On the one hand, unique jobs demonstrate the individual's ability to assert his idiosyncratic talents. On the other, they also point to the need to set oneself apart from others as a survival technique: when an individual has something unique to offer others, he is not easily substituted or replaced. Not only does the job seeker look for a unique service to offer; he also takes part in the creating of new needs, of furthering the differentiation of those to whom he caters. Both the consumer and the producer encourage individual differences in one another, but these differentiations are motivated by profit and interest in production, rather than in following the rules of one's own nature to find one's individuality (SG, 128).

Thus this need to establish difference does have a restricting aspect. Because contact with others is often brief, one must establish one's difference quickly and unambiguously. Often this leads to poses—such as pretentiousness or capriciousness—that have less to do with an actual attitude or characteristic than with the need for a firmly established difference and the niche this difference creates. Simmel writes:

> Die Entwicklung der modernen Kultur charakterisiert sich durch das Übergewicht dessen, was man den objektiven Geist nennen kann, über den subjektiven, d.h., in der Sprache wie im Recht, in der Produktionstechnik wie in der Kunst, in der Wissenschaft wie in den Gegenständen der häuslichen Umgebung ist eine Summe von Geist verkörpert, deren täglichem Wachsen die geistige Entwicklung der Subjekte nur sehr unvollständig und in immer weiterem Abstand folgt. (SG, 129)

> The development of modern culture is characterised by the predominance of what one can call the objective spirit over the subjective; that is, in language as well as in law, in the technique of production as well as in art, in science as well as in the objects of domestic environment, there is embodied a sort of spirit [*Geist*], the daily growth of which is followed only imperfectly and with an even greater lag by the intellectual development of the individual. (SE, 337)

In the city, the individual has the freedom to be an individual. This ability to be an individual, however, becomes a necessity for survival; one strives to be irreplaceable, to offer something no one else can. This distinction between "objective mind" and "subjective mind" parallels an argument Simmel makes earlier in the essay, namely that urban people are ruled by reason, in contrast to rural people, who are ruled by "Gemüt." That is, urban people are defined by outside influences and by their ability to present themselves to others and to react to the presentations of others, rather than by more regular and slowly developing emotional bonds. Yet Simmel's description of objective and subjective minds contains a critical tone that is lacking in his differentiation between "Verstand" and "Gemüt." The critique is implicit in the passage cited above, but becomes more transparent later in the same paragraph: "Diese Diskrepanz ist im wesentlichen der Erfolg wachsender Arbeitsteilung; denn eine solche verlangt vom Einzelnen eine immer einseitigere Leistung, deren höchste Steigerung seine Persönlichkeit als ganze oft genug verkümmern läßt. Jedenfalls, dem Überwuchern der objektiven Kultur ist das Individuum weniger und weniger gewachsen (SG, 129). ["This discrepancy is in essence the result of the success of the growing division of labor. For it is this which requires from the individual an ever more one-sided type of achievement which, at its highest point, often permits his personality as a whole to fall into neglect. In any case this overgrowth of objective culture has been less and less satisfactory for the individual" (SE, 337).] One's job represents a lack of deeper differentiation and individuality. It provides a shorthand way of distinguishing oneself, but the act of being different remains on a surface level. Here Simmel seems to criticize the lack of depth on the urban individual's part, a lack that earlier in the essay was handled more neutrally. Simmel continues his critique with the following observation:

> Es bedarf nur des Hinweises, daß die Großstädte die eigentlichen Schauplätze dieser, über alles Persönliche hinauswachsenden Kultur sind. Hier bietet sich in Bauten und Lehranstalten, in den Wundern und Komforts der raumüberwindenden Technik, in den Formungen des Gemeinschaftslebens und in den sichtbaren Institutionen des Staates eine so überwältigende Fülle krystallisierten, unpersönlich gewordenen Geistes, daß die Persönlichkeit sich sozusagen dagegen nicht halten kann. (SG, 130)

> One only needs to point out that cities are the proper arenas for a culture which has outgrown everything personal. In the buildings and educational institutions, in the wonders and comforts of space-transcending technology, in the formation of a communal life and in the visible state institutions one finds such an overwhelming wealth of crystalizing, depersonalized spirit that the individual personality cannot, so to speak, sustain itself in the face of it.

In the city, culture becomes something impersonal and overwhelming, and it is difficult for the individual to assert himself within this culture. Yet the city also offers the individual independence from others and the chance to be different. The word "Gemeinschaftsleben" [communal life] is ambivalent in the context of this passage—it allows for the possibility that society and community are not mutually exclusive, that even within the impersonal culture and technology a sense of community can exist. Or another reading is that living together in a city does not necessarily contain the qualities that are traditionally associated with community—intimacy and mutual dependency. I would argue that these two readings can coexist—community in the city does not mean the same thing that it does in the country. It does not disappear, but it takes on other qualities; one lives with others, but the relationships, the ratio of distance and proximity, change.

Simmel distinguishes between two kinds of individualism—"die Ausbildung persönlicher Sonderart" [the development of personal idiosyncracies] and "individuelle Unabhängigkeit" [individual independence]—that are equally important to one's social development. Although he has convincingly demonstrated the difficulty of satisfying the needs of both kinds of individualism, Simmel also claims that the city is the place where both may be possible. He writes: "Es ist die Funktion der Großstädte, den Platz für den Streit und für die Einigungsversuche beider herzugeben, indem ihre eigentümlichen Bedingungen sich uns als Gelegenheiten und Reize für die Entwicklung beider offenbart haben" (SG, 131). ["It is the function of the metropolis to make a place for the conflict and for the attempts at unification of both of these in the sense that its own peculiar conditions have been revealed to us as the occasion and the stimulus for the development of both" (SE 339).] By stating that there is the possibility of unifying these two desires, Simmel lessens his critique of objective culture: it may be difficult for the individual to develop into a differentiated individual because of the brief and superficial contact we have with others as well as the presence of an overwhelming objective culture. Yet the conditions that cause these phenomena also grant the individual the possibility of distinguishing himself from others and of interacting with the culture on a personal and independent level. The unique qualities of city life provide the city's inhabitants with the opportunity to be strangers in the sense that Simmel describes in his essay "Exkurs über den Fremden." But these qualities can also rob its inhabitants of anything but the most superficial assertion of individuality, and here, too, there are parallels to Simmel's description of the stranger: when others decide what it means to be an individual or a stranger, one no longer has the agency necessary to act on one's own.

Gesellschaft and Geselligkeit

These questions of agency and the individual in an urban environment are also explored in Simmel's "Soziologie der Geselligkeit" ["Sociology of Sociability"], a talk he gave in 1910 at the first German sociology conference. In this talk, Simmel searches for a balance between the individual as an autonomous figure motivated by personal desires, ambitions, and so on, and the individual as part of a larger society. Simmel explains that there are two very different definitions of society: the first postulates that it is only through society that human existence has meaning; the second views society as an abstract concept describing something that already exists. Rather than make an argument for or against these definitions, Simmel comes to the following conclusion about the debate: "Dieser Streit muss der Gesellschaft jedenfalls eine Realität in doppeltem Sinne lassen" (SS, 177). ["However one decides this conflict, he must allow society to be a reality in a double sense" (SE, 127).] Since each reality has close ties to a different definition of society, Simmel's insistence on their coexistence can be read as an attempt to find a new definition of society in which the two societies, and the needs they address, are allowed to interact. The first reality sees society as mystical and with a higher meaning; individuals are more closely rooted to reality through their connection with one another. This view depends on the notion of individuals "in ihrer unmittelbaren sinnlichen Existenz, die Träger der Vergesellschaftungsprozesse, die durch diese zu der höheren Einheit, die man 'eine Gesellschaft' nennt, zusammengeschlossen werden" (SS, 177) ["in their directly perceptible existence, the bearers of the processes of association, who are united by these processes into the higher unity which one calls 'society'" (SE, 127)]. This belief in a higher unity is linked to an unmediated existence; the individual is connected to this "sinnlicher Existenz," and this allows people to create a society that is greater than the individuals in it. The second reality is goal oriented. In this society everyone is motivated by their individual interests, and people come together in order achieve mutually beneficial goals. Simmel lists nation-states, churches, and families as some examples of this type of coming together. Since common interests or goals are what connect these people, the label of "society" is an after-the-fact nomenclature. That is to say, these people are not coming together to create a society. Instead, society is the by-product of people coming together to realize common goals. These two versions of society resonate with the conflict between notions of community and society that were prevalent at this time, particularly in the writings of another member of this conference—Ferdinand Tönnies. Yet rather than defining the first kind of society as community (Gemeinschaft) and the second as society (Gesellschaft), Simmel chooses to use the word "Gesellschaft" to describe both. By doing so, Simmel creates a framework in which there is, as is emphasized throughout the essay, no either/or proposition. It is not a question of either Gemeinschaft or Gesellschaft, with one representing a more "natural" and real way of being together, and the other representing a group of individuals who are bound together only through self-interest in a cold and abstract manner. Instead, both of these aspects are part of our understanding of Gesellschaft, and as such this framework contains no possibility for a "return," for a view of Gesellschaft and consequently of modernity as a condition of loss.

After Simmel sets up the two sides of Gesellschaft and the worldviews that create them, he works on redefining the concept. What Simmel proposes is that society is actually neither of these things, but it does involve both of these concepts and their realities. Simmel uses the example of the game (*Spiel*) to portray how society works. Games contain generalities that touch on the specifics of the individual but are also removed from them: "Ein Gemeinsames, Gleichartiges an seelischer Reaktion und seelischem Bedürfnis knüpft sich an all diese Mannigfaltigkeiten, sehr wohl zu unterscheiden von dem speziellen Interesse, das gerade ihren Verschiedenheiten gilt" (SS, 178). ["A common element, a likeness of psychological reaction and need, is found in all these various things—something easily distinguishable from the special interest which gives each its distinction" (SE, 128).] Simmel argues that a game's functionality stems from its roots in personal desires, but its form is removed from those roots, and only for this reason can the individuals involved play together. That is to say, this removal from the personal into the general is a necessary precondition of a game that otherwise would be too personal and not hold to the rules or formalities that structure a game. A game exists and is played for its own sake; these qualities are what create the requisite distance from the personal. Society functions in a similar way in that it exists for itself: "Typischer Weise aber verwebt sich in alle realen Veranlassungen zur Gesellschaftsbildung ein Gefühl für den Wert der Gesellschaftsbildung als solcher . . . " ["But typically all actual motives for society formation are imbued with a feeling of the worth of society formation as such"] (SS, 178). To understand how society functions, Simmel maintains that one must see society as Geselligkeit: ". . . so löst der Geselligkeitstrieb gleichsam in reiner Wirksamkeit aus den Realitäten des sozialen Lebens die Form des Miteinander, des bloßen Gesellschaftsprozesses als einen Wert und ein Glück heraus und konstituiert damit, was wir Geselligkeit im engeren Sinne nennen" (SS, 178) [". . . so also the impulse to sociability distills, as it were, out of the realities of social life the pure essence of association, of the associative process as a value and a satisfaction. It thereby constitutes what we call sociability in the narrower sense" (SE, 128–29)]. By emphasizing Geselligkeit rather than Gesellschaft, Simmel foregrounds the idea that our interactions with others are what create society—that society is something dynamic creating and created through relationships, rather than a static structure imposed on individuals. At the same time, these interactions necessitate distance between the individuals involved. In this model, Simmel attempts to find a role for the individual in society that protects the individual from too much exposure while still allowing for social interactions.[25]

According to Simmel, it is possible to have a society that is founded on interests such as those of a nation-state or commerce, what he calls a "durch irgend einen Zweckgedanken zusammengehaltene Gesellschaft" ["society held together by some purpose"] (SS, 179). But a society founded on the principles of Geselligkeit is one that is not directly related to these interests:

> Aber nur die gesellige ist eben "eine Gesellschaft" ohne weiteren Zusatz, weil sie die reine, prinzipiell über jeden spezifischen Inhalt erhobene Form all jener einseitig charakterisierten "Gesellschaften" in einem gleichsam abstrakten, alle Inhalte in das bloße Spiel der Form auflösenden Bilde darstellt. Von den soziologischen Kategorien her betrachtend, bezeichne ich also die Geselligkeit als die *Spielform der Vergesellschaftung* und als—mutatis mutandis—zu deren inhaltsbestimmter Konkretheit sich verhaltend, wie das Kunstwerk zur Realität. (SS, 179–80)

> But only the sociable gathering is "society" without the qualifying adjectives, because it alone presents the pure, abstract play of form, all the specific contents of the one-sided and qualified societies being dissolved away. Sociability is, then, the *play-form of association*. It is related to the content-determined concreteness of association as art is related to reality. (SE, 129–30)

In Simmel's insistence on the form of society and on its independent nature, there are parallels to Benjamin's notions of representation in *Ursprung des deutschen Trauerspiels*. As is the case in Benjamin's representation, in order for society to function, it cannot be rooted solely in our everyday reality, nor can it be completely removed from it and claim to exist on a higher plane. And Simmel's emphasis on the interactions between individuals as the foundation of society resonates with the importance Benjamin places on interpretation, on the dynamic nature of representation. Most importantly, in both cases there is an insistence on the absence of intent. The interactions between individuals is for the sake of society, not for personal interests, and as such, a lack of personal intent allows society to function as it does. Benjamin uses a similar approach in that he insists that the representation of the idea cannot be driven by the intent of the one creating the representation, because it would then become something subjective and personal, rather than a way to connect, albeit in a circumspect manner, to the idea and, through the idea, to truth. Society and ideas exist for themselves; individual desires and interests must be sublimated to successfully participate in the formation of society or the representation of an idea. This sublimation is not, however, a repression of those desires; rather, it is a way to express them while simultaneously participating in a society. Simmel uses the examples of conversation and storytelling to illustrate how individuals connect and interact with one another, while still maintaining a certain distance.

Simmel describes the ideal conversation in the following manner: "Nicht als ob der Inhalt der gesellschaftlichen Unterhaltung gleichgültig sei: er soll durchaus interessant, fesselnd, ja bedeutend sein—nur dass er nicht an sich den Zweck der Unterhaltung bilde, dass diese nicht dem objektiven Resultat gelte, das sozusagen ideell außerhalb der Unterhaltung bestünde" (SS, 188). ["Not that the content of sociable conversation is a matter of indifference; it must be interesting, gripping, even significant—only it is not the purpose of the conversation that these qualities should square with objective results, which stand by definition outside the conversation" (SE, 136).] Here again is the notion that the content is important, but only if it serves the purpose of creating an atmosphere and interactions conducive to society, not for other, outside goals. What is interesting is that Simmel then connects this notion of conversation with a particular position for the person talking:

> Die feinste gesellig erzählte Geschichte ist die, bei der der Erzählende seine Person völlig zurücktreten läßt; die ganz vollendete hält sich in dem glücklichen Gleichgewichtspunkt der sozusagen geselligen Ethik, in dem sowohl das subjektiv Individuelle, wie das objektiv Inhaltliche sich völlig in den Dienst an der reinen Geselligkeitsform aufgelöst haben. (SS, 189)

> The finest sociably told story is that in which the narrator allows his own person to remain completely in the background; the most effective story holds itself in the happy balance of the sociable ethic, in which the subjectively individual as well as the objectively substantive have dissolved themselves completely in the service of pure sociability. (SE, 137)

Benjamin maintains that writing is the medium through which ideas can be conveyed, more specifically in the form of a treatise (WB, 11). Since one of the key qualities of such writing is the lack of intention, such a genre necessitates a writer who is unobtrusive, who does not give great importance to a personal agenda or to conveying a subjective and personal experience. This position shows significant similarities to that of Simmel's storyteller. Here the story is the most important thing, and the story serves the purpose of Geselligkeit by achieving a balance between the subjective and the objective. The storyteller, in order to achieve this balance, must tell the story in a way that puts the story itself center stage. In other words, the storyteller as an individual must remain invisible so that he can serve as a storyteller in more abstract terms by maintaining a distance between himself and the story. This position of invisibility is deeply connected to the experience of modernity and the media that create this experience. Furthermore, this position connects the experiences of the urban individual to those of the stranger/outsider. The position of Simmel's stranger, for example, is one that depends on the stranger's impartiality; he is not involved in the personal interests and relationships of those around him in the same way that others of the community are. The result of this distance that defines his relationship to the others is that the stranger is to some extent an invisible entity. His personal qualities and personal interests cannot be foregrounded. If they are, he is not impartial, and the others will not recognize him as an objective intermediary. His interactions with others depend on being able to share general similarities that create interactions without entangling him too deeply in the personal lives of others. Thus the stranger, like those playing their roles in society, remains unknown; the stranger's mobility, his ability to interact with others and see what they do not, depends on his identification first and foremost as a stranger, and the same applies to Benjamin's flâneur. Anonymity creates a balance between the subjective and the objective that does not sacrifice either one of them. And in both Simmel's and Benjamin's writings, these kinds of negotiations between subjective and objective are not just vital to the positions of the stranger and the flâneur; they are also crucial to the individual living in modern society.

Simmel is careful to point out, however, that the individual still plays a key role in society, and not merely as a tool of that society. According to Simmel, Geselligkeit depends on personal qualities such as "Liebenswürdigkeit, Bildung, Herzlichkeit, Anziehungskräfte jeder Art" (SS, 180) ["amiability, breeding, cordiality, and attractiveness of all kinds" (SE, 130)]. These personal qualities must, however, remain somewhat impersonal: "Aber gerade darum, weil hier alles auf die Persönlichkeiten gestellt ist, dürfen die Persönlichkeiten sich nicht gar zu individuell betonen" (SS, 180). ["But precisely because all is oriented about them, the personalities must not emphasize themselves too individually" (SE, 130).] That is to say, boundaries are needed to keep the personal from becoming *too* personal because otherwise a community of people cannot be held together. Simmel places great importance on tact as a way of regulating these relationships, something we will see in Plessner's writings as well. The result of these impersonally personal interactions between individuals, regulated through tact, is what Simmel calls "eine sehr merkwürdige soziologische Struktur" (SS, 181) ["a very remarkable sociological structure" (SE, 130)]. According to Simmel, qualities that have an "objective meaning," such as wealth, social standing, fame, and exceptional talents, do not play a role in Geselligkeit. At the same time, those qualities that are too personal, such as mood and character, also do not play a role. A relationship built on personal qualities "wird zu einem durch einen Inhalt bestimmten Zusammensein" ["becomes an association determined by a content" (SE, 131)] and like one built on commercial purposes exists as an exchange of interests, rather than existing for its own sake. Tact allows interactions to be personal without being too personal, but also to be impersonal without going too far in that direction as well.

Simmel works against a notion of society being in opposition to a more "natural" community by redefining the notion of "künstlich," a move we will also see further developed in Plessner's writings about the organic and humans. Simmel contends that a society based on the principles of Geselligkeit is a democracy, but only because it is a balance between the objective and the subjective that does not allow for either of these in their most extreme forms, and the only way to achieve this balance is in a constructed world, "eine künstliche Welt." This world is, however, not about a loss of the natural; there is no Rousseauian alternative:

> Wenn wir jetzt die Vorstellung haben, in die Geselligkeit kämen wir rein "als Menschen," als das, was wir wirklich sind, unter Abwerfung all der Belastungen, der Hin- und Hergerissenheiten, des Zuviel und Zuwenig, womit das reale Leben die Reinheit unseres Bildes entstellt, so liegt das daran, dass das moderne Leben mit objektivem Inhalt und Sachforderungen überlastet ist. Diese im geselligen Kreise von uns abtuend, glauben wir zu unserem natürlich-persönlichen Sein zurückzukehren und übersehen dabei, dass auch dies Persönliche nicht in seiner ganzen Besonderheit und naturalistischen Vollständigkeit, sondern nur in einer gewissen Reserve und Stilisierung den geselligen Menschen ausmacht. (SS, 183–84)

> If we now have the conception that we enter into sociability purely as "human beings," as that which we really are, lacking all the

> burdens, the agitations, the inequalities with which real life disturbs the purity of our picture, it is because modern life is overburdened with objective content and material demands. Ridding ourselves of this burden in sociable circles, we believe we return to our natural-personal being and overlook the fact that this personal aspect also does not consist in its full uniqueness and natural completeness, but only in a certain reserve and stylizing of the sociable man. (SE, 133)

It is interesting that in Simmel's defense of a constructed or artificial world, he uses some of the criticisms against modern life to support his argument. He uses the depiction of modern life as too focused on rationality and objectivity (the use of the word "überlastet" [overburdened] serves as a nod of agreement to this assessment) to make the claim that it is only because of these circumstances that we view our ideal society as one in which we are completely ourselves without any artifice, without any boundaries between us. Yet this ideal is an illusion: the personal qualities that people value so much as being "natural" can only be conveyed to others through artifice, through "Reserve" and "Stilisierung."

According to Simmel, artifice is necessary because man is "ein ad hoc konstruiertes Elaborat" [an ad hoc construction]—he is a web of different strengths, possibilities, motivations, and relationships and is constantly changing according to those qualities that are dominant at a particular moment. According to this logic, it is impossible to ever fully incorporate all of these aspects of one's personality into one complete being that can be presented to the world, particularly since these aspects themselves change over time. Since society requires that our interactions with one another are not ruled by personal emotions, needs, and desires, Simmel argues that we are more complete and more ourselves when we follow the rules of Geselligkeit: "Die Diskretion, die dem anderen gegenüber ein erstes Erfordernis der Geselligkeit ist, ist ebenso dem eigenen Ich gegenüber erforderlich, weil ihre Verletzung in beiden Fällen die soziologische Kunstform der Geselligkeit in einen soziologischen Naturalismus ausarten lässt" (SS, 182). ["That discretion which is one's first demand upon others in sociability is also required of one's own ego, because a breach of it in either direction causes the sociological artifact of sociability to break down into a sociological naturalism" (SE, 131–32).] When one is part of a society and acts accordingly, one is not as torn by competing needs and personal emotions. This is not to say that one acts as an automaton; rather, the characteristics foregrounded in such interactions belong to the person in question but are not motivated by what he or she wants from others. There is a quality of disinterestedness in these interactions—not only for society's sake, but also for one's own. If one does not respect the boundaries that Geselligkeit creates through discretion or tact, the result is "soziologischer Naturalismus." Note that Simmel uses the adjective "sociological" for both possible outcomes, further emphasizing that the alternative to Geselligkeit is not a more natural way of being, but rather a construction that uses discourses of naturalism.

Society and Community: Plessner and the Need for Distance

Helmuth Plessner's work on the concepts of community and society has many parallels to Simmel's work on the stranger and urban life. Like Simmel, Plessner worked against a nostalgia for a preindustrial time of harmony. Whereas Simmel still sees some positive aspects in a slower-paced, more close-knit society, Plessner makes no distinction between urban and country spaces. This omission strengthens his case for the necessity of certain aspects of modern society; there is no alternative, and Plessner's examples support the contention that the more close-knit, immediate relationships of rural communities never existed. He also expands on Simmel's notion that estrangement is a natural part of every relationship in his examination of the ways individuals interact with one another.

Plessner's 1924 *Grenzen der Gemeinschaft: Eine Kritik des sozialen Radikalismus* (*The Limits of Community: A Critique of Social Radicalism*) is considered an unusual text in the position it takes on the definition of and relationship between the concepts of community and society. It was written as a reaction against an idealized imagining of community. Although Ferdinand Tönnies's 1887 work *Gemeinschaft und Gesellschaft* (*Community and Society*)[26] is not directly mentioned, it is clear that Plessner's text is a critique of the way that Tönnies had been received and interpreted, in particular the prevalence of the idea, which Tönnies's text does not explicitly refute, that society and community are two separate spheres and that the sphere of community contains all the desirable qualities of warmth, closeness, and harmony. In this view society is a threat to community; with its coldness, artificiality, and distance, society is a potential disruption to community's positive qualities. *Grenzen der Gemeinschaft* attempts to question the parallel constructions of "community versus society" and "real versus artifice."

Plessner's text was widely read when it was published. For the most part, the reviewers praised Plessner's intellect and the thought-provoking nature of his work. Yet they were also quick to dismiss this radical rethinking of the relationship between community and society. Their assessments may have differed in content, but most reviewers maintained that Plessner went too far in his praise of society and his warnings about the dangers of community. The critical reception demonstrates not only how entrenched the dichotomy of society/community was (and arguably still is), but also that a positive view of society requires a major shift in our understanding of how individuals interact and live with one another. Nicolai von Bubnoff writes of Plessner: "In seiner scharfen Kritik des Gemeinschaftsgedankens scheint mir der Verf. den Bogen zu überspannen und Licht und Schatten auf die beiden Grundformen menschlichen Zusammenlebens nicht ganz richtig zu verteilen" ["It seems to me that in his sharp critique of a communal mentality the author has gone too far and has not correctly allocated light and shadow to these two basic forms of human cohabitation"].[27] Ferdinand Tönnies carefully avoids the topic of society/community in his review, instead focusing on Plessner's treatise of social radicalism. He further distances his own work from Plessner's with the following comment: "Das geistreiche Büchlein gehört mehr zur Ethik als zur Soziologie" ["The ingenious little book belongs more to the field of ethics than it does to sociology"].[28] His one mention of the community/society dichotomy is to say that the book "bringt den Gegensatz des gemeinschaftlichen gegen das gesellschaftliche Wesen in ein helles Licht, würdigt aber, wie mir scheint, nicht in zureichender Weise das störende Hineinspielen feindseliger Beweggründe und Beziehung in den einen wie den anderen Typus" ["clearly illuminates the opposition of communal versus societal existence, does not, however, in my opinion, sufficiently recognize the disruptive role of hostile motives and a hostile relationship in the one type or the other"].[29] The review ends with a rather cutting dismissal of Plessner's project:

> Ich gebe dem Verfasser beinahe in jedem Punkte recht, meine aber, daß der Aufwand an Geist und Gründen nicht ganz in gehörigem Verhältnisse steht zu der Absicht, den sozialen Radikalismus zu bestreiten. Anders, wenn diese Absicht ihm nur willkommene Gelegenheit gewesen ist, sein philosophisches, auch philosophisch-soziologisches Verständnis zu bekunden. Dies ist ihm allerdings gelungen.[30]

> I agree with almost all the points that the author makes, but I believe that the mental and argumentative effort is out of proportion with the intention to fight against social radicalism. It is a different matter if this endeavor was merely an opportunity for the author to demonstrate his philosophical and philosophical-sociological understanding. In this he was successful.

Tönnies begins his review by separating the text's critique of community from its critique of social radicalism, a separation that undermines a crucial connection in Plessner's work. He maintains that Plessner's take on the antagonism between community and society, while interesting, lacks a nuanced portrayal of the two sides. He concludes by stating that Plessner's intellect is wasted on a topic such as social radicalism. The beginning of the review and its ending are connected to one another—Plessner's work can be considered a misguided project only if one reads it solely as a fight against social radicalism. Tönnies's review inadvertently highlights the central role that Plessner's critique of community plays in *Grenzen der Gemeinschaft: Eine Kritik des sozialen Radikalismus.* The text's full title shows the relationship between community and social radicalism. Plessner is not, as Tönnies implies, using a critique of community as a way to attack social radicalism. Instead, Plessner demonstrates how social radicalism is made possible by certain pervading discourses of community that are detrimental to social stability.

Siegfried Kracauer's review reveals his own position within the discourses of community and society. Kracauer praises Plessner's critique of "Gemeinschaftsfanatiker" and agrees that an idealization of community can be harmful. According to Kracauer, Plessner promulgates the idea that society is a necessary component of community. Kracauer does, however, find it difficult to place any further importance on society. He writes of *Grenzen der Gemeinschaft:* "Zu wünschen wäre eine stärkere Betonung der Aussage gewesen, daß die Sphäre der Gesellschaft nur dann zu Recht besteht, wenn eine wirkliche Gemeinschaft sie aus sich hervortreibt, daß sie aber die Gemeinschaftskräfte erstickt, wenn sie Selbständigkeit sich anmaßt und keine Grenzen mehr findet" ["One wishes for a stronger emphasis on the statement that the sphere of society can justifiably exist only if it emerges from a true community. If society, however, claims independence and no longer recognizes limits, it suffocates the strengths of the community"].[31] Here Kracauer offers his interpretation—in the form of a critique of Plessner—of the relationship between society and community. As Kracauer sees it, society is a means to an end, and the goal is a true community. Without community, society has no relevance. Although he finds Plessner's critiques of the dangers of idealizing community valid, it is clear that Kracauer still sides more with community than with society. He does not fear the limits of community; rather, he fears the dangers of a limitless society.

Despite the attention the text received, in subsequent years it was largely neglected until it experienced a renaissance in the 1990s. At the center of this resurgence of interest was Helmuth Lethen's *Verhaltenslehren der*

Kälte: Lebensversuche zwischen Kriegen [*Cool Conduct: The Culture of Distance in Weimar Germany*] and the debates this text provoked.[32] *Verhaltenslehren der Kälte* places Plessner's *Grenzen der Gemeinschaft* in the context of New Objectivity and sees it as celebration of a "cold" stance of society and repudiation of the "warmness" of community and the solidarity and human closeness that it offers. Although the emphasis is different, Lethen, in his reading of Plessner, reinforces the community/society dichotomy seen in contemporary criticism of *Grenzen der Gemeinschaft.* Lethen's reading has frequently served as the point of entry into Plessner's text, and in the process it has also tended to obscure other possible interpretations. Lethen sees New Objectivity as the transition from a culture of guilt to a culture of shame, in which our actions are no longer driven by inner morality, but by external judgments; the surface becomes the most important thing. As a way to cope one takes on armor (*Panzer*) in the form of specific codes of behavior Lethen names "Verhaltenslehren der Kälte" [literally: "behavior codes of the cold," but I will use "cool conduct"]. Lethen sees in Plessner's text a rewriting of seventeenth-century courtly codes of conduct in the context of New Objectivity. More specifically, Lethen argues that Plessner takes the writings of the Jesuit Gracián and reads them in such a way as to justify a life without depth, a life in which morals are replaced by tactical rules. All that matters is the surface and the ways in which we present our surfaces.

Joachim Fischer's essay "Panzer oder Maske: 'Verhaltenslehre der Kälte' oder Sozialtheorie der 'Grenze'" ["Armor or Mask: 'Cool Conduct' or the Social Theory of the 'Limit'"] provides a critical reading of Lethen's work.[33] Since Lethen insists that his reading comes not from subtext but from the "Logik des Textes,"[34] Fischer does a careful close reading of *Grenzen der Gemeinschaft,* not only to argue against Lethen's interpretation (with the implicit argument that Lethen's reading has little grounding in the actual text), but also to open up the possibility for other readings and applications of Plessner's work.[35] Fischer agrees that *Grenzen der Gemeinschaft* should be seen in the context of German modernity, but rather than a celebration of New Objectivity, he reads Plessner's view of modernity as an "Epoche der Autonomisierungen von Zonen oder Momenten wie Geist oder Körper" ["era of autonomizing zones or moments such as spirit or body"] that could lead to new possibilities, but with a corresponding lack of a sense of wholeness for those who live in this world.[36] The similarities this idea shares with Benjamin's and Simmel's examinations of modernity as a negotiation of fragmentation support Fischer's view. All three of them, albeit with different emphases and outcomes, view notions of totality and unity as ideas that produce an illusion of wholeness that is detrimental to our understanding of the world and our place in it. Furthermore, this wholeness cannot be lost, because it never existed. According to Plessner, attempts to achieve wholeness drive certain kinds of radicalism. As Fischer is quick to point out, it is not that Plessner is against Gemeinschaft; rather, he is against certain radical ideologies carried out in the name of Gemeinschaft.

One of the key points Fischer makes is that Plessner uses not the word "Panzer" (armor) but the word "Maske" and that this choice is a significant one. Lethen's use of "Panzer" implies a hard, impenetrable surface, one that not only prevents anything from entering, but also does not let anything out. Central to Plessner's notion of a mask, however, is that it provides the distance necessary to allow us to express ourselves. Rather than hindering the ability to be anything but surface, as Lethen contends, Plessner's mask is the very thing that allows us to interact and express at least a part of our inner selves. Simmel uses a similar notion of masks in his discussion of individuals and Geselligkeit. Simmel describes the mask as providing "unpersönliche Freiheit" (impersonal freedom) and a situation in which a person (in this case a woman) "nur sie selbst, aber doch nicht ganz sie selbst ist, sondern nur ein Element in einer formal zusammengehaltenen Vereinigung" (SS, 181–82) ["(is) herself, to be sure, but not quite completely herself, since she is only an element in a formally constituted gathering" (SE, 131)]. He contends that masks allow us to be more ourselves in that we are not only ourselves, but also an element of society and the relationships that create it; we see a continuation of such ideas in Plessner's work. In what follows, I will expand on Fischer's work and examine Plessner's notions of society and community through close readings of the text. In addition, I will explore the importance of eccentric positionality, as discussed in Plessner's *Stufen des Organischen und der Mensch* (*Levels of the Organic and Man*), for understanding the relationship between the outsider, society, and community.

The main argument of Plessner's text is that Gemeinschaft and Gesellschaft are not antagonistic opposites. Instead, Gemeinschaft cannot exist without Gesellschaft. Plessner maps out his idea in spatial terms by transforming the duality of Gemeinschaft/Gesellschaft into a model of overlapping spheres—Sachgemeinschaft/Blutgemeinschaft/Gesellschaft (community of the ideal/community of blood/society). In a Blutgemeinschaft the essential link between the members is blood, not only in terms of biological relationships, but also in the communion of like-minded souls. Affect and emotion are essential, as is the knowledge that these souls keep no secrets from one another. In fact, it is this conscious openness that produces the emotional connections. At the center of a Blutgemeinschaft is the concept of love. Plessner's critique of Blutgemeinschaften begins with this notion of love. He makes the distinction between "Liebe" and "Liebesgesinnung" [disposition to love]; the former takes place on an individual level, whereas the latter is for more general concepts such as "Volk" (the people) or "Menschheit" (humanity). Liebe does not need to be returned, but it does need what Plessner refers to as a "Gegenpol" [opposite pole] or "Gegenbild" [counterpart] (PG, 46). In other words, love needs something specific as its object. When the object is a vague concept such as humanity, only Liebesgesinnung is possible. In times of crisis, such as war, Liebesgesinnung can become Liebe, but otherwise concepts such as nation or people are too abstract for love. In the relationship between Liebe and Liebesgesinnung lies a central problem for a Blutgemeinschaft: "Zu einem Ganzen wird die Liebesintention immer gehen können, zu allen Elementen dieses Ganzen dagegen niemals" (PG, 47). ["The intention to love can be directed to the social totality. It can not embrace, on the other hand, each individual comprising that totality" (PGE, 90).] According to Plessner, a Blutgemeinschaft demands both general and specific love simultaneously, but a love for the whole does not translate into a love for all the individual elements of the whole. As a result, such an attempt more often than not leads to sentimental affect rather than love. The limit of a Blutgemeinschaft has to do with distance and proximity: "Die Chance ihrer Verwirklichung nimmt mit der Wahrscheinlichkeit der Liebe, d.h. mit wachsender Distanz zu individueller Wirklichkeit ab" (PG, 47). ["The chance of its actualization decreases with the probability of love—with growing distance to individual reality" (PGE, 90).] For this reason Liebesgesinnung always focuses on one person who serves as a catalyst and mediator of immediacy and true love among the members. A Blutgemeinschaft, then, is necessarily an exclusive sphere of intimacy. The opposition thus becomes the public, which represents all the people and things that do not belong but must be confronted.

Then there is the "Sachgemeinschaft" [community of the ideal/rationality], an example of which is rational communism, which uses conviction as its binding element. In this paradigm, ethnic and national differences can be overcome through rational conviction. And if one could be convinced of the "überpersönliche Sachzentrum des Wertgehalts" [central ideal of values that transcends the personal], then a borderless Gemeinschaft would be possible (PG, 51). In a Sachgemeinschaft there is reason instead of love, "Urbilder und Richtlinien aller Menschlichkeit" [archetypes and guiding principles for all of humanity] instead of a leader. The three central characteristics of a Sachgemeinschaft are (1) its impersonal nature (the Gemeinschaft is built on the "überindividuellem Geist" [a spirit that transcends the individual] rather than the "persönlichem Seinskern" [personal core being]); (2) unlimited expansion capabilities; and (3) "Arbeitscharakter" (the goal of the Gemeinschaft is to solve difficulties and strive toward absolute equality for all) (PG, 52). According to Plessner there are no better symbols of Sachgemeinschaft than the impersonal machines and machine-thinking of the industrial proletariat. In such a community, universal conformity is equated with rational efficiency. Plessner takes this idea one step further and claims that the relationship between socialist-communism and science is not only historical, but essential to socialist-communism.

The limit of a Sachgemeinschaft is the reality of individual life. Such a model lacks influence on one's everyday experiences. It is impossible to follow such principles all the time, since it would require knowing what exactly these principles are and also giving every decision equal consideration: "Ob ich den Schirm mitnehmen oder zu Hause lassen soll, ist niemals eine Angelegenheit, die gleichen Aufwand an Ernst lohnt wie er etwa der Frage zukommt, was ein Mensch für einen Beruf wählen soll" (PG, 54). ["Whether I should take my umbrella or leave it at home is never a matter of concern that deserves the same serious expenditure of effort as the question of what kind of profession a person should choose" (PGE, 97).] The mind is the place in which true conviction is formed. The difficulty is, however, that the mind is itself without end or borders, which makes it impossible for one to confine oneself within the principles of this conviction. Furthermore, for a Sachgemeinschaft to function, mind and body would have to act as one. But the mind and the body are not one, and the mind is incapable of completely dictating what the body should do. Thus there is a constant negotiation between the needs of the two, and unified actions are not often possible. The limit of a Blutgemeinschaft, then, is the necessity of a public, and that of a Sachgemeinschaft is the discrepancy between body and mind (PG, 55). Without a public there would be no intimacy; there would be no sense of a "Vertrautheitssphäre" [sphere of intimacy/familiarity] without a "Nichtvertrautheitssphäre" [sphere without intimacy/familarity].[37] And a Sachgemeinschaft can handle neither the irrationality of love nor the fragmented character of our existence.

Plessner's explanation of the relationship between Blutgemeinschaft, Sachgemeinschaft, and Gesellschaft is somewhat cryptic:

> Der Mensch muß, um sich zu vollenden und mit eigenen Mitteln aus der Verzweiflung seiner Innerlichkeit sich zu erlösen, von der Sphäre der Lebensgemeinschaft in die der Gesellschaft übergehen,

> um schließlich in der Sphäre der Sachgemeinschaft des Geistes und der Kultur die definitive Ruhe seines Selbstbehauptungsdranges zu finden. Freilich die meisten finden sie nicht und sehen sich einer dauernden Oszillation zwischen diesen drei Sphären überantwortet, wenn sie schließlich nicht aus der Summe und Art ihrer Erfolge und Mißerfolge ihre Begabung erkannt haben und in irgendeinem Dienst sich zu ihrem Sinn bescheiden. (PG, 92)

> To perfect and, through one's own efforts, rescue oneself from the despair of one's interiority, the person must move from the sphere of a life-based community to the sphere of society [*Gesellschaft*]; and, finally, he must move to the sphere of the ideal-based community of spirit and culture to find the definitive rest from his force to self-assertion. To be sure, most people do not find such peace and see themselves placed in a permanent oscillation between these three spheres, if they do not recognize their talents out of the sum and type of their successes and failures and commit themselves to some type of service in accordance with their abilities. (PGE, 144)

The description begins with a linear movement from Lebensgemeinschaft (another name for Blutgemeinschaft) into Gesellschaft and then into Sachgemeinschaft, only to then undermine it by bringing in the notion of oscillation. At first Plessner seems to describe the movements between the three spheres as one of a progression—the goal is to reach the peace of the Sachgemeinschaft, in which the individual's desires are stilled. Then he states that such a progression is nearly impossible: since most individuals are not self-aware enough to reach a stage where they understand the nature of their talents, they live in a state of oscillation that allows them to use those talents to the extent that they are aware of them. Although it may appear that Plessner is criticizing the state of oscillation as one of failure, in the context of the rest of the text and his other writings one sees that this is not the case. Rather than a failure, this fluctuation is a necessity, since this state is the only way to negotiate the conflicting and equally important desires that define our social interactions. Plessner emphasizes, as does Simmel, the dynamic nature of human relationships and the position of the individual. In both cases, this dynamic nature is rooted in an understanding of the individual as a being that is never complete.[38]

An example of our competing desires, as represented by the three spheres of community and society, is our attempt to connect to other people. We want an unmediated connection to another person. Acting according to this desire alone is not without its dangers; every naked expression of our psyche in public risks seeming ridiculous. When feelings or other psychic phenomena are expressed, they lose much of their weight, and others cannot empathize to the extent that would be necessary to understand the other person. What is needed is a "*Bekleidung mit Form,* damit es das auch an der Oberfläche bleibt, was es, in seiner unsichtbaren Tiefe genommen, ist" (PG, 72) [. . . it needs to be *clothed with form* so that it also remains on the surface what it is in its invisible depths (PGE, 119)]. The lack of this clothing is why heartfelt expressions often seem kitschy. The exception is simple expressions, such as the words of a child, but they are successful because nothing is lost in the communication with others; the sense of immediacy stems from the speaker's complete vulnerability. Only those aspects of the psyche over which we have some control run the risk of being ridiculous, but we cannot be vulnerable all the time because that would require a simplicity and lack of intention that we cannot maintain.

Why bother to express oneself at all, then? Because there is the possibility that others can experience what one has experienced and tries to express, and this possibility is a powerful motivation. Part of the difficulty in reaching other people is the relationship between the body and the soul. The body simultaneously expresses too much and too little of the soul:

> . . . woran wir nicht erinnert sein noch andere erinnern wollen, steht auf unseren Gesichtern mit dem Meißel der Natur verzeichnet, was aber nach unserem Willen sichtbar werden soll, muß sich mühsam ans Licht hervorkämpfen und die Gefahren der Wirkung auf andere bestehen . . . Eine derartige wesenhafte Unvereinbarkeit in der Einheit einer Person vereint zu sehen, hat etwas Lächerliches an sich. (PG, 74–75)

> . . . what we do not remember nor want others to remember is engraved on our faces with the chisel of nature. What should become visible according to our intention must, however, struggle with great effort into the light and withstand the danger of exposure to others . . . To see unified in the unity of a person what essentially can not be unified contains something of the ridiculous about it. (PGE, 122)

We are all to some extent caricatures of ourselves because of our limited control of how we are seen by others.

Plessner's use of the word "spirit" (*Seele*) in this passage is not to be read in the same way as it is used in the ternary structure of body, spirit, and mind. In the example above, the spirit represents internal desires, an inner self, and one's "true" personality, a combination of characteristics defined by nature and individual idiosyncrasies. The conflict described can be seen as existing within the realm of Blutgemeinschaft—it is the conflict between the desire to share emotions and connect with others, but at the same time not lose control over that expression. In this conflict one sees the impossibility of living according to the tenets of Blutgemeinschaft; the vulnerability and lack of reflection necessary are unattainable. Plessner places these concerns within the realm of society, in this case with the concept of "Würde" [dignity] in order to show us that this conflict is not one between two mutually exclusive desires, but rather one that requires constant negotiation and compromise.

Plessner emphasizes that the synonymous terms are not "Würde" and "Ehre" [honor], but "Würde" and "Harmonie." When someone finds us ridiculous, it hurts our sense of Würde because it reminds us of our failure to represent ourselves as a harmonious whole.[39] The realm of Würde is that of Gesellschaft; although it is nearly impossible to maintain a sense of wholeness in our interactions with others if we seek it exclusively within either a Blutgemeinschaft or a Sachgemeinschaft, Gesellschaft allows us to represent ourselves in an unreal space in which we are not required to show all of ourselves. We can therefore communicate and attempt to connect with others, but at the same time we are protected from exposing too much of ourselves and revealing our lack of wholeness.

Plessner calls the principle that guides us through our interactions with others "das Ethos der Grazie" [the ethos of grace] (PG, 80). This ethos is about a flexible balance, and its realm is that of the everyday. Grace is necessary because it guides us in society, which in this case is described as the traffic of everyday life in which we interact with many people who, whether due to lack of opportunities, time, or interest, remain at most acquaintances.[40] Plessner, like Simmel, uses the language of a game[41] to describe the ethos and defines it in the following manner:

> . . . die virtuose Handhabung der Spielformen, mit denen sich die Menschen nahe kommen, ohne sich zu treffen, mit denen sie sich voneinander entfernen, ohne sich durch Gleichgültigkeit zu verletzen. Die Liebenswürdigkeit ist ihre Atmosphäre, nicht die Eindringlichkeit; das Spiel und die Beobachtung seiner Regeln, nicht der Ernst ist ihr Sittengesetz. (PG, 80)

> . . . the virtuous mastery of forms of play where persons come close to each other without meeting and where they establish distance

> without damaging each other through indifference; amiability and not insistence is the atmosphere of this ethos of grace—its ethical law is the game and its observation, not seriousness. (PGE, 131)

With this ethos, forced "Ferne" becomes "Distanz," and "Indifferenz, Kälte und Roheit" [indifference, coldness, and rudeness] become "Höflichkeit, Ehrerbietung und Aufmerksamkeit" [politeness, reverence, and attentiveness] (PG, 80). There are clear similarities between Plessner's idea of grace and Simmel's notion of tact. Both provide a way for individuals to interact while achieving a balance between too personal and too impersonal, and to connect while respecting necessary boundaries that protect the group as a whole as well as the individuals involved in the interaction.

What is at stake here is mutual attention and respect. The reason this goal is so difficult to achieve is once again the opposition between soul and body—we want to be seen as little as possible, but we also want to be recognized. Another contributing factor is the pace of modern life, which does not allow individuals the attention they need.[42] Roles/masks are necessary to gain recognition but at the same time protect the self, since one receives the recognition not as an individual but rather in a specific role. This solution does not fully satisfy the need to be respected and understood as a unique individual, but it serves as a compromise because the individual does not completely disappear underneath his or her mask.

These roles must be must be removed from fundamental human necessities and physical reality because it is only through this level of abstraction that we can gain the proper amount of distance that is neither too far nor too close. When we respect the roles and forms, and also the distance they provide, we gain "Spielregeln," or game rules (again the game metaphor), and these allow us to "play" our roles; too little distance or "nackte Ehrlichkeit" [naked honesty] is "Spielverderberei" [being a spoilsport] (PG, 83). Simmel makes a similar argument about the realm of Geselligkeit. The rules both control interactions and create a space that is connected to our everyday reality but also somewhat removed from it. For both Plessner and Simmel artifice is a necessary component of this space.

Plessner sees a readiness to give up all progress in the name of Gemeinschaft, a readiness he finds self-destructive. What proponents of Gemeinschaft seem to ignore is that a true Gemeinschaft needs a leader/master in order to function because he is the link that allows for immediacy (PG, 43). Furthermore, Gemeinschaft requires an enemy, and every group that supports Gemeinschaft has a different idea of who the enemy is: "Seine Gesellschaftsfeindschaft spricht jeder von ihnen anders aus und orientiert sie nach anderen Zielen" (PG, 44). ["Each describes their animosity to the societal life order differently; each orients himself according to different objectives" (PGE, 86).] Those who support Gesellschaft (who are already small in number) have difficulties developing a rhetoric that combats these different orientations. According to Plessner, the notion that the distance Gesellschaft provides is not dehumanizing and a disintegration of human relationships is crucial to an argument for Gesellschaft. Distance is necessary in order to allow us to be individuals and also live in harmony with one another. Gemeinschaft is a dangerous ideal not only because such closeness and belonging to one another are impossible, but also because striving for it often leads to a radicalism that disrupts social order and makes it even less possible to be an individual.

One of the key differences between the orientations toward Gemeinschaft and Gesellschaft is the relationship to technology and artifice. Neither a community nor a society can function without these things, but those who are in favor of community see them as a necessary evil, only to be tolerated:

> Darum bleibt eine vorherrschend gemeinschaftlich sich empfindende Sozialordnung beispielsweise auf der Stufe der Werkzeugtechnik, da das Handwerk die größtmögliche Persönlichkeitsnähe und Beseelungsfähigkeit besitzt. Was hier der Tendenz nach zur Aufhebung der Künstlichkeit und Lebensfremdheit, des Unpersönlichen im ausgesprochenen Sinn, führt, macht den Reiz und das wahre innere Wesen, das Ethos der Gemeinschaft aus. (PG, 40)

> That is why a social structure that experiences itself predominately as a communal one remains, for example, at the level of tool technology, for the hand tool possesses the greatest possible closeness to one's personality and to the capability of animating life. What here leads to the tendency to abolish artificiality and interpersonal distance—the impersonal in an explicit sense—constitutes the stimulus and inner being, the ethos of community. (PGE, 80)

Those who share this "Ethos der Gemeinschaft" see artifice as something that leads to undesirable distance between individuals, something that should be kept at the absolute minimum necessary for the group to function. Those in favor of society seek the qualities that result from artifice: "Zum Grundcharakter des Gesellschaftsethos gehört hingegen die Sehnsucht nach den Masken, hinter denen die Unmittelbarkeit verschwindet. Die Gesellschaft gibt den bloßen Handgriffen und Hilfsmitteln notdürftigen Lebens über ihre Zweckmäßigkeit hinaus einen neuen Sinn . . ." (PG, 41).

["On the other hand, belonging to the basic character of the societal ethos is a longing for the mask behind which all immediacy disappears. Society (*Gesellschaft*) gives new meaning beyond mere utility to the chores and tasks necessary for life . . ." (PGE, 80).] Plessner is not proposing that everyone should be for society and against community, but by showing the limits of the ideals of community and the possibilities of society, Plessner argues against an ideology that claims community as the "ausschließlich menschenwürdige Form des Zusammenlebens" (PG, 41) ["exclusively human and dignified form of social life" (PGE, 81)].

The masks we wear around each other are not ways to hide our true selves; they are the only possibility we have to express ourselves. Plessner does not see the restrictions that society provides as a sacrifice of our ability to act according to our own will for the sake of the greater good, that is, social order and stability. In other words, society does not repress our "natural" desires and actions. The distance itself is a "natural" need that all humans share. In Plessner's model everyone is estranged from one another, but this state is not one that should be lamented, nor is there any room in Plessner's text for a nostalgic look at a time in which an unmediated relationship between individuals existed.

In a Gemeinschaft, individuality is given up for belonging, and differences are forgotten for the sake of what is common and in order to see others as equals in what Plessner calls the "Ethos der absoluten Rückhaltlosigkeit" [ethos of absolute transparency] (PG, 58). Of course, in reality this condition is never fulfilled. The reason is, as both Benjamin and Simmel also emphasize, that man is fundamentally "eternal potentiality": "Als geistig-seelische Wesen haben sie das ungeheuere Bewußtsein, selbst von den Bahnen ihres individuellen Gesetzes abweichen zu können oder wenigstens des Rechtes, sich gegen seine Definition aufzulehnen" (PG, 59). ["As a being of spirit and soul, humans have the enormous consciousness of the ability to deviate from the path of their own individual law, or, at least, the right to rebel against their own definitions" (PGE, 105).] Man is always more than he is because our soul is potential itself: "Denn sie [die Seele] ist mehr als diese geformte Wesenheit, sie ist der Urquell dazu, der Urgrund von Fähigkeiten, die Gestalt werden könnten, ohne Gestalt zu werden" [Because it (the soul) is more than a formed being, it is the source of this being, the primordial ground for abilities that *could* become shape without becoming shape] (PG, 59). Because the soul is always more than it is, there is no tie so strong that it cannot collapse.[43] Thus increased sensibility, civilization, and modernization do not cause one's need for distance and individuality; rather, this need results from the potential of one's soul and the impact this potential has on one's life.

One could argue that this drive toward individuality and egotism results from the needs of the body rather than, as Plessner claims, the spirit. In this line of thought, community appeals to one's spirit, thus the friction caused by these physical needs is curbed, creating harmony and avoiding war. Without this awakening of a conscience and the resulting social behavior, man would cause his own destruction in his bodily striving for power and dominance. The result of this line of thinking is, according to Plessner, "ein Asketismus aus Sozialfreundlichkeit, eine Lobpreisung der Armut und Schwäche, wie diese Ideale vom Urchristentum verfochten wurden und vom salutistischen Sozialismus und Kommunismus noch verfochten werden" (PG, 61) ["asceticism emerging from a socially friendly attitude, a praising of poverty and weakness, as this ideal was defended by primitive Christianity and still is by salutary socialism and communism" (PGE, 107)]. Plessner does not find this separation of body and spirit and their desires convincing. Instead he believes that both the fight for independent existence and the need for help from others come from the physiological makeup of all living beings and therefore that the same is also true for humans. Individualization comes from the consciousness that we have a spirit. Society exists to allow the needs of the body and soul to coexist through constant negotiation and compromise, rather than to suppress the one for the sake of the other.

Plessner's critique of psychology highlights the importance of the spirit's potential. According to Plessner, the problem with psychology is that it is grounded in the incorrect assumption that the physical is the only real and that the real is unambiguous and definable. Such a worldview does not allow for an understanding of the spirit and its ambiguity. Yet it is important to understand this ambiguity in order to better understand our relationship to others. The source of the ambiguity is that the spirit is simultaneously becoming and being (*Werden* and *Sein*). As a result the spirit[44] cannot be defined, yet because of this inability it needs definition or outside recognition. And if we define it and give it a concrete form, we lose the potential to be different—we are misunderstood even when we are understood: "Wir wollen uns sehen und gesehen werden, wie wir sind, und wir wollen ebenso uns verhüllen und ungekannt bleiben, denn hinter jeder Bestimmtheit unseres Seins schlummern die unsagbaren Möglichkeiten des Andersseins" [We want to see ourselves and be seen as we are, and in equal measure we want to hide ourselves and remain unrecognized. For underneath every certainty about our existences slumber the unutterable possibilities of alternative existences] (PG, 63). Of course, a certain amount of repression with regard to such considerations is unavoidable if we are to live our everyday lives, therefore a subconscious is vital to our existence. The less we think about our actions, the easier it is to make decisions and lead our life. And yet we cannot live without contemplating our actions and their potential consequences.

The Eccentric Positionality of Man

Throughout *Grenzen der Gemeinschaft,* Plessner works against the framework of binary oppositions. He breaks up the opposition Gemeinschaft/Gesellschaft by introducing the ternary structure Blutgemeinschaft/Gesellschaft/Sachgemeinschaft. He questions the divide between body and spirit by showing how the two interact within the realm of society. At the center of Plessner's argument against these oppositions is an argument against the dichotomy of interior truth and exterior reality. Plessner writes: "Mit seltsamer Logik führen die verschiedensten Richtungen der neueren Kultur auf die Entgegensetzung und Verfeindung von Innerlichkeit und Wirklichkeit, im großen von Gottesreich und Staatsmacht, in den Elementen von Seele und Körper" (PG, 23). ["With a strange logic, the different directions of the new culture lead to the opposition and estrangement between interiority and reality—writ large, between the kingdom of God and the domain of political power, writ small, in the elements of soul and the objectual body" (PGE, 58).] The notion that interior and exterior exist in an antagonistic relationship is, according to Plessner, a misunderstanding of the human condition. This argument is more fully developed in Plessner's *Stufen des Organischen und der Mensch: Einleitung in die philosophische Anthropologie.* In the chapter on the place of man titled "Die Sphäre des Menschen" Plessner explores the eccentric positionality of man as a way to rethink the individual's relationship to his environment. Even more so than in *Grenzen der Gemeinschaft,* one sees in this text that Plessner is working against a reading of subjectivity and objectivity that tends to privilege an originary unmediated existence that modernity has supposedly made impossible. He addresses this topic by looking at the subject/object relationship as it pertains to our position in the world. Plessner posits that the position of man is the position of eccentricity, of being outside the center—we never just are. Our relationship to the world and to each other is one of constant mediation. Rather than looking at the eccentric position as one that estranges us from ourselves and others, Plessner argues that it is what makes us human.

Our relationship to time plays a key role in understanding man's eccentric existence. According to Plessner, animals, unlike man, live in the "here-now," and as a result are not aware of their own position: "Das

Tier lebt aus seiner Mitte heraus, in seine Mitte hinein, aber es lebt nicht als Mitte" [The animal lives from its center and toward its center, but it does not live as center] (PS, 360). An animal experiences life in the present, without an awareness of the concepts of future, past, or present. As such, an animal cannot experience itself; it cannot live "as center." To be able to reflect, to be able to experience oneself as an individual, one must be able to step outside oneself, and according to Plessner, this ability remains exclusive to humans. Yet animals, because of this ability to exist in the "here-now," live an unmediated existence, something that is impossible for humans.[45] Plessner explores the impact our inability to live in an unmediated "now" has on our lives and our sense of self, and comes to the conclusion that action plays a central role in understanding this question. Plessner writes: "Als exzentrisch organisiertes Wesen muß er sich zu dem, was er *schon ist, erst machen* . . . Der Mensch lebt nur, indem er ein Leben führt" [As an eccentrically organized being man must *first create* what he *already is* . . . Man only lives by conducting/leading his life] (PS, 383–84). Because there is no a priori interiority, because our understanding of ourselves is mediated by our awareness of ourselves, we exist only through active participation in our own lives. Our interior and exterior selves are not competing with each other; our interior selves exist because of the actions of our external selves:

> Weil dem Menschen durch seinen Existenztyp aufgezwungen ist, das Leben zu führen, welches er lebt, d.h. zu machen, was er ist—eben weil er nur ist, wenn er vollzieht—braucht er ein Komplement nichtnatürlicher, nichtgewachsener Art. Darum ist er von Natur, aus Gründen seiner Existenzform *künstlich*. (PS, 384–85)

> Man's character forces him to conduct the life he lives, in other words to create what he is, because man only exists when he is actualizing. For this reason he needs a complement that is non-natural and non-organic. Thus he is by his very nature, because of the form of his existence, *artificial*.

This notion that man is by nature a construct fits in with Plessner's discussion of society and the ways in which we use masks and other social conventions to find a balance between our various needs and desires and create a place for ourselves in the world. This place is not something that is found or that one is born into; rather, it is constantly being created.

"Erfindung heißt auch Umsetzung aus der Möglichkeit in die Wirklichkeit . . . Der schöpferische Griff ist eine *Ausdrucks*leistung. Dadurch erhält der realisierende Akt, der sich auf die von der Natur dargebotenen Materialien stützen muß, den Charakter der Künstlichkeit" [Invention also means converting from possibility into reality . . . The reach to create is an effort to *express*. Thus the act of actualization, which must be supported by materials provided by nature, takes on the character of artifice] (PS, 397–98). That is to say, we shape the reality around us by giving form to materials that we did not create ourselves; our creations must conform to the facts of a reality outside our control. In this manner Plessner provides a way to balance the existence of an objective material reality with man-made artifice in a way that necessitates interactions between the two, rather than a model in which the two compete with one another. Plessner sees the a priori existence of the "Zwang zum Ausdruck" [need for expression] and comes to the conclusion that "der Mensch zum geselligen Leben geboren [ist]" [man is born for a sociable life] (PS, 399). We need to express ourselves; it is part of our fundamental existence. Expression requires artifice and therefore, according to this logic, artifice is also an essential part of what makes us human. And all of this has to do with the eccentric position, with our awareness of ourselves.

The outside reality and the form in which it is realized, however, are both tied to a particular historical moment: "Nicht die Ausdrucksform kann a priori sein, ebensowenig wie es der Inhalt ist, sondern allein die (nur anhand exzeptioneller Beispiele bloßgelegte!) Art und Weise, wie *zu* einem Inhalt seine 'Form' gefunden wird" [The form of expression cannot be a priori, much less the content; instead, it is only the manner (which is solely exposed in exceptional cases!) by which the 'form' for a content is found] (PS, 398). Since only the process through which content is given a form has an a priori existence, the particular form given to a content is not predetermined, thus man's contribution to the process is vital:

> Denn er selbst, das Subjekt, welches hinter (über) sich steht, *bildet* die Vermittlung zwischen sich und dem Objekt, damit er von dem Objekt weiß. Genauer: Das Wissen vom Objekt ist die Vermittlung zwischen sich und ihm. So tilgt die Vermittlung im Vollzug ihn, den Menschen, als das hinter sich stehende vermittelnde Subjekt, es vergißt sich (*er* vergißt sich nicht!)—und die naive Direktheit mit der ganzen Evidenz, die Sache an sich gepackt zu haben, kommt zustande. (PS, 404)

> For he himself, the subject, who stands behind (above) himself, *forms* the mediation between himself and the object so that he has knowledge of the object. More precisely: The knowledge of the

> object is the mediation between oneself and it. Thus carrying out the mediation effaces him, the person, as the mediating subject that stands behind him. The subject forgets itself (*he* does not forget himself!)—and the naive directness comes into existence, with all its evidence of having clutched the thing to itself.

One builds the relationship between oneself and an object, and that process is how one knows about the object at all: the mediating subject, which is oneself, disappears and the object appears to exist for itself, independently of the mediation, thus a relationship that is experienced as unmediated is produced. Although Plessner argues against the existence of immediacy, he does not dismiss the importance of a *sense* of immediacy and the corresponding feelings of warmth and intimacy. In his writings about society and community, these feelings and experiences are allowed room through the existence of a Blutgemeinschaft. In *Die Stufen des Organischen und der Mensch,* these sentiments are expressed in the notion of mediated immediacy. According to Plessner, all living things share this structure of mediated immediacy. With this assertion, Plessner complicates the notion of immediacy in "simpler" beings such as animals. In animals, the relationship to the outside world is mediated through the animal itself, but since it is not aware of this mediation (just as it is not aware of itself as a self), the interactions are experienced as unmediated. Plessner says of animals: "Es steht im Punkte der Vermittlung und bildet sie. Um von ihr etwas zu merken, müßte es daneben stehen, ohne doch seine vermittelnde Zentralität zu verlieren" [It stands in the point of mediation and forms it. In order to notice something about the mediation, it would have to stand next to the point, but without losing its mediating centrality] (PS, 401). Plessner claims that animals have relationships that are mediated but experienced as unmediated because animals just are; they occupy their positions without self-awareness, and it is only with self-awareness that one can recognize mediation. That is to say, there is no "primitive" unmediated existence in animals—their relationships are mediated like those of humans; the difference lies in the ability to be aware of this mediation. Insofar as humans occupy the position that they create, they also experience this mediated immediacy. Yet they are also outside this position because they are aware of it, which means that one simultaneously occupies and is outside this position. Existing within the position and existing outside it are not, however, mutually exclusive, and consciousness is the key to how these two forms of experience coexist. Since humans are conscious of themselves and their interactions with others, they create relationships. Yet at the same time, they also occupy the position from which they have these interactions; they are aware of themselves, but as themselves: "Infolgedessen ist der Mensch 'sich selber' nicht mehr verborgen, er weiß von ihm, daß er mit ihm, welcher weiß, identisch ist" [As a result man is no longer hidden "from himself"; what he knows about himself is that he is identical with the him who knows] (PS, 401). This simultaneous occupation of a position and awareness of ourselves in it leads to a complicated relationship with the outside world. We do not create the world outside of us, but we can only interact with it through our own consciousness.

Plessner claims that in the act of appearing in relation to the subject, an object reveals what is not revealed because an object represented is never completely the object, but at the same time it is the only way we can understand it. "Ein Wirkliches kann *als* Wirkliches gar nicht anders mit einem Subjekt in Relation sein, es sei denn von sich aus als das dem Subjekt Entgegengeworfene, als Objekt, d.h. als Er-scheinung, Manifestation von . . .: als vermittelte Unmittelbarkeit. Sonst verliert sich der Wirklichkeitscharakter, die Objektivität, wie es auch für das Tier der Fall ist" [Something real, *as* a real thing, cannot be positioned in relation to a subject in any other way than as something that emerges from itself in opposition to the subject, as object, i.e., as appearance, manifestation of, etc.: as mediated immediacy. Otherwise the quality of realness is lost, the objectivity, as is the case for the animal] (PS, 405, ellipsis and italics in original). Objectivity is tied to an awareness of oneself as subject, and the outside world as object mediated by that subject, something that can only be accomplished by an eccentric position, which is why for animals objectivity does not exist. Yet the eccentric position allows one to see that what is perceived as unmediated is in fact mediated, since the eccentric position allows for self-reflection. This awareness of mediation introduces potential instability into the relationship between man and the world around him because in that moment of awareness, doubt creeps in about the validity of this mediated understanding of the world. Without a belief in an objective reality separate from a subjective experience, reality itself is questioned. "Darum kommt es notwendig zu diesem Schein der Unmittelbarkeit, von dessen Haltlosigkeit uns die Reflexion überzeugt" [Thus it necessarily results in this appearance of immediacy, of whose instability reflection convinces us] (PS, 406). Plessner insists that to understand how we interact with the world, we must find a model that allows these two impulses to coexist. Man simultaneously creates and exists in the position from which he interacts with others, therefore his relationship to others is indirect or mediated but is experienced as direct and unmediated, because otherwise these interactions would not have the authenticity of objectivity to make them believable. A balance must exist between the position and our awareness of the position, of subjectivity and a belief in objectivity, in order for us to function and interact with the world around us.

There are similarities between Plessner's notion of the eccentric position and Simmel's work on the city. Simmel focuses more on how we react to the conditions of the city, but he states that the external conditions and reactions shape our inner selves. He does, however, contrast the city life with that of the country, allowing for the possibility of a life that is closer to the model of one rooted in family, community, and the land. Even in the country the external and internal are linked, but relationships in the country are different from those in the city, and the advantages of the city in terms of individual freedom are at the price of a certain warmth, stability, and security. Plessner does not provide an alternative to the constructed existence he maps out, just as he does not connect his description with a particular place or mode of existence. Through this lack of specificity, Plessner emphasizes the universal nature of the eccentric position and its impact on the individual and his social interactions. In his exploration of Geselligkeit, Simmel takes a similar approach by emphasizing human interactions and their necessarily artificial qualities. But the most important similarity between Simmel and Plessner in this context is the notion of continuity. Artifice is not a modern phenomenon; it does not mark a break from a previous natural existence. Instead, it is a fundamental characteristic of humans and their interactions with others. Even though Simmel claims that urban life has changed aspects of everyday life, he maps the urban experience onto a universal and timeless narrative of the individual's struggle to define himself. Modernity in these texts is an experience not of break and loss, but rather of continuity and promise.

Plessner further undermines the concept of a "natural" and unmediated community in his redefinition of homelessness. He states that man is by definition homeless, even when that does not seem to be the case:

> Wohl hat es Zeiten gegeben (und wird auch wieder Zeiten geben), die nicht davon sprachen und in denen das Bewußtsein der konstitutiven Heimatlosigkeit des menschlichen Wesens durch starke Bindungen an Scholle und Familie, an Haus und Ahnen überdeckt war. Aber auch sie hatten keinen Frieden, es sei denn, sie suchten ihn. (PS, 383)

> There have certainly been times (and there will again be times) that did not speak of it and during which the consciousness of the constitutive homelessness of human existence was hidden by strong ties

> to the soil and to family, to a house and ancestors. But even these times did not have peace unless they sought it out.

A sense of belonging, whether through the land or family, does not erase the homeless state; one is merely less aware of one's intrinsic homelessness. This sense of home does not in and of itself create peace and satisfaction. Such feelings exist because we seek them out and thus they are created by our desire for them; they are not to be "found" in a family or in our ties to a place. This understanding of homelessness fits well with Plessner's arguments about the dangers of a community based on notions of "natural" bonds. At the same time, Plessner once again is careful not to dismiss notions of belonging; he notes that homelessness and feelings of belonging are not mutually exclusive. Instead, he insists that these important feelings are of our own making rather than belonging to something to which we must subjugate ourselves.

The themes of *Heimat* and *Heimatlosigkeit* also appear in *Grenzen der Gemeinschaft*. There Plessner writes against a neo-Platonian view of the world in which our bodies lead isolated and lonely existences while our spirits exist on a plane of harmony and Gemeinschaft (PG, 24). He describes the concept of return and renewal that often results from the belief in such a division:

> . . . die beständigen Anreizungen zur Erneuerung der Gesellschaft, die Revolutionen, in denen die kräftig gewordene Tiefenschicht eines Volkes das Bestehende nicht nur stürzen will, um sich selbst an die Macht zu bringen, eine universalhistorische Selbstverständlichkeit, sondern um den Menschen aus seinen Wurzeln, die ihn mit seiner wahren Heimat, mit dem unsichtbaren Geisterreich zu verbinden, zu erneuern. (PG, 25)

> . . . the constant incitements to renew society, the revolutions in which the lower stratum of the people, who have grown powerful, do not want to destroy the status quo in order to come into power—a universally understandable motive—but rather to rejuvenate man from his roots, roots that connect him to his true home, to the invisible realm of the spirits.

The passage continues with an attack on Rousseau, who serves as exemplary of such a position: "Großes ist von ihm ausgegangen, aber etwas Furchtbares hat sich durch seine Lehren in den Köpfen verfestigt, der Glaube an die Erneuerungsmöglichkeit des Menschen durch bewußten

Rückgang auf die Quellen der menschlichen Natur" (PG, 25). ["He has given rise to great things; but, something terrible has lodged itself in the head through his teaching, namely, the belief in the possibility of being able to renew mankind through a conscious return to the sources of human nature" (PGE, 60).] A desire for renewal through return presupposes a previous existence in which we transcended the separation that our physical bodies now cause. It also implies that the way we live now is something to be fought against, that we have been separated from our "true home" and are alienated from nature. Plessner's argument against this stance is that we always were and always will be homeless and the state to which people like Rousseau's followers wish to return never did exist and never will.

In regard to the notion of homelessness, Plessner and Kracauer stand in opposing camps. Although they agree that it is the state in which the modern individual finds himself, they differ in their opinion about the "naturalness" of this condition. Kracauer sees the urban and modern individual's life as one of loss—we once lived in a world of unmediated relationships with one another but are now isolated atoms that cannot connect. He describes modernity as a new artificial state. According to Kracauer, we are homeless and will remain so because we are unaware of our artificial existence. Kracauer represents the neo-Rousseauian rhetoric that Plessner strives against. Seen in relation to each other, however, nuances from both are foregrounded and complicate this reading of their works. Kracauer despises society and its alienation, but privileges the outsider position that allows him to recognize how meaningless life in a society is. This position is created within modernity, thus showing the possibility of being an individual who does not live unaware of his artificial surroundings. Yet Kracauer then uses this position to criticize the conditions that made it possible. When brought together with Kracauer's writings, the aspects of Gemeinschaft in Plessner's writings are foregrounded. One sees that although Plessner argues for the necessity of artifice and society, he sees it as a way to protect the aspects of community that we also need. He speaks of masks as a way to protect our inner selves, and in his belief in sovereign individuals one sees that his views are not as far removed from Kracauer's as may first appear to be the case. Where the two differ is in their opinion of whether or not an individual can exist within a modern urban environment. There Simmel treads the middle ground between Kracauer and Plessner—he sees the big city as a place of unequaled possibility, but he is also aware of the sacrifices that are necessary and the dangers of losing oneself in the attempt to assert one's individuality.

Kracauer's Detective: The Fiction of Strangers

In works such as the collection of essays *Denken durch die Dinge: Siegfried Kracauer im Kontext,* there is a tendency to see Kracauer's work as a progression from a mourning of a lost whole to an embracing of the individual and fluidity. I agree that both of these elements exist in Kracauer's earlier writings, but rather than seeing them in conflict with one another, I see them both as crucial elements of his views on modernity. Nostalgia and loss are not the antithesis of Kracauer's modernity, but an important component thereof. Rather than standing in opposition to the freedom and independence that modernity offers, these qualities help form the underpinnings of the modern outsider. Seeing them in this light, we gain a better understanding of the relationship between the outsider's position and notions of a transcendental and timeless truth. As Caren Kaplan has shown in her exploration of the relationship between modernism and postmodernism, the maintaining of a strict division hides the continuities between these two traditions.[46] In a similar way, insisting that modernism was a clear break from what came before it is a misrepresentation of the ways in which romantic discourses of the stranger and the concept of a transcendental mysterious truth interact with discourses of modernity. Furthermore, focusing on those aspects of Kracauer that celebrate the individual and a more fragmentary existence can be seen as an attempt to present Kracauer and his writings as more "modern," which in this context means a view of modernity that is more in keeping with postmodern sensibilities. Thus if we insist on a clean break between discourses of romanticism and modernity, the lines between modernity and postmodernism blur, contributing to an uprooting of discourses of modernity from their sociohistorical context.

In her essay "Vielschichtige Oberflächen: Kracauer und die Modernität von Weimar" ["Multilayered Surfaces: Kracauer and Weimar Modernity"], Dagmar Barnouw distances Kracauer from Benjamin and aligns him with Plessner and Robert Musil:

> Kracauer dagegen teilte mit einer relativ kleinen Gruppe von Weimarer Intellektuellen wie Robert Musil und Helmuth Plessner das Realitätsprinzip einer Pluralität von unabhängigen, kritischen Stimmen, die weniger an ihrer intellektuellen Identität und deren jeweiliger "Wahrheit" interessiert waren als an einem besseren Verständnis schwieriger zeitgenössischer Realitäten, vor allem auch Fragen politischer Macht in einer technokratischen Massendemokratie.[47]

> In contrast, Kracauer shares with a relatively small group of Weimar intellectuals such as Robert Musil and Helmuth Plessner the reality principle of a plurality of independent, critical voices that were less interested in their intellectual identity and their respective "truth" than in a better understanding of difficult contemporary realities, especially questions of political power in a technocratic mass democracy.

Barnouw emphasizes the traces of a pluralistic understanding of reality that are to be seen in Kracauer's Weimar writings. Furthermore, she presents the other elements of Kracauer's writings, those that connect Kracauer to Benjamin, as aspects of Kracauer's thinking that he "overcomes" later. In contrast, Kracauer's interest in Plessner demonstrates how forward-thinking Kracauer was: "Mit dem Begriff 'Takt' verweist Kracauer hier bereits auf ein Verhalten, das er vier Jahrzehnte später in seinem letzten Buch *History* dem (idealen) Historiker als dem essenziell 'Fremden' zuschreibt" [With the term 'tact' Kracauer already refers here to a position that many decades later in his last book *History* he ascribes to the (ideal) historian as the essential 'stranger'].[48] In the next paragraph Barnouw writes, "Die Plessner-Besprechung endet mit einer für den Kracauer der Weimarer Periode charakteristischen Einschränkung" [The Plessner discussion ends with a reservation characteristic for the Weimar-era Kracauer][49] as a way of prefacing Kracauer's critique that Plessner ignores the need for Gemeinschaft. Looking for connections to Kracauer's later works as a way to redeem his Weimar writings leads to a reading of his Weimar writings in which only those aspects that can be read as traces of his future works or as indicators of his future progress are foregrounded. It is an attempt to make Kracauer "modern" in opposition to the more neo-Romantic Benjamin.

According to Barnouw, Kracauer's writings about film and photography stood against the ideal of absolute objectivity because everything was fluid and changing. She claims that in these writings one can see an interest in the historical specificity of the Weimar Republic and modernity in its complexity, since the focus is an articulation of a world shared by others, not a privileging of one's own outsider position.[50] To explain the emphasis Kracauer places on the documentary value of film and photography while not privileging an objective perspective, Barnouw argues that interpreting the tension between the represented and the representation is still about a connection to a shared world—a reality outside of oneself—but is not necessarily objective in an absolute way. I argue that rather than explaining a shared experience, Kracauer uses an unobtrusive observer position in order to establish a position that implies one is merely describing what already exists rather than participating in the creation of this reality through one's own interpretation. The reality may not be absolute, but in Kracauer's writings it is objective in a more authoritative manner than Barnouw allows for. In this regard I agree with Gertrud Koch's assessment that Kracauer already positioned himself as an extraterritorial observer of the world around him in the 1920s, rather than doing so only in his later writings.[51] With this position, Kracauer enacts the distance and lack of intent that are so important in Benjamin's and Simmel's writings.

I find that Kracauer's emphasis on modernity as loss is critical to understanding his earlier writings, and not something that can be ignored. It can be read as a denial of transcendence in the modern world. The wholeness that once was, echoes of which can be seen in spaces such as the church, has been replaced by the meaningless and isolating hotel lobby. Kracauer's writings are filled with attacks on people deluded into thinking otherwise, such as the little shopgirls in the movie theater, or those who see the hotel lobby as a place where people come together and connect to one another. The modern experience means irrevocable loss, but even more importantly, it is the unawareness of this loss. There is little in the way of a "solution" to this situation to be found in Kracauer's writings, nor could one for the most part argue that Kracauer celebrates the fragmentary, individual, and fluid reality that is also modernity. Yet Kracauer's own position as the detached observer relies on these other discourses in order to exist. The notion that the outsider can provide a more objective viewpoint, that the distance between him and others affords him a position of privilege, depends both on romantic notions of loss and genius and on a belief in individual agency and universal alienation. Kracauer describes a world in which individuals are alienated and there is no higher power or greater meaning, yet this fragmentary existence is simultaneously a universal experience that is shared by all. In his writings, Kracauer positions himself as very much part of the fragmentation and loss of the modern experience, but he is different from the others in that he can see this reality for what it is and understand the impossibility of a return. Yet he can see our existence for what it is only because he occupies a position built on the very discourses that he criticizes.

Written between 1922 and 1925, the chapter entitled "Hotelhalle" was the only section of *Der Detektiv-Roman* published during Kracauer's lifetime. As Gertrud Koch writes, Kracauer's goal is "das Phänomen des Detektivromans als eine 'Übersetzung' menschlicher Existenz zu analysieren" [to analyze the phenomenon of the detective novel as a 'translation' of human existence].[52] The text's exploration of the detective novel genre is first and foremost an analysis and critique of society. Kracauer claims that in modern society, our connection to an absolute reality or truth has been lost, thus relegating us to a pseudolife that leaves us isolated from others and prevents us from interacting in a meaningful way with our surroundings. The detective novel, with its formulaic plots and conventions, highlights and exaggerates the concept of an artificial society. And when one recognizes this artificiality in the detective novel, it becomes easy to see it as a "translation" of our own existence.

In this text, the natural/real manifests itself in two ways.[53] First, it is what we have lost. According to this text, there was a time when we had an unmediated relationship with our world and those around us, but now we live as estranged individuals. This world in which we find ourselves is artificial because there is no connection to anything. The second manifestation is a bit more subtle—the artificial is also real in the sense that it is the state in which we find ourselves and is therefore our current reality. This text creates discourses about the stranger and alienation that are rooted in the belief that the artifice of modernity and the loss of reality create this state of being. It then hides the constructed nature of these discourses by presenting estrangement and artifice as universal phenomena that exist independent of any construction. It is not that Kracauer *defines* everyone as alienated and homeless: in his text everyone *is* alienated and homeless, and it is an experience *everyone* has. The artificial reality of modernity is an objective truth that can be identified if one has the right tools. Like Plessner, Kracauer argues that artifice is real, but for Kracauer this condition is created by the loss of an authentic reality. These two levels of the real/natural play an essential role in forming the discourses from which the stranger is created, for the stranger is simultaneously removed from and a part of these alienated masses. Instead of looking at reality as a construction, I will examine how important it is to our sense of reality that, as Plessner points out in his concept of mediated immediacy, we forget it is a construction. Kracauer mourns the loss of the real, but he does so by presenting the current artificiality using discourses of objective reality. Kracauer's choice of the detective novel as a way to explore discourses of modernity is significant.[54] The fact that detective novels are works of fiction foregrounds the lack of truth and reality in society. The detective himself is unreal—he is after all a literary figure, and the world in which he finds himself is that of fiction. Kracauer's reading of the detective novel implies, however, that the world outside fiction, the "real" world, is no less fictional.

There are parallels between Kracauer's text and Georg Lukács's *Theorie des Romans,* published in 1920. In *Theorie des Romans,* Lukács explores the genre of the novel and the connections between the genre and the society that produces it. According to Lukács, the novel contains no connection to totality, and in its fragmentation it demonstrates the fragmented nature of modern society. Lukács sums up his own text in a foreword written in 1962: "Die Problematik der Romanform ist hier das Spiegelbild einer Welt, die aus den Fugen geraten ist."[55] ["The problems of the novel form are here the mirror-image of a world gone out of joint."[56]] Like Kracauer, Lukács sees modern society as one defined by loss; for Lukács the epitome of the lost unmediated relationship to reality and each other is to be found in ancient Greek society and in the Greek epic. The primary difference in the projects is that ultimately Kracauer's outlook is far more pessimistic than Lukács's: Lukács sees the novel as a representation of loss, but also as a source of newfound possibilities in terms of agency and creativity. Kracauer does not see hope for redemption and renewal. This pessimism is not a constant in Kracauer's writings on modern culture. Like Lukács, Kracauer saw the positive potential of forms of mass entertainment, but always with some ambivalence. A well-known example is his attitude toward film and his anti-Kino, pro-Film stance. Kracauer saw great potential in film to be a truly egalitarian cultural phenomenon, one not only enjoyed by the masses but also serving to represent and educate them. Yet he also saw films as a danger; a person could walk into a movie theater and be captivated by the illusion, forgetting that it is an illusion and becoming complacent. He writes about the little shopgirls who escape their dreary reality by watching films that fill them with false hopes and reinforce a passive role in society.[57] In the case of *Der Detektiv-Roman,* pessimism gains the upper hand and the positive aspect of the detective novel, that it leads to an awareness of the artificial nature of modern life, does not seem to outweigh the persistence of artifice.

Influenced by the works of Søren Kierkegaard and Anatole France, Kracauer discusses his views of reality in terms of higher and lower spheres and the *Gesamtmensch* (complete person). The world is divided into various spheres; the higher the sphere, the closer it is to reality. Kracauer also discusses the relationship between the higher and the lower spheres as that between Gemeinschaft and Gesellschaft, with Gemeinschaft existing in the higher spheres, Gesellschaft in the lower ones. The inhabitant of the higher spheres/Gemeinschaft is Kierkegaard's Gesamtmensch, someone with a real relationship to the absolute. In a Gemeinschaft, tension is caused by the fact that the Gesamtmensch participates in both the world of the absolute and that of the conditional. This tension and an awareness thereof define the real and are the foundation of Gemeinschaft. The

Gemeinschaft itself is also in between worlds—between the ephemeral and the eternal, the natural and the supernatural. It is dynamic: the middle in which man lives is constantly being created, constantly in flux. In this model, the real is the tension created by the dynamic relationship between the conditional and the absolute. The unreal or artificial is a result of the loss of this tension, a world in which only the conditional exists. Like Benjamin, Simmel, and Plessner, Kracauer defines man's existence as constant becoming, and his descriptions of the negotiations between the absolute and the conditional have similarities to Plessner's eccentric positionality. Yet unlike Plessner's conception of artifice, in which artifice is real and necessary in order to create and occupy this position, Kracauer posits that artifice indicates the absence of the real. Gesellschaft is only a means to an end—Gemeinschaft—and is a tool to be discarded when the goal is reached. When this purpose is lost and Gesellschaft is all that exists, then there is only artifice existing for its own sake, and this state removes man from himself and reality.

Kracauer's Gemeinschaft does, however, place importance on outsiders. There are "besondere Einzelne" [special individuals] whose role is to create and maintain a relationship with the absolute for the entire Gemeinschaft by taking their leave of the others. Although their particular manifestation is historically defined, the role remains the same. One example of this group is monks. According to Kracauer, distance from others leads to the ability to serve as a conduit between the absolute and the others; through them the others also live in awareness of the absolute. Monks live to serve the community, but they can only do so if they are not really a part of it (SK, 112). As we will see later, in society we find the detective who is also an outsider, but one who no longer has a connection to the absolute.

The main difference between those who live in the higher spheres and those who live in the lower ones is that of consciousness. Those in a Gemeinschaft are aware of their paradoxical situation; they experience and name their situation. Those in the lower spheres/Gesellschaft are not aware and live what Kracauer calls "d[as] entwirklichte[] Leben" [the life lacking reality] (SK, 115). The more estranged from reality life is, the greater the need for art. In the higher spheres, art confirms reality. In the lower ones it takes on a pedagogical role: the artist becomes an educator and prophet who points the way to possibly understanding the existence of the absolute. Kracauer states that the detective novel is not art, but it also shares this educational aspect in that it shows society (Gesellschaft) "ihr eigenes Antlitz reiner, als sie es sonst zu erblicken vermöchte" [its own face more clearly than it would otherwise be able to see it] (SK,

116). The detective novel can serve this function because it is created by a consciousness that is not limited to the Gesellschaft that is its context, but rather reaches beyond it. It takes the idea of a society ruled by an autonomous ratio and completes it with a consistency that does not exist in society, thereby highlighting the constructed nature of what we consider to be reality.

The world of the detective novel lacks tension; its inhabitants are not conscious of their estranged state. Instead, this world is controlled and understood by a constructed rationality that further disconnects it from the absolute. It is a world in which everything is accessible to the "abgelösten Intellekt" [detached intellect] of the detective. His thinking lacks nuance because it is not called for—this world is a single-faceted one. Because of his insistence on unlimited autonomy, the detective is removed from the others, but unlike the monk he is not connected to the absolute. In his eyes, people are fixed atoms that no longer have meaning besides what they bring to the larger pattern. There is no true individuality and, consequently, no true togetherness. Gone is the consciousness of the paradox that results from negotiating the simultaneous existence of the conditional and the absolute. With the absence of an absolute authority, man must create the structures that hold a society together, but they are a poor substitute for what has been lost. As a result, ethics becomes legality, and morality becomes convention. Instead of sharing and immediacy, there is a *Verkehrsnetz* between pseudopeople. Kracauer describes the interactions as "Schienenstränge[], die unzählige zerstreute Punkte in verlassener Welt verbinden" [railroad tracks that connect countless scattered points in a forsaken world] (SK, 119). The use of train and traffic imagery (*Schienenstränge, Verkehrsnetz*) implies a causal link between how people interact and the modernization/mechanization of the environment, which serves to dehumanize not only interactions between people, but also the people themselves.

Throughout the text there is an emphasis on the inability of the individual to truly be an individual in the lower sphere. This point is made particularly clear in Kracauer's discussion of the spirit. According to Kracauer, the spirit or inner self is not a priority in the *Ratio*-driven world of the detective novel; it is important only inasmuch as it helps further the plot. An example would be that jealousy only exists as an explanation of motive, not as an integral part of a character. All focus is placed on actions and surfaces; the true individual cannot exist. Specific qualities are turned into typical ones; a lawyer acts a certain way because that is the way lawyers are "supposed" to act. The lack of an interior, of individuality, is also what makes deception possible in the detective novel. One needs only to take on the necessary characteristics to be recognized as a certain "type" of person, and the result is that correct behavior hides illegal actions (SK, 125). And since in the end the criminal is caught, the norms are further reinforced because those who break them are ultimately identified and removed from society. There are similarities here to Simmel's work on the city—Simmel points out that in our need to become easily distinctive to others, we actually run the danger of becoming conventionally different instead of developing into unique individuals. What Kracauer is criticizing in his analysis of the detective novel's characters is that the city necessitates easily recognizable codes of behavior and appearance; he cannot, unlike Simmel, see the value of an environment in which such conventions are possible. Simmel focuses on our desire to differentiate ourselves within the fast-paced city and sees this need as a possibility for individuality, whereas Kracauer focuses on the stifling nature of norms and the resulting lack of difference.

Kracauer uses the detective novel as a "Zerrbild" [distorted image] of society. One could therefore assume that this world is not "real," as it is a world of fiction. But according to Kracauer, the detective novel exaggerates qualities that exist in the world outside it. The fictional quality of the detective novel is only a more extreme version of unreal modern society. In other words, the fictional blurs into the unreal reality that the inhabitants of the modern world experience. Fiction is fact because it highlights the artifice of reality. Although Kracauer is analyzing a construction—the detective novel—he seeks to turn his observations about it, and thus his observations about modernity, into objective truths. One strategy Kracauer uses is his focus on the detective novel's structure and the genre's identifying characteristics. He sees genre as a group of texts that share certain characteristics; these commonalities objectively exist and can be seen by everyone. He then conflates this approach with his way of presenting the modern world—he is merely stating a truth that exists outside of him. This approach is complicated by the fact that genre is itself a construct used to explain man-made objects, but if we are to believe that our current reality is one in which authenticity and truth are absent, then an explanation of this artifice from an outsider position is modernity's objectivity. And this objectivity is what allows him to make an argument for the lack of truth and reality in the world around him—the one truth is the absence of truth. Just as an explanation of genre compiles texts and then creates a definition of them, thus to some extent treating the texts as objective realities that exist outside of oneself, Kracauer views the artificial constructs around him and explains them to his readers while still claiming that this world around him, although constructed, is not his construct. One could argue that Kracauer takes this approach one step further by positioning himself as an observer; he claims to describe what is around him without having an effect on it. Within the genre analogy, this means one finds commonalities that already exist and that defining the genre is descriptive rather than creative in nature. By disavowing the observer's power to create and thus relinquishing claims to individual agency, Kracauer's description gains authority. The self-effacement of the narrator, in this case Kracauer—the small importance given to the person of Kracauer himself in his writings—is the precondition for the objective authority of his writings.

The detective is an interesting figure because he is somewhat removed from these questions about construction, unreal and real. He moves within the world of the detective novel, but he is also separate from it. The detective is the personification of *Ratio*. Kracauer makes it clear that the detective is not a follower of *Ratio,* but rather that *Ratio* defines him. Without it the detective is nothing; he has no self other than as the embodiment of *Ratio*. The detective's main purpose is to maintain a logic that is itself only a simulacrum of real logic, a "Pseudo-Logos." The detective has autonomy, but this independence actually takes away agency and power rather than bestowing it. He moves alone within a world of people who are unconnected and who are governed by social norms that have lost any meaning other than to hide the fact that there is no meaning. Autonomy makes the detective into a god, but a powerless one who rules in an unreal world. His limited power consists in making sense of events by interpreting them from the position of *Ratio;* through interpretation the detective plays an important role in maintaining the illusion of reality. The detective is not aware of his position as a pseudogod in a pseudoworld, but the detective novel makes the reader aware of it. Kracauer's comparison of the detective to other outsider figures, such as the monk, points to the potential power of the detective while simultaneously emphasizing his powerlessness. For example, the detective is "a secularized priest" who listens to the confessions of criminals but provides neither justice nor absolution (SK, 142). For the monk, confessions and meditations help him provide the masses with a connection to the absolute; the detective's solitary meditations are a result of a *Ratio* whose only goal is to fulfill itself. Both the detective and the monk need to be separated from the others, but for the detective this separation only emphasizes his lack of connection to others, whereas for the monk this separation creates connections.

The detective lives outside communal life; he is not connected to the absolute, but in his role as a pseudogod he is necessarily set apart from the others. Certain generic plot devices and characteristics underscore this separation. For example, the detective is always unmarried. At most he has a housekeeper. He is seen as a neuter being—he is neither erotic nor unerotic but rather "ein unaffizierbares 'Es,' dessen Sächlichkeit sich aus der Sachlichkeit eines Intellekts erklärt, der durch nichts beeinflußbar ist, weil er gründet im Nichts" [an imperturable 'it' whose neutered state can be explained by the neutrality of an intellect that cannot be influenced because it is rooted in nothingness] (SK, 145). Here Kracauer connects the grammatical "Neutrum" with the idea of being neuter sexually and with a position of neutrality. According to Kracauer, detective novelists use various devices to make the detective's solitary existence "aesthetically palpable." For example, in an Anglo-Saxon detective novel, the detective is given puritanical traits and is depicted as a model of ascetic life. Other novels find some sort of psychological basis for the detective's separation from others by turning the detective's a priori solitude into something that results from an event or situation in his life. Yet the reasons given are not central to the detective's identity but rather an afterthought. Kracauer maintains that the detective's position begins with a separation from others—and this isolation itself, not the reasons for the isolation, defines him.

For the reader of detective novels, the detective represents the dangers of living in an artificial world. Kracauer's blurring of the fictional world and characters of the detective novel with those of the outside world creates a way for him to show the reader of his text the world as he sees it, as an objective artifice. On a metalevel, the text takes on its own outsider position in order to show the reader the world as it is; the text creates a mirror so that society can see itself by explaining how the detective novel serves this function. The outsider, in his many manifestations throughout the text, serves as the lens through which one sees things as they are; he provides a way to make others conscious of their own state. The detective is powerless in his own world, but as a tool to examine society, he opens up the possibility of power and potential intervention. In Kracauer's text, the figure of the detective is simultaneously a powerless pseudogod and a tool for Kracauer's own position as an outsider observer. These two levels of existence and the tension between the powerlessness and the power of the detective raise questions about the ultimate purpose of the outsider. In this text, as in many others he has written, Kracauer occupies the position of the privileged outsider. He sees what the others cannot, namely that modern society no longer has a connection to an absolute truth or reality. What Kracauer finds most reprehensible are the societal structures that allow the modern individual to live a pseudoexistence, the structures that foster complacency. Yet does the outsider himself need to be aware of the real in order to accomplish these goals? Is Kracauer stating that the detective cannot be a true outsider because he is not aware, and at most can serve as a tool for a real outsider such as Kracauer? But if the detective novel's world is representative of society and the detective's powerlessness is largely due to the artificial reality of society, how can a true outsider exist? The central question is how to achieve a critical position within an environment that seems to preclude such a position. As Kracauer's text demonstrates, perhaps there is no solution, only a careful balancing act that allows for both positions—that of the unknowing alienated stranger and the critical outsider—while simultaneously putting them into question.

By taking the idea of a rationalized society to its extreme, the detective novel world becomes one for "den bindunglosen Intellekt" [the disconnected intellect], a world in which one lives next to others, not with them (SK, 105–6). How Kracauer understands the relationship between the real and the artificial can be seen more clearly in the chapter about the hotel lobby. Kracauer compares the spaces of the hotel lobby and the church. In this comparison, the hotel lobby is both a fictional and a real space, and in both instances a microcosm of artificial society. The main difference between the hotel lobby and the church is that in the latter everything has meaning, while in the former there is only the illusion of meaning. The similarities between the two spaces only further emphasize their differences. In a church there is prayer; in the hotel lobby, trivial talk. In both there is quiet or peace (*Ruhe*), largely because in both spaces one sees the others as equal to and similar to oneself. But whereas in the church this quiet and equality result from inner contemplation and speech is extinguished in order to allow for "das andere Wort," in the hotel lobby not even reciprocal consideration between the occupants exists. Instead it is the flattening of differences that causes the quiet—everyone is the same and therefore there is no need for communication.

Anonymity exists in both spaces. In the church, one gives up one's name in order to be united with others and connect with the mystery/the absolute. Here Kracauer makes an interesting claim about strangers—he states that by giving up one's name and any marker of being different from the others one becomes "fremd genug, um sich als Brüder zu finden, sie nur so weit enthüllt, daß sie sich ungekannt und namenlos zu lieben vermögen" [estranged enough that they find themselves among brothers, exposed just enough so that they are capable of loving each other without knowing each other and without names] (SK, 134). In other words, the anonymity of the church actually brings people closer to one another rather than alienating them. The church provides a way of being a stranger without estrangement; in fact, being a stranger is how one becomes the ultimate nonstranger, a part of a "we." His description of the relationship between individuals is similar to Plessner's—distance creates the possibility of connecting to others—but has a very different outcome. Kracauer is proposing an anonymity that erases the need for individual identities because of an unmediated connection between individuals. And this kind of connection, according to Kracauer, is not possible in the modern world. In the hotel lobby there is the "isolation of anonymous atoms" (SK, 135). The inhabitants of the hotel lobby are not individuals to begin with; whatever traces of individuality they possess are mere conventions. Therefore, they have nothing to renounce, and the anonymity of the hotel lobby does not contain any potential to connect people to one another. Kracauer once again questions whether such people can actually be considered people; he calls them mannequins and emphasizes their lack of interior:

> Besäßen sie ein Innen, es entbehrte der Fenster, und sie vergingen in dem Bewußtsein unendlicher Verlassenheit, statt wie die Gemeinde um ihre Heimat zu wissen. Als bloßes Außen aber entschwinden sie sich selber und drücken ihr Nichtsein durch die schlecht-ästhetische Bejahung der zwischen ihnen gesetzten Fremde aus. Die Darbietung der Oberfläche ist ihnen ein Reiz, der Hauch des Exotischen streift sie angenehm. Ja, um die Ferne zu bekräftigen, deren Definitivum sie lockt, lassen sie sich abprallen an einer Nähe, die sie selbst heraufbeschwören. (SK, 135)

> If they possessed an interior, it would have no windows at all, and they would perish aware of their endless abandonment, instead of knowing of their homeland as the congregation does. But as pure exterior, they escape themselves and express their nonbeing through the false aesthetic affirmation of the estrangement that has been installed between them. The presentation of the surface strikes them as an attraction; the tinge of exoticism gives them a pleasurable shudder. Indeed, in order to confirm the distance whose definitive character attracts them, they allow themselves to be bounced off a proximity that they themselves have conjured up . . .[58]

Here proximity is only a way of emphasizing the distance between people instead of a certain amount of distance actually bringing people closer together, as is the case in the church. The real danger of the distance between the inhabitants is that they are not only unaware of the alienation they are experiencing, but also enjoy the distance between one another because it creates a sense of the exotic and excitement; one enjoys presenting a surface to others and being presented with surfaces. There is no desire to connect to anyone or anything in a more intense manner. The hotel lobby inhabitants have no home (*Heimat*), yet they do not seem to feel their homelessness. In the hotel lobby, the absolute is replaced by a superficial sense of mystery that serves as a veil to cover up the artificiality of their lives.

In his discussion of the hotel lobby Kracauer mentions a specific detective novel, Sven Elvestad's *Der Tod kehrt ins Hotel ein*. He quotes a section of the novel in which the narrator claims that the hotel lobby is not only a world unto itself, but also no different from the world outside it: "So bestätigt es sich wieder einmal, daß ein großes Hotel eine Welt für sich ist, und diese Welt ist wie die übrige große Welt. Hier treiben sich die Gäste in ihrem leichten, sorglosen Sommerdasein herum und ahnen nicht, daß sich mitten unter ihnen seltsame Geheimnisse bewegen."[59] [Once again it is confirmed that a large hotel is a world unto itself and that this world is like the rest of the large world. The guests here roam about in their lighthearted, careless summer existence without suspecting anything of the strange mysteries circulating among them.[60]] The Elvestad quote serves to reinforce Kracauer's reading of the hotel lobby and also to strengthen the ties between the hotel lobby and the detective novel, the hotel lobby and society, and also the detective novel and society. The description is, however, treated not as a "Zerrbild" of society, as Kracauer describes detective novels to be, but rather as a straight description, a move that further blurs the borders between "Zerrbild" and "Abbild" [reproduction] (SK, 136). It is telling that in this rare citing of a specific detective novel Kracauer chooses to undermine the notion that the detective novel provides an exaggerated picture of society and instead chooses a passage that essentially reinforces the ideas he has developed about society in his reflections about the hotel lobby. In this quote, there is none of the positive aesthetic that Kracauer praises as one of the most useful things about the detective novel. In fact, the style of Elvestad's observations differs so little from Kracauer's that one could almost say that Kracauer's text is just as much a detective novel as Elvestad's. The differences between the hotel lobby, the detective novel, and society are further diminished by the constant emphasis on the artificiality of one's life in the hotel lobby and, when society is seen as an extension of the hotel lobby, then of modern life in general. Modernity is a state of deceptive surfaces that hide the reality of an artificial and alienated existence. An acknowledgment of this reality, and the search to escape it by taking the outsider position made possible by modernity's artifice, are central features of the texts we will explore in the next section.

Benjamin's flâneur, Simmel's stranger, Plessner's masked individual, and Kracauer's detective are all anonymous symbols of modernity, and their anonymity is the source of their privilege. At the same time, this anonymity is inextricably linked to the universality of the positions. Anonymity helps these figures position themselves in abstraction and thus create a universality that is about the erasing of specificity. The figures navigate the intersections of the historically specific and the atemporal abstract to create a universal modern condition that is part of a historical continuum. Considerations such as class, race, history, and politics are rarely directly addressed. In this chapter, I explored some of the ways in which these omissions impact these figures of urban modernity and the positions they occupy by demonstrating how the move toward ahistoricity is rooted in a historical moment. The following chapter looks at the stranger's position in relation to questions of German Jewish identity and how the abstract and ahistorical position of the urban stranger interacts with and reacts against other conceptualizations of outsiderness.

Chapter 2

The Traveler and the Wanderer

In considering the distinctions between travelers, wanderers, and strangers, it is important to return for a moment to the relationship Simmel describes between the stranger and mobility. What marks Simmel's stranger is his potential mobility; he could leave but he chooses to stay. The connection between mobility and the stranger's privileged position changes when potential and actual mobility intersect, namely in the cases of travelers and wanderers. Both travelers and wanderers are strangers, but they have made other choices than those made by Simmel's stranger. The traveler chooses to be a temporary outsider, never allowing for the possibility of becoming an integral member of his new surroundings. Like Simmel's stranger, he comes from elsewhere, but unlike him, the traveler has the intention of returning home. The wanderer does not stay, but he also does not go back. Instead he continues moving to other places where he is also a temporary stranger. Of course, these distinctions between stranger as insider, stranger as traveler, and stranger as wanderer are fluid. The possibility of being more than one kind of stranger simultaneously is demonstrated in Alfred Döblin's 1925 *Reise in Polen* (*Journey to Poland*) and Joseph Roth's 1927 *Juden auf Wanderschaft* (*The Wandering Jews*). These two travel texts add an element into the discourses about the stranger, namely that of Jewish identity. West European travelers/narrators observe both assimilated and Orthodox Jews in Eastern Europe. Thus we have narrators who themselves are both insider-strangers (assimilated Jews from Western Europe)[1] and travelers and who are fascinated by Orthodox Jews, whom they define as wanderers.

As is implicit throughout the texts, and explicit in Roth's title, the figure of the Wandering Jew is linked to East European Jews. In the early twentieth century, this figure is evoked in debates about nation, national identity, diaspora, and religion in relation to Jewish identity. During this time, Jewish writers and artists also used this figure to explore the idea that wandering is not solely the result of persecution but could also be a choice. Döblin's and Roth's texts examine East European Jews, their traditions, and their identity and raise the possibility that for Jews a concept of home and authenticity are possible only when they accept their fate as wanderers, potential or otherwise.

Another name for the Wandering Jew is the Eternal Jew; "eternal" refers to both the fact that the figure wanders forever and the fact that he is always a Jew. Discourses of time, mobility, and Jewish identity intersect. In *Reise in Polen* and *Juden auf Wanderschaft* this intersection is thematized on several levels. On a stylistic level, Döblin's text creates a timeless "now" through various narrative techniques, including a self-effacing narrator and montages of the past, present, and future. On a thematic level, both Roth and Döblin travel to what they view as a static past in which Jewish identity is tied to timeless traditions and the absolutes of religion. The texts also explore notions of history and nation and raise questions about the possibility that Jews can have a history without a nation, or perhaps that Jewish identity can exist only when the notion of belonging to the linear narrative of history is relinquished.

In what follows, I will first examine the narrator/traveler position that Döblin creates in his text. The self-effacing and anonymous nature of the narrator resonates with the strangers we encountered previously, but the genre of the travel narrative relies on the reader's identification with the narrator and his experiences in a way that further complicates notions of the individual and individual agency. I will then turn to the subject matter of these two texts—East European Jews. Following the trail of scholars like Martin Buber, Döblin and Roth viewed East European Jews, in particular the Hasidim, as a possible source of renewal and rejuvenation but also as a representation of the authenticity that assimilated West European Jews have lost through modernity. The Hasidim represent an existence that is no longer possible for the West; their authenticity depends on their isolation from the corrupting influences of Western modernity. Thus another mode of timelessness is introduced, one that removes the Hasidim from history so that they can maintain a primitive authenticity and experience unmediated and thus more "natural" relationships with one another. The questions of history and where Jews fit into history, if they fit at all, play crucial roles in creating and understanding the relationship between the Hasidim and their environment, particularly in terms of nation and history. I will examine an alternative model of Jewish history offered by the Russian historian Simon Dubnow, not only to provide a counternarrative to those of Döblin and Roth, who would predicate Jewish authenticity on an absence of history and its implications of progress, but also to foreground the conflicts and interactions between these notions of Jewish identity, religion, national identity, and history. Finally, I will return to the notions of community and society and investigate them within the context of these debates.

On the Move: Travels of a Disappearing Narrator

In *Practice of Everyday Life* (1984), Michel de Certeau defines spatial practice as the ability to change a space by one's interactions with it. He focuses on the possibility of an individual experience within the Foucauldian discourses of discipline. His most famous example of these disruptions and negotiations of discourses within the context of space is the individual walking in the city. Like Certeau's urban pedestrian, Döblin interacts with his surroundings in ways that both appropriate and subvert the discourses that shape the way we see the world around us. Yet Döblin's text also complicates this notion of agency. *Reise in Polen* privileges the experience of space over a clear-cut narrative about Poland and its people; the reader experiences the narrator's travels as if the reader him- or herself were traveling. Nevertheless, the spontaneity and the possibility of choice that are so strongly associated with Certeau's pedestrian take on a different form in this travel text.

Certeau creates a distinction between spatial practices and their representation by comparing the act of walking to a speech act:

> The modalities of pedestrian enunciation which a plane representation on a map brings out could be analyzed . . . Walking affirms, suspects, tries out, transgresses, respects, etc., the trajectories it "speaks." All the modalities sing a part in this chorus, changing from step to step . . . These enunciatory operations are of an unlimited diversity. They therefore cannot be reduced to their graphic trail.[2]

Certeau emphasizes that walking can be represented, can be mapped out, but its enunciations are not the same thing as the representations thereof. Nevertheless, we attempt to "read" the movements from what Certeau refers to as the "graphic trail" because that trail consists of traces of movement, of what movement has left behind. Döblin's text highlights the connections between the act and its representation; the reader is interested in Döblin's interactions with the spaces of Poland, and without these experiences the text would lose its claims to truth and authenticity. Yet at the same time, through the representation of experience, the text attempts to create new spatial practices that involve the reader, that allow the reader to also walk through Poland. A further complication is that the reader is in fact traveling on someone else's journey—he or she does not have the possibility of choosing a different path, of going left instead of right. A closer inspection of the text will show that the experiences are created through careful stylistic choices that give one the sense they are the spontaneous reactions and interactions of the traveler, but that are instead created by the author writing about the traveler. Thus the agency of the reader as traveler is created through the spontaneous quality of the experiences, but this spontaneity is itself a literary construct.

In 1924 Alfred Döblin—doctor, novelist, and journalist—journeyed through Poland and wrote a series of articles about his experiences for the *Vossische Zeitung*. The articles for the *Vossische Zeitung* might have provided the basis for *Reise in Polen,* but *Reise in Polen* contains significant deviations from the newspaper articles. Even things that the reader would take for granted, for example that the route explained in the book is the one the narrator[3] took and is one that could also be taken by the reader, prove to be uncertain; the articles for the *Vossische Zeitung* outline a route that differs from that of the book.[4] The changes that have a greater impact on the narrative and the reception of the text are the stylistic ones. Döblin's writing style has been a subject of much discussion in critical reception of his works. The style of *Reise in Polen* hints at the montage style that will later appear in *Berlin Alexanderplatz.* Claudia Sonino points out in her study of West European Jews in Eastern Europe that, like *Berlin Alexanderplatz, Reise in Polen* is a product of conscious style: "Auch der parataktische Stil . . . bei dem jede hierarchische Struktur wegfällt, d.h. jede vorher festgelegte Wahrheit oder jedes Dogma, ist das Ergebnis einer subtilen, bewussten Schreibweise, ist ein Stil, den Döblin sich allmählich aneignet, wie das Manuskript der Reise in Polen bezeugt" [Even the paratactic style . . . through which every hierarchical structure falls away, i.e., every previously established truth or every dogma, is the result of subtle and self-conscious writing, a style that Döblin gradually made his own, which the manuscript of the journey to Poland makes evident].[5] Sonino claims that Döblin's stripped-down style leads to a nonhierarchical text, which precludes the possibility of a set truth or dogma. I would argue, however, that the style leads to a *sense* of neutrality, rather than actually attaining such a position. *Reise in Polen* achieves its authority through an ostensible disavowal of any position of authority. The text's "neutrality" is what enables it to convey a particular look and viewpoint that readers take as their own. The care that Döblin exercised in the narration of this story, his conscious manipulation of the text and its language, increases a sense of spontaneity and immediacy even as the act belies the possibility of these qualities.

What I am concerned with is not proving that the text is a carefully constructed narrative, but rather with why the reader can so easily forget this fact, and why this forgetting is critical to experiencing the text. This effect relies on a constructed present that contains a multitude of times, created in part by eliminating temporal adverbs and other temporal markers, and in part through the juxtaposition of various time frames. The shifts in time, often denoted by a change in verb tense, are also shifts in discourses and, as such, shifts in the ways one experiences space. Ethnographic, historical, and travel discourses serve as modes of perception that layer different ways of shaping and interpreting one's surroundings. And by experiencing various times simultaneously, one is both within these spaces at these times, and also in a new space and time that encompasses the others. Bringing together these various discourses and times creates a sense of objectivity through a sense of impersonal subjectivity. The result is a text that allows the reader to travel—the reader sees the world through someone else's eyes and yet is made to feel that they are his or her own.

The text expresses on a stylistic level a desire for authenticity, for an active memory that is the embodiment of unmediated experience. The diegetic and stylistic levels converge to produce a text that explores the relationship between experience, memory, and authenticity in the larger context of modernity and Jewish identity. The result is a narrative that tries to capture or create the timeless authenticity that the narrator sees as the definitive Jewish characteristic. *Reise in Polen* utilizes changes in verb tenses to create a juxtaposition of present, past, and future that is simultaneously a combination of the three and a timeless "now" that does not belong to any of them but is tied to one geographical space. The historical discourse is marked by the use of past tense. Occasionally the information is attributed to an outside source. For example, Döblin cites "an official Polish Almanac from 1924" as a source of three paragraphs of statistics interspersed with commentary about the significance of the numbers (AD, 21–22). Often, however, there is no transition into or out of these historical sections, nor is there a clear citation of the source materials used. The following passage is exemplary of these shifts in discourses:

> Männer wie Frauen, vom reinen Typus, mit hellen und braunen Haaren. Die Männer massiv, kräftig, ja es sind ganz gewaltige Exemplare darunter. Neben dem Hotel Bristol liegt ein Ministerpalais mit tiefem grünem Vorgarten. War früher Magnatenschloß,

der Radziwill, dann Sitz des russischen Gouvernements. Ein Bronzestandbild des Fürsten Paskewitsch stand davor, Paskewitsch Eriwanskij, ein Geschöpf von Härte und Grausamkeit.

Es gab eine Revolution der Polen im Jahre 1830/31 . . . Mißlang alles; in der Nähe Warschaus, bei Grochow, erlagen die unglücklichen Polen dem Russen Diebitsch, und noch mal bei Ostrolenka. Auf Diebitsch folgte dieser Paskewitsch. Der gab den Rest, Warschau, Polen war hin.

Die Polen haben nichts vergessen. Sein Denkmal haben sie beseitigt. Vor dem neuen Sitz der polnischen Regierung aber stehen jetzt zwei lebendige Schutzleute in schwarzer Uniform mit großem Säbel und heruntergeschlagenem Sturmband. Lebende Kolossalgestalten. Ich betrachte sie jedesmal, wenn ich das Hotel verlasse. (AD, 14)

Men and women, of a pure type, with light or brown hair. The men massive, powerful—why, there are some enormous specimens among them. Next to the Hotel Bristol lies a ministerial palace with a vast green front lawn. It used to be a castle belonging to magnates, the Radziwills; then it became the residence of the Russian governor. A bronze statue of Prince Paskevich stood in front of it: Paskevich Erivansky, a harsh, cruel creature.

The Poles had a revolution in 1830/31 . . . The whole plan failed. At Grochow, near Warsaw, the unfortunate Poles were defeated by the Russian Dibich; and they were defeated once again near Ostrolenka. Dibich was followed by that Paskevich. He dealt the coupe de grâce. Warsaw, Poland were lost.

The Poles have forgotten nothing. They got rid of his monument. But now, in front of the seat of the Polish government, two live policemen in black uniforms stand with large sabers and turned-down chin straps. Living colossi. I scrutinize them each time I leave the hotel. (ADE, 3–4)

The first two sentences are laden with adjectives, and the only verb is "to be." This description creates a static picture, much like those one would find in an ethnographic study, an impression strengthened by the words "Typus" and "Exemplare." There is a timeless quality to this picture; because there are almost no verbs, one is literally outside of time. And the idea that these individuals are part of a "type" abstracts them from actual people Döblin sees on the street and makes them interchangeable examples of a group. The qualities that make them different from others, that deviate from the "pure type," are not important. Here we see the world through the eyes of an ethnographer, interested in generalizations and scientific categories of identification.

The next sentences explore the relationship between time and a geographical space in a historical discourse with names, dates, and places. The first sentence is in the present tense and describes where the minister's palace is situated. The next one moves into the past to mention the building's former functions. Then comes a description of a monument, which we later find out is no longer standing. The one sentence pertains to a building that still exists in the present, the other to a statue that no longer exists, yet there is no distinction made between the two: they are both described in the past tense. Then there is a description of the revolution of 1830–31. Like the two preceding sentences, this passage is in the simple past. Nothing in the grammar distinguishes the past of the building from the past of the revolution, although the building existed before and after the revolution. Through the lack of differentiation in the grammar, the various pasts coexist. The narrative creates different layers of time that are connected by their relation to a geographical location, thus creating a space in which these different times come together to form a single narrative.

Various pasts converge with the present and future in the next paragraph; the monument may be gone, yet now there are guards who not only stand where the monument once was, but who themselves resemble statues; the narrator describes them as "lebende Kolossalgestalten" [living colossi]. The whole sentence consists of only those two words with no verb, similar to the characterizations of Polish physiognomy earlier in the text. In this description of the present, the narrator suddenly appears in the text again; he sees the guards every time he leaves the hotel. This sentence introduces a present that implies a future; he sees them as he leaves the the hotel, and he will see them every subsequent time he does so. Yet this present/implied future and in fact all the present tense of the text is simultaneously a past and a present. It is "now" in the narrative and for the reader, but it is also something that has already happened to the narrator and has been written down.

In this passage, as in other parts of the text, shifts in time are expressed through verb tenses or the absence of verbs altogether, but no particular time is privileged in the text, nor any particular discourse. The effect is a seeming lack of hierarchy between the different discourses. This lack of distinction creates an authority and objectivity that appear to emerge from the text rather than from the narrator. The historical discourse seems to impart objective facts: the descriptions in which the narrator disappears convey the sense of unmediated impressions. Both give the reader the feeling of being directly connected to the facts and experiences. This sense of immediacy allows the text to make "organic" arguments, arguments that seem to grow so naturally out of the impressions and experiences that deliberation does not play a role. In fact, they do not seem like arguments at all; rather, they seem to be conclusions that "arise" out of the text.

The narrative performs the act of creating spaces by connecting temporalities, geographic locations, and specific discourses of perspective, then allows readers to experience these spaces as their own. The narrator blends into the experience/space and becomes a part of it, erasing the traces of his agency in order to give readers a sense that it belongs to them. The act of narration creates a new experience in which the reader becomes the traveler, at times traveling with the narrator, at times replacing him. The position of the narrator is also ambiguous in this regard. In the historical or the descriptive sections, the first person sometimes disappears altogether, strengthening the impression that readers are traveling and seeing with their own eyes. Yet even when the narrator disappears, he is always present. He is present in the places and events he chooses to describe, in the way he creates a picture of a particular place and experience and from this picture draws conclusions about the people who live there, about the events that unfold. The narrator's simultaneous presence and absence is foregrounded in the beginning of the text:

> Ich—bin nicht da. Ich—bin nicht im Zug. Wir prasseln über Brücken. Ich—bin nicht mitgeflogen. Noch nicht. Ich stehe noch am Schlesischen Bahnhof. Sie stehen um mich herum, aber ich bin dann eingestiegen, sitze auf dem grünen Polster, zwischen Lederkoffern, Handtaschen, Plaids, Mänteln, Schirmen. Ich bin gefangen. Der Zug trägt mich fort, hält mich fest, schwankt mit mir über die Schienen in die Nacht . . .
>
> Ich—bin nicht da. Die Zeitung liegt auf meinen Knien. (AD, 11)

> I—am not here. I—am not in the train. We pelt across bridges. I—have not flown along. Not yet. I am still standing in the terminal, Schlesischer Bahnhof. They stand around me, but then I get into the train, I sit on the green cushion, amid leather valises, satchels, plaids, coats, umbrellas. I am caught. The train carries me off, holds me captive, rocks me along the rails into the night . . .
>
> I—am not here. The newspaper lies on my lap. (ADE, 1–2)

Here the narrator describes a displacement that happens to the traveler when his body and consciousness do not occupy the same space. There is a disconnect between the physical reality and the narrator's perception of it. The "I" of the text and the verb "to be" ("Ich—bin") are separated; the dash performs the disconnect between the narrator and his being. It is significant that the word that almost always follows "bin" is "nicht." Beginning the text with such a displacement, with the repeating pattern of "ich—bin nicht," can also be read as a performance of the narrator's position in the text: "I—am not" can be seen as an act of disappearing, of not being. The constant use of the first person draws attention to the presence of what is absent. The last two sentences of the excerpt above illustrate this interaction between presence and absence: the narrator is not there, but there is a newspaper on his knees. Even as he feels disoriented and displaced, he is still there; his presence is what makes his absence palpable.

A discourse of implied objectivity allows for the possibility of an impersonal subjectivity in Döblin's text. *Reise in Polen* suggests that there is a reality that can be known. The world the narrator sees is one that "really" exists; what the narrator "sees" are people, places, and events that would exist even without the narrator's presence. The narrator's personality is not a necessary component of his viewpoint; he could be anyone, including the reader. Yet the viewpoint is subjective; for example, there are events that the narrator does not understand, and he occasionally mentions his inability to speak to or understand the people around him. This combination of impersonal and subjective creates a universal and abstract outsider/traveler, a position that resonates with a large audience. The narrator's position is itself in flux and is continually being constructed through the act of narration. One aspect, however, does remain constant—the narrator is always an outsider. He often makes his presence known in order to emphasize his position as a stranger—to describe, if not an absence, a lack of belonging.

The position is one that allows for a viewpoint privileged by being less involved in the world it describes. This viewpoint does not preclude biases or subjective opinions, but it does lend them a sense of objective authority they would not otherwise have. For example:

> Ich, weder zu den Aufklärern noch zu dieser Volksmasse gehörig, ein westlicher Passant—auf mich machen diese "Aufgeklärten" den Eindruck von Negern, die mit den Glasperlen paradieren, die ihnen die Matrosen schenken, mit den schmutzigen Stulpen an ihren schlenkernden Armen, mit dem eingebeulten, funkelnagelneuen Zylinder auf ihrem Kopf. Wie arm, wie schäbig, unwürdig und seellos verwüstet die westliche Welt ist, die ihnen diese Stulpen schenkt; woher sollen sie es wissen. (AD, 251)

> I, neither an Enlightener nor a member of these national masses, a Western European passerby—I view those "Enlightened" ones like Africans who flaunt the glass beads they've gotten from sailors, the dirty cuffs on their dangling arms, the brand-new dented top hats on their heads. How poor, how shabby, how unworthy and soullessly devastated the Western World is, giving them those cuffs; how are they supposed to know. (ADE, 191)

The narrator first situates himself as belonging neither to the one group nor to the other, but rather to a third outside group. He then proceeds to share his opinion about certain assimilated Jews. The two parts of the sentence, separated by a dash, depend on one another; his position is what gives his viewpoint weight. The second sentence comments on the unworthiness and soullessness of the colonizing Western world from which these assimilated Jews take their cues. The last part of the sentence, this time separated from the first part with a semicolon, excuses their blindness, for they are not in a position to be able to see the West for what it is. The first describes how the narrator sees them from his privileged position; the second describes what cannot be seen from the vantage point of the assimilated Jews.

The narrator is aware that his outsider position is necessary in order for him to see what he sees. Before he leaves Krakow for Zakopane, he writes: "Zu lange bin ich schon in Krakau. Endlich kommt der Punkt, wo man alles kennt, was einem zugänglich wird, und wo es heißt: entweder weggehen oder sich einleben, sich gefangen geben. Da besteige ich den Wagen" (AD, 277). ["I've been in Cracow too long already. You finally reach the point where you know everything that's available to you, and you have to decide; either move on or settle in, surrender. So I climb into the wagon" (ADE, 211).] For him, the notion of settling down and becoming part of his new surroundings is the same as being trapped. One must continue to travel in order to maintain the necessary distance; mobility is essential to the narrator's freedom. Here, as in many other sections of the text, the train—a symbol of modernization and modernity—represents this mobility; in order to escape the trap of becoming part of Krakow, the narrator steps into the train.[6]

Buber's Hasidism

The carefully constructed narrative of *Reise in Polen* allows the reader to travel to Poland, to see "firsthand" how East European Jews live. Before we turn our attention to the portrayals of East European Jews in this text and in Joseph Roth's *Juden auf Wanderschaft,* however, it is important to note that these depictions of East European Jews are themselves West European. The fascination West Europeans had with East European Jews tells us much more about Western Europe, particularly about assimilated, secular, West European Jews, than it does about the historical realities of East European Jews, their traditions, and their religious practices. As Paul Mendes-Flohr convincingly argues in his collection of essays *Divided Passions,* the popularity of portrayals of the Hasidim in West European culture had much to do with the fact that these portrayals focused on the philosophical and aesthetic aspects of the Hasidim, rather than the religious. That is to say, these depictions resonated with their audience, which was comprised primarily of Jews who were "estranged from Judaism," because they served to provide more positive portrayals of Jews without demanding that the reader embrace a more religious way of life. Debates about Jewish identity in these texts are conducted first and foremost on the level of culture and cultural critique, and less on the level of debates about religion. I mention this here not to belittle the importance of these depictions and debates, but rather to emphasize how integrated they are in West European discourses of the time, particularly those of cosmopolitanism, renewal, and loss. As with the texts discussed in the first chapter, I argue that it is not a coincidence that the texts I examine here emphasize the universal and timeless aspects of East European Jewish religion and identity, as these aspects resonate with the position of the privileged outsider, even as they also complicate it. More importantly, these notions of timelessness and the universal nature of Jewish spirituality are themselves constructs and should be examined as such.

Döblin's *Reise in Polen* and Roth's *Juden auf Wanderschaft* can be seen within the larger context of creating positive images of East European Jews that simultaneously critique West European Jews and West European culture, as well as try to rehabilitate them by linking them to more positive images of Jews. Since Martin Buber's writings on East European Jews, particularly his 1906 *Geschichten des Rabbi Nachman,* are so influential in this context, it is vital at this point to look at them in more depth. Of particular relevance is how Buber emphasized the universal and timeless aspects of the Hasidic "Oriental"[7] wisdom in order to appeal to a Western audience, a move that resonates with the positions taken by Simmel and Plessner to legitimate their views on urban modernity. As others have pointed out, Buber's immense popularity, not only with readers of his generation but also subsequent ones, stems from the ahistoricity of his approach. Aschheim writes of Buber's role in popularizing Hasidism to German Jews: "Hasidism fitted admirably into the *Erlebnismystik* of the time. More than anything else it was a spiritual phenomenon, and it functioned for Buber and his readers with an elasticity that the concrete historical phenomenon lacked."[8]

Buber provided an alternative to the view of Jews and Judaism as calculating and without spirituality. Working against common perceptions of the "Oriental" origins of Jews as something to be ashamed of and purged for the sake of acculturation and acceptance among West European Jews, texts such as Buber's sought to reappropriate and reclaim these Oriental roots as a source of renewal. Buber's writings achieve these goals, making East European Jews and in particular Hasidism palatable for West European Jews by integrating them into New Romanticism and Expressionism. This integration is even to be seen in the books' art nouveau cover designs.[9] Additionally, in his retelling of Rabbi Nachman's Hasidic tales, Buber removed language and cultural references that were too distinctly Jewish, or more specifically too East European Jewish, in order to avoid alienating his West European audience, both Jewish and non-Jewish.[10] Mendes-Flohr sums up Buber's project with the following description: "This dialectic between the subjective experience of unity and a commitment to extend that experience to the objective realm—between what Hasidism referred to as *hitlahavut and avodah*—characterized, according to Buber, the most fundamental sensibility of the Jew, and as such it constituted the abiding significance of Judaism for mankind."[11] Thus Buber foregrounded those aspects of Hasidism that most resonated with New Romanticism's and Expressionism's notions of renewal through art by projecting an inner and unifying reality onto the outside world. As with the texts discussed in the first section, the topics of universality and timeless truths are rooted in a particular cultural and historical context. The writings about Hasidism and Jewish spirituality are produced within a Western context for a Western audience and as such are very much products of West European modernity.[12] With this emphasis on unity, Buber created an image of Hasidism that emphasized the universal nature of Jewish spirituality, linking it not only to these West European aesthetic movements, but also to the many "Oriental" mystical traditions.

At the heart of these debates about Jewish identity are questions of history and national identity. Within the questions of history, Christian biblical studies on Judaism as well as the secular approaches of Kant and Hegel played important roles. Mendes-Flohr characterizes Kant's and Hegel's influences in the following manner:

> Each treated the religion of Israel typologically, that is, as representing a specific type or mode of religious consciousness and apprehension of truth; and both found Judaism, especially in comparison to Christianity, to be a typologically inferior religion. Further, both considered Judaism historiosophically, assigning it to a specific historical stage in humankind's cognitive and spiritual development. In emphasizing that the stage assigned to Judaism was preparatory to that stage entrusted to Christianity, both Kant and Hegel were clearly presenting a secular version of Christian *Heilsgeschichte.*[13]

Buber's writings focused on the spirituality of the Hasidim in a way that emphasized their spirituality and the continuing relevance of Judaism for the modern world as a source of renewal and can be seen as one of the alternatives to this model of thinking about Judaism and history. Yet Buber did so in part by removing Jewish spirituality and Jewish culture from history by emphasizing their universal aspects. For example, by eliminating temporal markers in his retelling of Hasidic legends, Buber emphasizes the timelessness of the story and its subject.

Influenced by the work of historian Simon Dubnow,[14] Buber sees Jewish spirituality, more specifically Jewish mysticism, as a long and continuing tradition. We will now take a closer look at the introduction to his *Die Geschichten des Rabbi Nachman,* an introduction that makes up about half of the text. It provides background information about Jewish mysticism and explores the themes of timelessness, absolute truth, renewal, and loss in relation to Jewish culture and identity. According to Buber, Jewish mysticism provides insight into the essential character of Jews, something so fundamental to Jewish identity that it has always existed:

> Es ist eine bedeutsame Eigentümlichkeit des Juden, die sich in den Jahrtausenden kaum gewandelt zu haben scheint, daß sich die Extreme bei ihm aneinander entzünden, schneller und mächtiger, als bei irgend einem anderen Menschen. So geschieht es, daß mitten in einem unsäglich begrenzten Dasein, ja gerade aus seiner Begrenztheit heraus plötzlich mit einer Gewalt, die nichts zu bändigen versucht, das Schrankenlose hervorbricht und nun die widerstandlos hingegebene Seele regiert. (MB, 6)

> It is a significant peculiarity of the Jew, which hardly seems to have changed in thousands of years, that with him one extreme quickly and powerfully enkindles another. Thus it happened that in the

> midst of an unspeakably circumscribed existence, indeed out of its very limitations, there suddenly broke forth the limitless which now governed the soul that surrendered itself to it. (MBE, 4)

Buber describes the ability to live in extremes, to experience the "limitless," as an enduring facet of the Jewish character; the unchanging nature of the limitless or absolute has a direct correlation to the unchanging nature of the Jewish spirit. Buber frequently uses vague time references such as "in the time of the Talmud" (MB, 9) or even "from time immemorial" (MB, 5–6) to further emphasize the constancy of Judaism and the Jews. Numerical dates are often not much more precise: for example, "between the seventh and ninth century" (MB, 9). Within this context, Buber positions Rabbi Nachman in the following way: "Er steht am Ende einer ununterbrochenen Überlieferung, deren Anfang wir nicht kennen" (MB, 5). ["He stands at the end of an unbroken tradition whose beginning we do not know" (MBE, 3).] With this sentence, Buber establishes that Jewish mysticism's origins are so old they cannot be pinpointed to a historical time or a geographic location, and that Nachman both represents this tradition and its end. He represents the end because the people around him are not receptive to his teachings; Hasidism has been corrupted, and Nachman, one of the few who stays true to the continuous tradition, cannot stem the decline. It is interesting that Buber's symbol of Jewish spiritual renewal is one who is ultimately unsuccessful in revitalizing the Jewish spirit.

Buber's own project is one of salvaging universal truths that have been lost. In the foreword to *Die Geschichten des Rabbi Nachman,* Buber mentions that since Nachman did not write down any of his teachings himself, the writings we have are transcriptions and recollections from his students: "Die Geschichten sind uns in einer Schülerniederschrift erhalten, die die ursprüngliche Erzählung offenbar maßlos entstellt und verzerrt hat. Wie sie uns vorliegen, sind sie verworren, weitschweifig und von unedler Form" (MB, foreword). ["The tales have been preserved for us in the notes of a disciple, notes that have obviously deformed and distorted the original narrative beyond measure. As they lie before us, they appear confused, verbose, and ignoble in form" (MBE, foreword).] Buber's description of the stories is in keeping with his representation of Nachman as a man who was misunderstood by those around him. Implied is that the student could not accurately write down the stories because he did not understand them, and this lack of understanding is typical for those who heard Nachman's stories. The question Buber finds himself asking is: if even his students did not understand him, how could one expect others to have done so? Buber writes of the relationship between Nachman and the people around him: “Rabbi Nachman hatte sein Werk nicht gewirkt. Er war der Zaddik gewesen, den er meinte: ‘die Seele des Volkes.’ Aber das Volk war nicht sein geworden” (MB, 32). [“Rabbi Nachman did not accomplish his task. He had become the zaddik whom he meant, ‘the soul of the people’; but the people had not become his” (MBE, 34).] He ends his introduction with the following words:

> Sie [die jüdische Mystik] war die Blüte der Exilseele; sie verdarb aber auch am Exil. Die Juden waren nicht stark und nicht rein genug, sie zu bewahren. Es ist uns nicht gegeben zu wissen, ob ihr eine Auferstehung gewährt ist. Aber das innere Schicksal des Judentums scheint mir daran zu hangen, ob—gleichviel, in dieser Gestalt oder einer anderen—sein Pathos wieder zur Tat wird. (MB, 32)

> It [Jewish mysticism] was the flowering of the soul of the exile; but it also withered in exile. The Jews were not strong enough and pure enough to preserve it. It is not given to us to know whether a resurrection will be granted it. But the inner destiny of Judaism seems to me to depend on whether—no matter if in this shape or another—its pathos will again become deed. (MBE, 34)

Buber sees his mission as one of “restoring” these stories, finding the timeless truths within them, truths that the people around Nachman were not receptive to. In the quote above, Buber tentatively expresses the hope that perhaps now is the right time to receive such wisdom. Yet he also points out that the renewal has yet to happen, and even the form in which it could happen is not certain. Although Hasidism may not be the answer, it contains what Buber sees as the key component of a renewal—the combination of pathos and action.

According to Buber, one of the few important developments in Jewish mysticism was the emergence of Hasidism:

> Die Verkündigung der Freude in Gott wirkte nach einem Jahrtausend freudenbarer, freudenfeindlicher Gesetzesherrschaft wie eine Befreiung. Dazu kam, daß das Volk sich bisher einer durchaus unfruchtbaren, wirklichkeitsfremden, tatenlosen, aber nie angezweifelten “geistigen Aristokratie” von Talmudgelehrten gegenüber gesehen hatte. Nun wurde es mit einem Schlage von diesem Gegensatze erlöst und auf den eigenen Wert gestellt. Nun wurde ihm gesagt, nicht das Wissen entscheide über den Rang eines Menschen,

> sondern die Reinheit und Weihe seiner Seele, das ist: seine Gottnähe. (MB, 17–18)

> The proclamation of joy in God, after a thousand years of a dominance of law that was poor in joy and hostile to it, acted like a liberation. In addition, the people up till then had acknowledged above them an aristocracy of Talmud scholars, alienated from life, yet never contested. Now the people, by a single blow, were liberated from this aristocracy and established in their own value. Now it was said to them that it is not knowledge that determines the quality of a man, but the purity and devotion of his soul, that is, his nearness to God. (MBE, 15)

For Buber Hasidism's defining characteristic is a disavowal of asceticism in favor of a religion founded in joy. Unlike a religion based on elitism and intellectualism, Hasidism insists that each individual is responsible for his or her spirituality. This emphasis on individual agency fundamentally changed the people's relationship to God. There is no more need for intermediaries, and the old hierarchy is gone. Yet, as Buber himself points out, this approach ultimately fails because although it appeals to the masses, this way of life is possible for very few individuals. The criteria that define the few are now different, because it is not about social standing or education, but nonetheless not many can live "near God."

The main reason that so few can follow the teaching of Hasidism is that it is, according to Buber, a form of mysticism that strives to bring the absolute into everyday reality. On the one hand, one can see this endeavor as one that brings the two worlds together and emphasizes the importance of everyday life for spirituality. On the other, these glimpses of the absolute are fleeting and result from moments of extreme crisis:

> Das Wandern und das Martyrium der Juden haben ihre Seelen immer wieder in die Schwingungen der letzten Verzweiflung versetzt, aus denen so leicht der Blitz der Ekstase erwacht . . . Das Pathos erniedrigt sich oft genug zur Rhetorik; diesem Sündenfalle waren die Juden von jeher ausgesetzt, und nicht immer bloß die mittelmäßigen. Aber immer wieder macht sich das Pathos frei und ist reiner und größer als zuvor. (MB, 8)

> The wandering and martyrdom of the Jews have time and time again placed their souls in a vacillation of ultimate desperation, from which ecstasy's lightning easily breaks through . . . Pathos

> often enough stoops to rhetoric; this flaw was one that Jews have always been susceptible to, and not just the mediocre ones. But time and time again the pathos breaks free and is purer and greater than before.

The persecution that Jews have suffered, the resulting moments of deep desperation: these are, according to Buber, the necessary prerequisites to the kind of pathos necessary for a connection to the absolute.[15] Buber defines Jews by their suffering, but as a precondition for their joy. Yet these extreme states cannot be maintained for prolonged periods of time, and Buber warns of the possibility of pathos becoming rhetoric, of experience being diluted by words.

Buber marks one of the most significant moments in Jewish mysticism as Poland, more specifically the Ukraine, in the eighteenth century:

> Polen hatte eine feste, durch die fremde, verachtende Umwelt in sich gestärkte jüdische Gemeinschaft, und zum erstenmal seit der spanischen Blüte entwickelte sich hier ein eigenes Leben in Werken und Werten, eine dürftige und gebrechliche aber selbständige Kultur . . . Und dann war der Jude hier nicht, wie in den übrigen polnischen Ländern, ein Städter, der in dem engen rabbinischen Studium vertrocknete oder in der Atmosphäre der geschäftigen Masse verflachte, sondern zumeist ein Dörfler, einsamer und sich selbst näher, begrenzt im Wissen, aber ursprünglich im Glauben und stark in seinem Traume von Gott. (MB, 14)

> Poland had a solid Jewish community, strengthened by an alien, disdainful environment. For the first time since the Spanish blossoming an idiosyncratic life developed through activities and values, a meager and fragile but independent culture . . . And unlike in other Polish lands, the Jew here was not a city person, dried out by narrow rabbinical studies or flattened by the atmosphere of the busy masses, but rather a villager, lonely and closer to himself, limited in knowledge, but authentic in belief and strong in his dream of God.

Whereas in the previous quote Buber emphasizes the notion of suffering and crisis, here he underscores the importance of separation to the development of Jewish spirituality. Not only are the Jews in the Ukraine separate from the non-Jews, forcing them to create a community that is defined in great part by its separation from those around them; in addition, these Jews are removed from modernity in the form of cities, intellectualism, and commerce. Here as throughout the text, Buber conflates individual agency with anti-intellectualism and a celebration of the primitive and ancient.

In his descriptions of Rabbi Nachman, Buber repeatedly emphasizes how Rabbi Nachman embodies the teachings of those who lived a few generations before him, like his forefather, the famous Baal Schem (MB, 21). Yet as a representative of these spiritual truths, of a chance to challenge the false teachings of the Zaddik, Rabbi Nachman is ultimately unable to connect to others; to paraphrase Buber, Jewish mysticism was born in exile and, through Rabbi Nachman, also dies in exile, since Rabbi Nachman is separated from the world around him through his knowledge. Thus a central paradox is foregrounded—an unmediated relationship to the absolute potentially produces a community built on an awareness of the spiritual in the everyday, yet this awareness, since it is so difficult to achieve, often alienates one from the others. In Buber's model the timelessness of Nachman's wisdom made it difficult for him to exist in his own time. Nevertheless, Buber asserts that this symbol of renewal, although already a symbol of loss, is simultaneously one of a possible future renewal. Döblin and Roth, although clearly influenced by this portrayal of Jewish mysticism, in particular with the notions of timeless truths and of a deeper connection to an absolute reality, shift the focus from the idea of the Hasidim as a symbol of both the past and the future to one of the Hasidim as a preserved past that exists in the present. They emphasize the connection between isolation and mysticism, and in their writings they create a geographic and temporal space for the Hasidim that is removed from their surroundings. This move is in keeping with a change in the relationship between the West and the East. Whereas Buber looks to the East to rejuvenate the West, Döblin and Roth use the East to critique the West and to emphasize that what has been preserved in the East is, because of modernity and assimilation, irrevocably lost in the West. We will now take a closer look at their works and the interactions and conflicts between various discourses of time, space, and mobility that together create both the worlds of the traveler/narrator and of the East European Jews they observe.

Heading East

Alfred Döblin's *Reise in Polen* and Joseph Roth's *Juden auf Wanderschaft* are often contrasted with one another. Roth's text is seen as a personal, clearly opinionated text that creates a romantic, pathos-laden, and nostalgic picture of East European Jews. Döblin's text, on the other hand, is read as a collection of carefully crafted, unmediated impressions that allows readers to come to their own conclusions about what is "seen" on the journey.[16] Roth makes a comment about the narrator's lack of definitive position in *Reise in Polen* in his review of the book for the *Frankfurter Zeitung*. He writes: "Döblin hat eine wohltätige Frechheit. Er will keine 'Verantwortung' vor den abstrakten Autoritäten tragen. Er hat keine 'Grundsätze.' Er stellt das Prinzip hinter die Anschauung. Er kann höhnisch sein, und man wird ihn niemals als Lästerer empfinden. Sein Witz ist kühl. Seine persönlichen Erlebnisse werden nicht privat" [Döblin has a benevolent audacity. He does not want the abstract authorities to hold him 'responsible.' He does not have any 'principles.' He subordinates the principle to the outlook. He can be scornful, and no one will ever perceive him to be a detractor. His wit is cool. His personal experiences never become private].[17] Roth's insight is that Döblin's text is not without opinions, but they do not seem to belong to the narrator. He describes Döblin's impersonal subjectivity as a refusal to take responsibility for his own opinions. His observation that Doblin's experiences are personal but not private captures the fine line the text navigates between the impersonal and the personal, the subjective and the objective.

Considering the very different reception these two texts have received, the similarities between them are surprising. As much as Roth may have criticized Döblin's text for the distance between the narrator and narration, Roth occupies a similar position in his own text. He often uses the third person to present his opinions as fact, and the reader learns very little about the narrator or his relationship to East European Jews and their culture. In other words, the credibility of Roth's portrayal of East European Jews depends on discourses of objectivity and distance. A closer look at Döblin's text also reveals that the distanced but subjective narrative position serves to bring the reader closer to the experiences portrayed; it is the narrator's distance that allows the reader to become a traveler, to have what at least seems to be a more intimate relationship with the travel experiences. Both texts rely on a distanced outsider position in order to accomplish two things—allow the reader to become a traveler and emphasize or even create the separate space that the Hasidim occupy. The authority of the narrative position simultaneously brings readers closer to the experience and reminds them of the limits of their intimacy with the subject, due to the nature not of the medium, but of the subject.

One of the ways in which Döblin creates this distance is through the use of ethnographic discourses. Döblin sets out to learn more about East

European Jews in Poland in order to gain insight into Jewish identity and the interactions between Jews and non-Jews. Döblin's representation of the Hasidim acknowledges their existence, but as one that belongs to the past and bears little connection to the Western present, both geographically and temporally. He searches in Poland for insight into Jewish identity, and brings these images of East European Jews back to the West, but creates a temporal and geographical divide between the two groups that makes it impossible to see East European Jews as an example to emulate.

As Assenka Oksiloff and others have shown, the "primitive body" was an object of great interest in the early twentieth century—both in the realm of scientific study and in the popular imagination.[18] *Reise in Polen* can be seen as part of this tradition, as Döblin's view of Poland and its people is clearly influenced by the ethnographic discourses of the time. For example, Döblin often describes physical attributes in detail, and he pays close attention to those characteristics that are "typical" for a people. And in general, Döblin is primarily interested in individuals for what they can tell him about the people as a whole, in bringing these people to life for his audience, but in a way that emphasizes their distance from the audience's reality. Central to this project of "reviving" the East European Jews as "dead," to use Mary Louise Pratt's terminology,[19] is their separation from the other peoples in Poland—in terms of culture, religion, and time. These demarcations are made most clear when Döblin visits Jewish ghettos. In Warsaw, Döblin's description of the "Judenstadt" focuses on those elements he finds strange: they wear dirty kaftans, many have red hair, the married women wear wigs, the men have heavy beards. Close attention is paid to the German-sounding names of many of these Jews, which bear little resemblance to German surnames. For example, he lists the Jewish names he sees on store signs: "Waiselfisch, Klopfherd, Blumenkranz, Brandwain, Farzstandig, Goldkopf, Gelbfisch, Gutbesztand. Man hat den Menschen des geächteten Volkes Spottnamen angehängt. Ich lese weiter [The members of the ostracized nation have been saddled with derisive nicknames. I read on (ADE, 52)]: Goldluft, Goldwasser, Feldgras, Oksenberg" (AD, 74). Two pages later we find another list of names: "Die gewaltigen Stofflager. Ich lese die Namen [The massive textile warehouses. I read the names]: Seidenstrumpf, Butterfaß, Tuchwarger, Spiegelglas. Dann Jakob Natur, Israel Gesundheit" (AD, 76). Such lists appear throughout the book, and they emphasize the distance between Jews and non-Jews in several ways. First, the names are of German origin, not Polish. Already there is one step of separation between Jews and Poles. Furthermore, they are not typical German last names; Döblin interprets the names as evidence of how much the Jews are despised by referring to them as "Spottnamen" [derisive nicknames]. The fact that the names are not of the Jews' choosing, that they are "angehängt" [saddled with], also points to a clear discrepancy in power. These names serve as a reminder of how Jews are asked to assimilate (in this case by taking on the naming conventions of the majority culture) but also constantly reminded that they are not equals.

When he sees Jews who do not conform to his notions of what is Jewish, these examples are "less" Jewish:

> Jüdische Frauen gehen in der Menge; sie tragen schwarze Perücken, einen kleinen schwarzen Schleier darüber, vorn eine Art Blume. Einen schwarzen Schal haben sie um. Merkwürdig ein großer modern gekleideter junger Mann mit seiner eleganten Schwester; stolz geht er und trägt eine Judenkappe auf dem Kopf. (AD, 74–75)

> Jewish women pass through the crowd; they wear black wigs, small black veils on top, a kind of flower in front. Black shawls. A tall young man in modern clothes with his elegant sister looks strange; he walks proudly, with a skullcap on his head. (ADE, 52)

The women who are "typically" Jewish are labeled "jüdische Frauen." The man and his sister are separated from these women with the commentary "merkwürdig" [strange], denoting that their appearance is somehow unexpected and atypical. Furthermore, they themselves are not marked as Jewish; only the man's "Judenkappe" is. Modern clothes and elegance point to a worldliness that disturbs Döblin because it makes it difficult to separate Jews from non-Jews. In the same paragraph, he writes: "Ein polnischer Schutzmann leitet auf dem Damm den Wagenverkehr. Dieses Nebeineinander zweier Völker. Junge Mädchen schlendern Arm in Arm her, sehen wenig jüdisch aus, lachen, sprechen jiddisch, tragen sich bis auf die feinen Strümpfe polnisch" (AD, 75). ["A Polish policeman directs vehicular traffic in the roadway. This contiguousness of two nations. Young girls stroll arm in arm, they don't look very Jewish, they laugh, speak Yiddish, their clothes are Polish down to the fine stockings" (ADE, 52).] Although "nebeneinander" [contiguousness] denotes proximity, it also emphasizes the distance that separates—the one is next to the other, but there is no interaction. This distance is further emphasized by referring to Jews and Poles as two peoples. In the next sentence we once again have examples of people who do not, according to Döblin, look very Jewish—the young girls speak and laugh in Yiddish, but wear Polish clothing.

In his description, Döblin keeps the Jewish and the Polish qualities separate, even though they apply to the same people. Yet in this description and others, it is evident how much effort is involved in keeping Polish and Jewish qualities separate; Döblin creates the separation through his narrative rather than "merely" describing a preexisting situation.

This separation is also a geographical one. As Döblin leaves the Judenstadt, he remarks: "Draußen sind die Geschäfte geschlossen. Langsam flanieren Kaftanträger über die stille Straße. Wie ich mich dem Theaterplatz nähere, ändert sich rasch das Bild. Ich bin in Polen, in einer wogenden großen polnischen Stadt" (AD, 80). ["Outside, the stores are closed. Men in caftans slowly amble along the hushed street. As I approach Theater Square, the tableau quickly changes. I am in Poland, in a surging Polish metropolis" (ADE, 56).] The Jewish space, that of the "kaftan-wearers," is marked by its slowness and quiet. The shift is marked as rapid, and the new space is Poland, more specifically a Polish city. "Wogend" [surging] also adds to the sense of movement that defines the urban, Polish, non-Jewish space. Here Döblin has mapped temporal qualities onto a geographic location, and he, as a traveler, moves from one to the other. When he does encounter Jews in a space that is not exclusively Jewish, it is almost always in the presence of farmers, whose shabby appearance and backward ways are constantly foregrounded. By connecting the Jews to the farmers, Döblin creates a distinction between rural and urban spaces, even within a city. Jews and farmers belong to a rural space that is everything the city is not—slow, old-fashioned, poor, uneducated: in short, primitive.[20]

Although Döblin attempts to separate the Jews from all that is modern and urban, his first encounter with the "primitive" elements of Jewish culture leaves him unsettled. He observes the inhabitants of the Judenstadt as they prepare for Yom Kippur, or the Day of Atonement. He hears cries, singing, and moaning and observes women clutching gravestones and appealing to their dead relatives. All Jews—those elegantly dressed and those not—take part in these rituals. Döblin flees from the masses of people:

> Ich bin durchschauert, wie ich dies gesehen und gehört habe. Wie ich mit der Elektrischen zurückfahre, die Hoteltreppen aufsteige, in meinem Zimmer sitze, kann ich mich lange nicht besinnen. Es ist etwas Grauenhaftes. Es ist etwas Urnatürliches, Atavistisches. Hat das mit Judentum etwas zu tun? Das sind leibhaftige Überbleibsel uralter Vorstellungen! Das sind Überbleibsel der Angst vor den Toten, der Angst vor den Seelen, die herumschweifen. Ein Gefühl,

> den Menschen dieses Volkes überliefert mit ihrer Religion. Es ist der Rest einer anderen Religion, Animismus, Totenkult. (AD, 92–93)

> Cold shivers run up and down my spine when I see and hear these things. I ride back on the trolley, climb the hotel stairs, sit in my room; it takes me awhile to collect my thoughts. This is something horrible. It is something primordial, atavistic. Does this have anything to do with Judaism? These are living vestiges of ancient notions: These are vestiges of the fear of the dead, the fear of wandering souls. A feeling handed down to the members of this nation with their religion. It is the remnant of a different religion, animism, a cult of the dead. (ADE, 66)

Döblin cannot accept that what he has witnessed is part of the Jewish religion. He insists that these practices are not Judaism but rather another religion. He emphasizes the separation of time between the Jewish religion and these beliefs with the use of the prefix "ur-"—"Urnatürliches," "uralt." Although the Jews do not occupy the same temporal space as the urban Poles, they also do not belong to the temporal space of these beliefs. Only remnants of this older religion are to be seen; the Jews have progressed, but not far enough to be free of this "Totenkult." Döblin insists on the timeless qualities of Jewish mysticism, and his descriptions of East European Jews use ethnographic discourses that place them into the category of "primitive natives," but he is also insistent that there is a difference between a superstitious, cultlike primitivism and the essential nature of the East European Jews and their beliefs. This distinction between different notions of "primitive" is important, as it gives the reader a better sense of what this essential nature is by comparing it to what it is not. It also implies that Jewish beliefs have evolved over time. There may be elements of an older belief system still present, but these are just traces that, according to Döblin, do not belong there, and Jewish religious beliefs have for the most part outgrown them. Within this paradigm, one could surmise that Jewish customs and beliefs are capable of change, and when there is a lack of change it is by choice rather than because of a lack of ability. In other words, the East European Jews may for the most part be "primitive" not through ignorance of what modernity is, but rather through their rejection of it. What is most interesting about this passage is Döblin's need to escape from this world and the alienation he experiences during this escape. He lists the steps of his departure—taking the tram, climbing the steps, sitting in his hotel room. But he cannot connect himself to these actions, and the next sentence returns the reader to this unsettling ancient world. Unlike the clean transition when Döblin walked toward the Theaterplatz, here he takes the one world with him into the other, and as a result cannot fully be part of his own experience of moving through the various spaces. His mode of travel is a modern one, yet the impressions of this ancient world stay with him.

Joseph Roth claims to hold the scientific objectivity of disciplines like anthropology in disregard. In the foreword to *Juden auf Wanderschaft,* Roth writes: "Dieses Buch ist nicht für Leser geschrieben, die es dem Autor übelnehmen würden, daß er den Gegenstand seiner Darstellung mit Liebe behandelt, statt mit 'wissenschaftlicher Sachlichkeit,' die man auch Langeweile nennt" (JR, 7). ["This book has not been written for readers who would blame the author for treating the subjects of his account with love, and not with that 'scientific detachment' better known as indifference" (JRE, 2).] Here Roth signals his subjectivity and affection for his subject with a dismissal of cold scientific objectivity. Yet his positive portrayals of East European Jews depend on distance and the sense of objectivity this distance provides. Similar to that in Döblin's text, the narrator's position in Roth's *Juden auf Wanderschaft* is one that privileges an outsider position and that separates the narrator from his surroundings. Roth uses the position of the narrator to legitimize a different model of an outsider from his own, one that creates a community. Roth almost always refers to the Jews he sees in the plural to emphasize a collective identity. It is not a coincidence that the title of the text is also in the plural; Roth turns the solitary figure of the Wandering Jew into a wandering people. In opposition to Benjamin's flâneur or Simmel's stranger, the East European Jews are a group of outsiders, removed from the culture and time of the people around them. Furthermore, they do not wear Plessner's masks; their strength comes from the ability to live naked existences in which all are connected to one another through their relationship to God. Yet at the same time, Roth's position as a narrator is none of these things. When covering the topic of Jewish religion and mysticism, Roth often situates the narrative in a nonspecific time and geographical location in order to emphasize the enduring and unchanging qualities of these traditions. Nevertheless, the book does rely on discourses of objectivity in order to provide a position of authority for the narrator and his narrative. The narrator remains anonymous and, if not fully impartial, at least without a personal vested interest in his subject. As is the case with *Reise in Polen,* we are not told whether or not the narrator is Jewish, and throughout the text it is clear that he does not identify himself as a member of any of the East European Jewish groups he meets. It can be inferred from Roth's intended audience that he is West European, but he does not include himself in his descriptions of West Europeans either; there is no "we" in this narrative, only "they" and the occasional "I." The narrative is seldom in the first person, and when it is, the purpose is to emphasize that the narrator witnessed the events he describes; the "I" authenticates the experience. And in these circumstances, as is the case in Döblin's text, the emphasis is on how others see the narrator, particularly on how the narrator does not belong in his surroundings.

While Roth maintains that his encounter with the Hasidim does not resemble the study of exotic natives, his descriptions recall ethnographic writings and their particular viewpoint. For example, he describes various rituals and traditions, such as a dance at a festival: "Die Chassidim faßten sich bei den Händen, tanzten in der Runde . . . ergriffen die Thorarollen und schwenkten sie im Kreis, wie Mädchen und drückten sie an die Brust, küßten sie und weinten vor Freude. Es war im Tanz eine erotische Lust" (JR, 40). ["The hasidim took each other by the hand, they danced in a ring . . . picked up their Torah scrolls and swung them around like partners, clasped them to their bosom, and kissed them and shed tears of joy. There was eroticism in their dance" (JRE, 39–40).] The narrator is also quick to point out that this primitivity he observes is a source of vitality and health: "Das war nicht der Tanz eines degenierten Geschlechts. Es war nicht nur die Kraft eines fanatischen Glaubens. Es war gewiß eine Gesundheit, die den Anlaß zu ihrem Ausbruch im Religiösen fand" (JR, 39). ["It wasn't the dance of a degenerate race. It was more than the energy given by a fanatical faith. It was a kind of health that took the occasion to break out into religion" (JRE, 39).] The positive portrayal of these qualities is a pointed critique of the West as a place where people have lost their connection to God and religious traditions. The narrator implies that Westerners could learn something from their more "primitive" neighbors, all the while emphasizing that it is their isolation from modernity that gives the Hasidim their vitality and authenticity.

According to Roth, the contact that West Europeans have with East European Jews, primarily through East European Jewish immigrants living in the West, creates a familiarity with them that makes East European Jews seem to be an uninteresting subject of study: "Man betrachtet die Juden, weil sie überall in unserer Mitte leben, als bereits 'erforscht' " (JR, 32–33). ["The Jew, because he lives everywhere in our midst, has ostensibly already been 'researched' " (JRE, 32).] Roth's descriptions of the Hasidim are in part an attempt to rectify this conception that Westerners already know all they need to about East European Jews. Like Döblin, Roth maintains that the East European Jews one sees in the West are not "authentic" East European Jews, as they have been corrupted by Western Europe. There is much to admire about East European Jews, but first one must learn more about their culture and traditions, and in order to do so, one must travel to Eastern Europe.

Döblin echoes these sentiments in an introduction he wrote for a later edition of his book. He writes that Berlin's first twentieth-century pogrom, which took place in the Scheunenviertel in November 1923, was the impetus for his journey:

> Ich fand, ich müßte mich einmal über die Juden orientieren. Ich fand, ich kannte eigentlich Juden nicht. Ich konnte meine Bekannten, die sich Juden nannten, nicht Juden nennen. Sie waren es dem Glauben nach nicht, ihrer Sprache nach nicht, sie waren vielleicht Reste eines untergegangenen Volkes, die längst in die neue Umgebung eingegangen waren. Ich fragte also mich und fragte andere: Wo gibt es Juden? Man sagte mir: In Polen. Ich bin darauf nach Polen gefahren. (AD, 352)[21]

> I felt I had to get my bearings about the Jews. I realized I didn't know any Jews. I had friends who called themselves Jews, but I could not call them Jews. They were not Jewish by faith or by language; they were possibly remnants of an extinct nation that had long since integrated into a new milieu. So I asked myself and I asked others; "Where do Jews exist?" I was told: Poland. And so I went to Poland. (ADE, xii)

Here we see Döblin connecting notions of ethnography and space with one another—it is impossible to find an "authentic" Jew in the West, but in Poland they are still to be found. And in order to understand the intersections between location, religion, language, and culture, he must travel to Poland and see for himself. In his travels he seeks to find the essence of Jewish identity, to travel back in time to discover the "Ur-Jews"—the Hasidim—in their natural habitat.

Encounters with Wunderrabbis

Through their narrative positions in *Reise in Polen* and *Juden auf Wanderschaft,* Döblin and Roth make it clear that East European Jews, in particular the Hasidim, are everything that West European Jews are not, and this distance between narrator and subject also foregrounds the impossibility for West European Jews to find an authentic existence. We will find in these texts that, as is the case in Buber's Hasidic tales, the timelessness of East European Jewish identity is inextricably linked to Jewish mysticism. This relationship is the source of authenticity; it allows East European Jews to live outside of time and history, separate from their surroundings.

Döblin's encounters with Hasidim reinforce the importance he places on a timeless Jewish identity. In Krakow, Döblin returns to the theme of elements of ancient beliefs embedded in Jewish life, but now he sees this as a desirable trait; the tie to mystic beliefs is part of the connection the Jews have to the "Kern" [core] of Jewish identity. While in Krakow, Döblin visits the Jewish quarter Kazimierz. He sees the men going to pray and walks the streets with his guide. But a large portion of the description is dedicated to legends about the Hasidim that were told to Döblin. More specifically, they focus on a particular aspect of Hasidism—kabbalistic teachings and legends.[22] These stories have no temporal markers; they are allegories that convey certain mysterious and timeless truths. The mystical aspects of Hasidism fascinate Döblin. In reference to the various incantations, amulets, and what he calls superstitions (*Aberglauben*), he writes:

> Es ist konzentrierte Kabbalistik. Wächst aus dem alten Glauben einer Verbundenheit, ja Identität von Wort und Realität, ist Ausfluß eines alten mystischen Gefühls. Eine große alte Denkweise. Wie fern, oder heimlich nah, winkt Hegelsche Vorstellung: "Was ist, ist vernünftig." Die von heute begnügen sich, die Ebene des Historischen zu studieren: im sichtbaren animalischen Leben entstehen Worte und Zeichen. Hier zeugt im Anfang das Wort. Der Faust des deutschen Goethe beginnt damit, daß er diesen Satz ablehnt; er ist kein alter, kein echter Faust. Welche Mischung von Naivität und Tiefsinn. (AD, 255)

> It's concentrated cabbalism. It stems from the old faith in a connection, nay, identity between words and reality; it emanates from an ancient mystical feeling. A great ancient way of thinking. The Hegelian notion beckons from far away or intimately near: "Whatever exists is rational." Modern-day people are content to study the state of history: words and signs issue forth in visible animal life. Here, in the beginning, the word begets. The Faust of the German Goethe begins by rejecting that proposition; he's not an ancient, not a genuine Faust. What a blend of naïveté and profundity. (ADE, 195)

Döblin uses "wachsen" [grow/stem from] to connect kabbalah to an older belief system; the verb connotes a sense of natural progress and creates the image that the older beliefs are the roots that nurture kabbalah. Now "alt" is used to signify ties to mystical truths about the relationship between words and reality. In this passage, Döblin dismisses the historical as not being about life. Although the Hasidim's status as a primitive people is apparent in words such as "Naivität" and "altes mystisches Gefühl," it is also clear that these qualities are what create a connection between words and reality. The reference to Hegel opens up the possibility that what Western Europe considers rational may be less so than the seemingly irrational Hasidim. According to Döblin, history is just words in relation to the visible and superficial manifestations of reality, while Hasidic rituals and beliefs are living words that stem from an ancient tradition. Döblin also mentions Goethe's *Faust.* These comparisons to figures of West European thought and culture create a stark contrast between sterile, rational words and words that are infused with life and reality. The references to an old mystical feeling and to the rejection of history reinforce the notion that the Hasidim do not belong within history; they are a part of something older and more real. Instead of a temporal gap between the Jews and certain aspects of their culture, Döblin now sees the mystic and irrational elements of the Hasidic beliefs and traditions as a connection to an otherwise lost truth and authenticity.[23]

In this more or less enclosed Hasidic space, Döblin's separation from the others is constantly foregrounded. Döblin travels to Gura Kalwarja to visit a famous "Wunderrabbi." He describes the villagers thus: "Ihre Blicke sind mißtrauisch, abweisend. Es hilft nichts, daß mein Begleiter unaufhörlich auf jiddisch mit ihnen redet. Es beschnüffeln uns immer neue. Ich bin, kommt mir vor, unter eine exotische Völkerschaft geraten; man will mich nicht, mich und meinen Begleiter, wir sind ihnen Eindringlinge" (AD, 103). ["Their eyes are distrustful, chilly. It doesn't help that my companion speaks Yiddish to them nonstop. New ones keep sizing us up. I feel as if I've come upon an exotic tribe; they do not want me, me or my companion, they regard us as intruders" (ADE, 75).] By the end of his visit, his position as a complete outsider remains unchanged: "Ich komme mir im Dorf wie verjagt vor, kann die aufdringlichen und spöttischen Blicke der Neugierigen auf der Straße nicht ertragen. Ich will weg, bin froh, als ich den Bahnhof sehe" (AD, 108). ["In the village, I feel virtually expelled, I can't stand the obtrusive and derisive looks of the rubberneckers in the street. I want to leave, I am delighted to see the railroad station" (ADE, 79).] Döblin feels on display; there is no possibility for him to belong in this environment. His brief and confusing meeting with the rabbi also emphasizes the gap between Döblin and the Hasidim of the village.

After a harrowing experience of being caught in the middle of the crowd of people waiting for an audience with the rabbi, Döblin and his guide enter his room and find the rabbi sitting at a table by the window. After the guide speaks to the rabbi, he relays to Döblin a message from the rabbi: "Plötzlich sagt mein Begleiter: 'Er läßt Ihnen sagen, Sie möchten etwas fragen'" (AD, 105). ["All at once, my companion says: 'He says you can ask him something'" (ADE, 77).] Döblin's reaction is one of confusion:

> Ich denke: unmöglich; das ist ja gar nicht meine Absicht; ich will mit ihm sprechen, doch nicht fragen. Aber schon spricht der Rebbe wieder, leise; kein Wort dieses ganz besonderen Jiddisch kann ich verstehen. Dann habe ich plötzlich seine Hand, eine kleine schlaffe fleischige Hand, an meiner. Ich bin ganz erstaunt. Kein Druck der Hand; sie schiebt sich an meine heran. Ich höre ein leises "Scholem," mein Begleiter sagt: "Wir gehen!" Und langsam gehen wir. (AD, 105–6)

> I think to myself: Impossible, that's not what I'm after; I want to speak to him, not question him. But the rebbe is already speaking again, softly; I can't understand a single word of this very special Yiddish. Then, suddenly, I have his hand, a small slack fleshy hand, on mine. I am astonished. No pressure from his hand; it moves over to mine. I hear a quiet "*Sholem,*" my companion says: "We're leaving." And slowly, we leave. (ADE, 77)

After they leave the room, his guide explains that the rabbi was reluctant to see him and thought that perhaps Döblin was a lawyer who wanted to investigate him; he could not understand why Döblin would want to speak with him and ask him questions. As with the descriptions of his interactions with the villagers, the first-person singular is used often in Döblin's account of his meeting with the Wunderrabbi. This frequent use of the pronoun "I" is unusual when Döblin finds himself in non-Jewish spaces. There is a shift in his position to his surroundings, his experiences, and his narrative in these two spaces, illustrating the vast difference between the two worlds. He can disappear as a narrator in the Polish spaces because they are spaces of modernity in which he can be an anonymous outsider. But in this village, which represents a community removed from that modernity, Döblin has no way to interact with his environment comfortably; this world is too different from his own.

The isolation of the rabbi and his followers from the world around them is emphasized through a reference to the Middle Ages. When Döblin arrives in Gura, there are men waiting to greet the many pilgrims who were also in the train:

> Die Männer und Knaben aber, die die Reisenden erwarten und ihnen entgegenkommen, sind von einer ganz besonderen Art . . . Ich bekomme ein Bild, was Schläfenlocken sind, welch stolzer Schmuck. Wie diese Männer, Jünglinge, Knaben im sauberen schwarzen Kaftan schreiten, in hohen schwarzen glänzenden Mützen, sehen sie schwärmerisch-romantisch, mittelalterlich aus. Ihre Gesichter sind von besonderem Ausdruck, von einer ernsten Stille. Manche blicken ungewöhnlich frei und stolz. (AD, 102–3)
>
> But the men and boys who await the travelers and come to meet them are a very special breed . . . I get a picture of what earlocks are; what a proud adornment. How proudly these men, youths, boys stride along in clean black caftans, in high shiny black caps; they look romantic, rapturous, medieval. Their faces have an extraordinary look, an earnest stillness. Some of them boast free, broad expressions. (ADE, 75)

Döblin finds that the pride these men have in their appearance and the care with which they dress (expressed through adjectives such as "sauber" and "glänzend") sets them apart from other Jews. And it is these qualities that Döblin also associates with the Middle Ages. Implied is that their clothing and attitude more closely resemble that of their ancestors than the Jews Döblin normally encounters and that this constancy, this lack of change, has preserved the Jews' more admirable qualities.

In this world so unlike his own, Döblin relies on others to navigate his surroundings. The mediated nature of his interactions is foregrounded through the frequent mention of his guide, his inability to communicate on his own, and the need for outside interpretations to understand what he has seen and experienced. This absence of immediacy further demonstrates how impossible it is for Döblin to belong in the world of the Hasidim. He does not understand his encounter with the Wunderrabbi until his guide explains the conversation that he had with the rabbi on Döblin's behalf. Almost all the interactions Döblin has with the villagers and with the Wunderrabbi's followers are indirect; the guide speaks to them, and Döblin observes him as he does so. After the audience with the rabbi, Döblin observes him and his followers at a large table eating a meal: "Die Frommen beobachten ihn und seine Gäste, seine Bewegungen, haschen nach jedem Wort, erläutern es sich gegenseitig. Der größte Gewinn ist, Schirujim zu essen, Überbleibsel von der Schüssel des Zadik. Sie schlagen sich darum. Bisweilen gibt der Zadik selbst einem von seiner Schüssel" (AD, 107). ["The pious observe him and his guests, his movements, seize upon every word, elucidate it to one another. The biggest prize is eating *Shirayim,* leftovers from the tsadik's plate. They fight over them. Occasionally, the tsadik himself hands someone a scrap from his plate" (ADE, 78–79).] This description, although matter-of-fact and neutral, demonstrates a lack of knowledge; the word "Schirujim" is used, but no explanation is given of its significance. It is not until Döblin returns to Warsaw that he receives an explanation for what he has observed. There he and his guide receive an invitation from a follower of the rabbi of Gura who tells them:

> Essen und trinken: wir denken darüber anders als ihr. Ihr denkt, ihr eßt für den Körper. Wir denken das nicht. Wir sehen im Essen und Trinken etwas Geistiges, das zum Geist beiträgt. Das Brot und der Wein sind vielleicht nichts oder nicht viel. Aber wenn es an den Zadik herankommt, verändert es sich und wird etwas Besonderes. Der Zadik ist nicht wie der und jener Mensch. Er ist heilig, durch sein Lernen und durch den Vater und den Großvater, von denen er herkommt. Er ist näher an Gott als andere Menschen. Wenn der Zadik den Fisch berührt oder auch nur ansieht bei seiner Tafel, dann geht etwas von seinem Geist auf den Fisch über. Und nimmt man davon, so hat man von dem Geist aufgenommen. (AD, 109)

> Eating and drinking: our attitude toward them is different from yours. You believe that you eat for the sake of your bodies. We do not believe that. We see eating and drinking as something spiritual, something that contributes to the mind. Bread and wine may be nothing, or nothing much. But when they reach the tsadik, they change and become something special. The tsadik is not like just anyone. He is holy, because of his learning and because of his father and grandfather, from whom he issues. He is closer to God than other people. When the tsadik touches the fish or merely looks at it on his table, something of his spirit goes over to the fish. And if someone else partakes of that fish, then he absorbs something of the rebbe's spirit. (ADE, 80)

The mention of his guide at the beginning of this story[24] undermines the sense of immediacy created by the direct quote, as it reminds the reader that the follower's words were translated not by Döblin, but rather by the guide, as has been the case throughout Döblin's interactions with the rabbi and his followers. Thus several interventions are occurring simultaneously—the follower intervenes to explain what Döblin saw the previous day, and the guide intervenes to translate this explanation for Döblin, and then Döblin writes down his version of this translation for the reader. The seemingly unmediated experience the reader has in other parts of the book is absent here; the central role of the guide and other intermediaries increases not only the distance between Döblin and the world around him, but also the distance between the reader and this world.[25]

Roth has similar difficulties finding his place in the world of the Hasidim, as can be seen in the stark contrast between the descriptions of the Hasidim in which he does not play a role and the ones in which he has direct contact with them. Like Döblin, Roth sees the Wunderrabbis as the key connection to the world of Jewish mysticism; they are a visible reminder to others that this world exists.

> Er weiß mehr, als er sagen darf. Er weiß, daß über dieser Welt noch eine andere ist, mit anderen Gesetzen, und vielleicht ahnt er sogar, daß Verbote und Gebote in dieser Welt von Sinn, in einer anderen ohne Bedeutung sind. Es kommt ihm auf die Befolgung des ungeschriebenen, aber desto gültigeren Gesetzes an. (JR, 35)

> He knows more than he is permitted to say. He knows that there is another world above this one, which is differently constituted, and he may even sense that certain commands and interdictions that make sense in this world are of no consequence in the other. What matters to him is following these unwritten, but all the more valid, laws. (JRE, 35)

In this passage it appears that the two worlds and the two sets of laws are not connected with one another. Unlike Kracauer's model, in which everyday life (or, as he calls, it the lower sphere) gains meaning only when it is connected to the absolute (higher sphere), in Roth's description everyday life and its rules are meaningless in the other sphere. The spiritual world is less accessible than the material one, for its laws are not written, but it is also more valid and more authentic. For Roth, the Wunderrabbis also represent the continuity of Jewish mysticism. This is expressed in the text both directly and indirectly. An example of the former is the following description: "Die Würde des Wunderrabbis vererbt sich seit Generationen vom Vater auf den Sohn" (JR, 33). ["The calling of wonder-rabbi has been handed down from father to son for generations" (JRE, 32).] Indirectly, Roth emphasizes the unchanging qualities of the Wunderrabbi with an absence of temporal markers; everything is in the present. Roth describes how the Wunderrabbi lives, and by using the present tense he gives the reader the impression that every day is the same; the present is the same as the past and the future, thus the description is in a timeless present. The description of the Wunderrabbi resembles that of a figure in a fairy tale, combining a sense of wonder with this impression of timelessness:

> Aus weiten Gegenden kommen sie zu ihm. Er hört in einem Jahr die merkwürdigsten Schicksale und kein Fall ist so verwickelt, daß er nicht einen noch komplizierteren schon gehört hätte. Der Rabbi hat ebenso viel Weisheit, wie Erfahrung und ebenso viel praktische Klugheit, wie Glauben an sich selbst und sein Auserwählt-sein. (JR, 34)

> People come to him from far afield. In the course of a single year, he hears the most extraordinary stories, and no case is so complicated that he hasn't already heard one that was still more so. The rabbi has wisdom and experience in equal measure; he has as much practical common sense as he has confidence in himself and his mission. (JRE, 34)

Roth emphasizes the continued validity of this kind of mysticism in his comparison of the Wunderrabbi's wisdom to that of modern science:

> Das Stadium des Wissens hat er schon hinter sich. Der Kreis ist geschlossen. Der Mensch ist wieder gläubig. Die hochmütige Wissenschaft des Chirurgen bringt dem Patienten den Tod und die schale Weisheit des Physikers dem Jünger den Irrtum. Man glaubt nicht mehr dem Wissenden. Man glaubt dem Glaubenden.
>
> Viele glauben ihm. Er selbst, der Rabbi, macht keinen Unterschied zwischen den treuesten Erfüllern der geschriebenen Gebote und den weniger treuen, ja, nicht einmal zwischen Jude und Nichtjude, nicht zwischen Mensch und Tier. Wer zu ihm kommt, ist seiner Hilfe gewiß. (JR, 35)

> He has left the stage of [knowledge] behind him. The circle is unbroken. Man is once more a believer. The arrogant science of the surgeon kills the patient, and the empty [wisdom] of the physicist

> leads his students into error. One no longer believes the knower. One believes the believer.
>
> Many believe in him. He himself, the rabbi, does not distinguish between the most faithful followers of the Scriptures and the somewhat less faithful ones, no, nor even between Jew and *goy* or man and beast. Whoever comes to him is assured of getting his help.[26] (JRE, 34–35)

Rather than seeing religion and science in a linear timeline, with science gradually replacing religion, Roth describes the relationship as a circle, and the belief in mysticism as a return to true wisdom; science is a temporary detour and mysticism the enduring truth. Not only is mysticism timeless, it is also universal. The Wunderrabbi, the holder of this eternal wisdom, treats everyone as equal and sees similarities rather than differences between all those who come to him. Nevertheless, as Roth points out frequently, such a universal outlook is possible, paradoxically, only if the Wunderrabbi and his followers are kept separate from others, if differences are recognized and maintained. The timeless, universal wisdom that can erase differences and connects everyone to each other has as a necessary precondition an acceptance of strict boundaries through difference.

When Roth sets out to visit one of the Wunderrabbis himself, however, the experience is disappointing. Here the narrator places himself in the story; instead of descriptions that are told in the third person and opinions expressed as generalizations, references to Roth in the first person occur frequently in this section. It is also told in the past tense, further separating this singular event from the timelessness of the Wunderrabbis and their wisdom. All of these stylistic choices emphasize how much Roth does not belong in this world. The description of his own appearance is a telling example: "Ich trug einen kurzen Pelz und hohe Reitstiefel und sah aus, wie einer der gefürchteten Beamten des Landes, auf deren Wink man eingesperrt werden kann. Deshalb ließen mich die Leute vorgehen, sie machten mir Platz und wunderten sich über meine Höflichkeit" (JR, 36). ["I had on a short fur coat and high riding boots. I no doubt looked like one of the feared local officials, a signal from whom was enough to get someone thrown into prison. Therefore people let me pass. They moved aside for me and were surprised that I thanked them" (JRE, 36).] In this description of his appearance, Roth not only establishes the separation between him and the others; he also establishes the power dynamic between them. The reader is reminded that the position of the traveler is privileged; his interactions with his environment often differ greatly from those of an "average" inhabitant. Even with the use of the first person, we are given little insight into the narrator's character or personal history; instead the emphasis is on how others see him and how much he does not belong. These themes continue in Roth's brief interaction with the Wunderrabbi himself.

Because his clothes lend him importance in the eyes of the others, Roth is allowed to circumvent the long wait and use an entrance reserved for the very wealthy and important, the entrance through the kitchen. Although he seems to have more control over his environment than Döblin had during his encounter with a Wunderrabbi (for example, Roth does not need an intermediary to negotiate his audience with the rabbi), his meeting, like Döblin's, does not go as he had planned:

> Er fragte mit starker Stimme nach meinen Wünschen und sah mich nur einen Augenblick flüchtig an, um dann in den Hof hinauszusehen.
>
> Ich sagte, ich hätte ihn sehen wollen und von seiner Klugheit viel gehört.
>
> "Gott ist klug!" sagte er und sah mich wieder an.
>
> Er winkte mich an den Tisch, gab mir die Hand und sagte mit dem herzlichen Ton eines alten Freundes: "Alles Gute!" (JR, 39)

> He asked in a clear voice what I had come about, cast a quick look in my direction, and then gazed out into the courtyard again.
>
> I replied that I had heard much about his wisdom and had wanted to meet him.
>
> "God is wise!" he said, and looked at me again.
>
> He beckoned to me to come to the table, shook my hand, and, with the heartfelt tone of an old friend, bade me: "Farewell!" (JRE, 38–39)

Like Döblin, Roth wants to have a conversation with a Wunderrabbi, to experience firsthand the wisdom of his words. And this rabbi, like the one Döblin interacted with, leaves Roth in confusion; the encounter only emphasizes the lack of common ground. The man who went in the room before him, a wealthy merchant, spends a long time with the rabbi, and when he comes out, Roth notices how happy he is, even though he was a bit pale and nervous before he entered the room. In contrast, Roth spends a very short time with the rabbi and leaves disappointed and uncertain of what has just happened. Despite his privileged position, Roth does not belong; the comparison with the wealthy merchant underscores how

Roth, privileged or not, remains an outsider and how he cannot experience the wisdom of the rabbi firsthand, as the rabbi's followers can. It is a world that depends on a separation from Western assimilation and modernity, and for these reasons Roth cannot enter.

For Döblin and Roth, religion is the key to an authentic Jewish existence, a religion rooted in ancient traditions and beliefs, not bound by modern notions of rationality and logic. It is no surprise, then, that they are fascinated by the Hasidim, particularly by the more mystical aspects of their teachings. They insist that authentic East European Jews cannot exist in Western Europe. According to both, modernity, nationalism, and assimilation/secularization lead to the inevitable decline of Jews who are exposed to these phenomena. An attack on West European politics and cultures plays a crucial role in justifying the necessity for a separate space for East European Jews. They conflate the assimilated, secular West European Jew with modernity and attack him for all that he has lost in order to become this modern individual. West European Jews are inauthentic, no longer capable of connecting to an absolute truth. Here a critique of modernity similar to Kracauer's is projected onto a Jewish context in which the church is replaced with the synagogue and the West European Jew can no longer enter. As with Kracauer's comparison of the hotel lobby and the church, the West European Jew's loss becomes apparent only when we see an example of its opposite. If modernity means the loss of the real, then East European Jews have access to the real only because they are removed from modernity; they are connected to timeless truths because they are removed from history. This removal from time is accompanied by a removal from questions of national identity, and both texts implicitly and at times explicitly connect secularization with a strong national identity and with assimilation/acculturation. Thus the assimilated West European Jew stands as a symbol for modernity, in particular West European urban modernity, and the religious East European Jew symbolizes a different model of a universalized outsider position, one that is primitive, exotic, and kept separate from the others. Rather than a Simmelian stranger who interacts with others, whose privileged position relies on making others aware of distance through proximity, East European Jews occupy a position that relies on minimal contact with others so that they can "preserve" their authenticity and protect it from the corrupting influences of modernity. In this model, Western modernity is not universal and timeless, but rather locked into history and unable to reach any sense of absolute truth, whereas East European Jews are part of a timeless tradition. These texts shed light on the complex role mobility and time play in the positioning of the stranger. Not only is the mobility of the traveler critical to the position of objective observer that Roth and Döblin take in their travel texts; it is also used to explore the possibility of a different kind of mobility, one based in an identity that excludes nationality, in a rootlessness that defines East European Jews. This mobility is tied to a freedom from time, or rather to an unbroken and unchanging relationship to an earlier time and a more "authentic" Jewish identity. In these texts, the "authentic" East European Jew has ties to an absolute truth through religion; modernity means assimilation into history and an integration into the binary of national identity versus religious identity.

The abstract, anonymous outsider still plays a crucial role in Alfred Döblin's *Reise in Polen* in the role of the self-effacing narrator, but so do other notions of timelessness and other definitions of outsiders. Döblin's look at East European Jews offers a model of Jewish identity that celebrates a rootlessness and atemporality that allows for an authenticity lost to the West. Yet as the narrator praises East European Jews for their authentic existence and criticizes West European Jews for their loss of this kind of authenticity and truth, he simultaneously occupies an outsider position that relies on the West European culture he finds lacking. The narrator occupies a position of objectivity and anonymity that draws on discourses of urban modernity in order to legitimize a different model of being an outsider, one that has not experienced the struggles with authenticity that mark the urban stranger. The temporal and spatial divides that separate the traveler from his surroundings in general and East European Jews in particular remind the reader that this authentic existence can be observed, but for the narrator, and by extension for West European Jews in general, it is impossible to return to this state.

Roth also utilizes his exploration of East European Jews as a way to critique the West, while maintaining the separation between the two. Roth's *Juden auf Wanderschaft* begins with a description of the book's intended audience, a description that maps out what he sees as the potential difficulties of presenting East European Jews in a positive light for a West European audience because West Europeans lack the proper frame of reference:

> Der Verfasser hegt die törichte Hoffnung, daß es noch Leser gibt, vor denen man die Ostjuden nicht zu verteidigen braucht; Leser, die Achtung haben vor Schmerz, menschlicher Größe und vor dem Schmutz, der überall das Leid begleitet; Westeuropäer, die auf ihre sauberen Matrazen nicht stolz sind; die fühlen, daß sie vom Osten viel zu empfangen hätten, und die vielleicht wissen, daß aus Galizien, Rußland, Litauen, Rumänien große Menschen und große

> Ideen kommen; aber auch (in ihrem Sinne) nützliche, die das feste Gefüge westlicher Zivilisation stützen und ausbauen helfen—nicht nur Taschendiebe, die das niederträchtigste Produkt des westlichen Europäertums, nämlich der Lokalbericht, als "Gäste aus dem Osten" bezeichnet. (JR, 8)

> The author has the [foolish] hope that there may still be readers from whom the Eastern Jews do not require protection: readers with respect for pain, for human greatness, and for the squalor that everywhere accompanies misery; Western Europeans who are not merely proud of their clean mattresses. These are readers who feel they might have something to learn from the East, and who have perhaps already sensed that great people and great ideas—great but also useful (to them)—have come from Galicia, Russia, Lithuania, and Romania; ideas that would help shore up and expand the firm foundations of Western civilization. These are readers who have already perceived that these "visitors from the East'—as the local news report, the meanest product of Western Europe, likes to call them—are not just pickpockets.[27] (JRE, 2)

This passage is ostensibly a description of the readers Roth hopes to reach, but it is also an attack on all those who do not belong to this category. The dig at people who consider themselves morally superior because of their hygiene is an example of the disdain Roth directs at those who view East European Jews as lowly thieves.

Although Roth claims that his intended audience is already sympathetic toward East European Jews and their cause, the mention of widespread stereotypes and also the phrase "törichte Hoffnung" [foolish hope] express his doubts that such an audience exists. The discrepancy between his intended audience and the reality of the situation serves as an implicit justification for the text as a whole: it connects the perception of East European Jews in Eastern Europe to their treatment in the West. Following this logic, if one were to have a more positive view of East European Jews in their "homes," they would then also have a higher status in the West. What Roth does not discuss, but can be inferred from the text, is the sentiment that if East European Jews were valued for their contributions, then West European Jews would not suffer from being associated with them. Roth does not address "Westjuden"; rather, he speaks to "Westeuropäer." It is important that non-Jews also see East European Jews, and in connection with them West European Jews, as valuable members of a society, as a people who have their own culture, beliefs, and identity.

Much of this "rehabilitation" of East European Jews' image in the West follows in the footsteps of Buber's writings about the Hasidim. And like Buber, Roth maintains that this connection to a timeless truth connects the Hasidim not only to one another, but also to millennia of Jewish culture and religion. Thus the timelessness of their religious beliefs is connected to a timeless Jewish identity.

Buber searched for those elements of Jewish mysticism that would appeal to a Western audience by making them attractively exotic. In other words, the Hasidim are to be seen as unique and different, but in ways that resonate with Western ideas of renewal and the rebirth of culture. Roth, on the other hand, connects what he sees as the positive attributes of East European Jews with a critique of Western culture, particularly Western notions of national identity. Roth does not actually disagree with the stereotypes of East European Jews in the West as being poor and often living in squalid conditions. What he does disagree with is the notion that these East European Jews and their daily lives represent fundamental and essential aspects of East European Jewish identity. Roth seeks to demonstrate that East European Jewish immigrants are the victims of their circumstances, of an environment (in this case Western Europe) that minimizes their rights and their agency and gives the majority of them no choice but to live as they do—focusing on their daily survival and making decisions based on necessity. By viewing East European Jews in several environments, most importantly in their "home" of Eastern Europe, Roth argues that the plight of East European Jews in Western Europe is the fault of West European culture and politics. Thus Jews can preserve the timelessness of their culture and identity only by remaining separate from the West.

When Roth's writings about Hasidim in Eastern Europe are put in the context of the urban outsider and his position in society, *Juden auf Wanderschaft* can be read as skepticism about the possibility of an advantageous minority position. While discussing East European Jews in the West, Roth emphasizes the importance of not being influenced by Western notions, of remaining to some extent unassimilated in the dominant culture, since assimilation means a loss of autonomous identity. Simmel also writes about the stranger position as one based on the agency gained from distance, from not seeing the world as the others do. The difference between the two is that Simmel foregrounds the interactions between the stranger and his environment, whereas Roth sees such interactions as a loss of agency and autonomy rather than an assertion thereof. For Roth, interactions between East European Jews and West Europeans simply reinforce the discrepancies in power; the only possibility East European

Jews have to attain power is assimilation, but this is not a successful option. Thus, according to Roth, the solution is a disengagement with Western culture. As the text moves to East European Jews in Eastern Europe, the themes of distance and separation become more insistent. In the texts explored in the previous chapter, the authors establish the legitimacy of the outsider position by rooting it in discourses of modernity so that the similarities between the stranger and those around him are foregrounded. The stranger is different, but in ways that others can relate to. For Roth, East European Jews can attain an advantageous stranger position only through difference, through the renunciation of similarities between them and others. Yet Roth makes these arguments from a narrator position that is rooted in the discourses of modernity that he rejects, a position of anonymity, mobility, and privilege. Taking on the position of a West European, and writing for a Western audience, Roth has written a text that simultaneously asks its readers to identify with the East European Jews, but also to recognize that it is impossible for a West European Jew to fully enter a world untainted by Western notions of nation, progress, and modernity. Roth's position as an outsider legitimizes the exclusive nature of East European Jews and reinforces the notion that they are bound together by their rejection of the outside world, rather than solitary in the way of the narrator, and by extension West Europeans in general.

For Roth the main difference between "aufgeklärten" [enlightened] Jews and the Hasidim is that the former group does not believe in mysticism. Roth's depiction of mysticism is that it creates a world that is timeless; he conflates the timelessness of the teachings with the timelessness of those who practice them. And this world connects its inhabitants to one another, just as it separates them from others. Roth offers various Jewish religious traditions as examples of times when communities are simultaneously naked and anonymous in relation to the other members; the anonymity that Kracauer describes in the church is also to be found in these villages. But there is a loss of agency as a result; such moments can occur only through collective actions in which everyone acts in the same way and for the same reasons. By connecting these moments to particularly important religious holidays, Roth implicitly acknowledges that it is impossible to sustain such a community continuously, something that Plessner also argues for in his defense of society. Roth does not spend much time describing the Hasidim in their daily routines, preferring to write about these moments of heightened awareness and belonging. The one exception is a passage where he mentions that although the East European Jews present a united front to outsiders, there is in fact much infighting:

> Dem Fremden und dem Feind stellen alle Ostjuden eine geschlossene Front entgegen, oder eine scheinbar geschlossene Front. Nichts dringt an die Außenwelt von dem Eifer, mit dem einzelne Gruppen einander bekämpfen, von dem Haß und der Bitterkeit, welche die Anhänger des einen Wunderrabbis gegen die des anderen aufbringen und von der Verachtung, die alle frommen Juden gegen jene Söhne ihres Volkes hegen, die sich äußerlich an die Sitten und die Tracht ihrer christlichen Umgebung angepaßt haben. (JR, 29)

> To outsiders and enemies, Eastern Jews like to present a united front, or what appears to be a united front. Nothing gets through to the outside world of the zeal with which individual groups fight one another, the hatred and the bitterness with which the supporters of one wonder-rabbi assail those of another, or the contempt all devout Jews have for those sons of their tribe who have conformed to the customs and dress of their Christian surroundings. (JRE, 29)

Here Roth moves from a discussion about Hasidim to one about East European Jews as a whole; he asserts that one can consider them a cohesive group only because of their interactions with non-Jews. Thus they are only united in reaction to how outsiders see and treat them. In the second sentence, Roth moves from a discussion of infighting to the ways in which more traditional and religious Jews view assimilated Jews, and after several more sentences about how reprehensible Orthodox Jews find assimilated Jews, Roth concludes:

> Aber es ist eben die Pflicht der Juden, nicht von den Menschen, sondern von Gott eine Milderung ihres Schicksals zu erwarten. Jede, noch so äußerliche Assimilation ist eine Flucht, oder der Versuch einer Flucht aus der traurigen Gemeinschaft der Verfolgten; ist ein Versuch, Gegensätze auszugleichen, die trotzdem vorhanden sind.
>
> Man hat keine Grenzen mehr, um sich vor Vermischung zu schützen. Deshalb trägt jeder Jude Grenzen um sich. Es wäre schade, sie aufzugeben. (JR, 30)

> Anyway, it remains the obligation of the Jews to look to God, and not to their fellow man, for some relief of their position. Any form of assimilation, even the most superficial, constitutes flight or attempted flight from the sad society of the persecuted—an attempt to gloss over differences that aren't so easily gotten rid of.

> There are no longer borders that protect against miscegenation. Therefore every Jew erects borders around himself. It would be a shame to give them up. (JRE, 29)

The text shifts from attributing such opinions to the Orthodox Jews to generalizations without attribution to emphasize the universal validity of the statement. Even in this discussion of the heterogeneity of East European Jews, the emphasis is on how important it is to remain separated from outsiders. According to Roth, what really connects the East European Jews to one another is less a reaction to the outside world than a rejection of it. The East European Jews can fight with each other as much as they want about which rabbi is the one who should be revered; the only real danger to their identity is assimilation. Religion, then, is the way to keep East European Jews together and separate them from the others. West European Jews, with their secularism and assimilation, turn instead to a national identity—an identity that, according to both Roth and Döblin, is doomed to fail. In this argument against nationalism and national identity, history and religion play crucial roles. We will now take a closer look at the relationship between these concepts.

Can the Jews Be a Nation?

Early in his text, Roth explores East European Jews' conceptions of the West, or rather their misconceptions. According to Roth, when East European Jews think about the West, they think about freedom, technological advances, and a culture rooted in Goethe and Schiller. Not only do they fail to recognize the hypocrisy and the brutality of the West; they also fail to see the advantages of their home:

> Dagegen sieht der Ostjude nicht die Vorzüge seiner Heimat; nicht die grenzenlose Weite des Horizonts; nichts von der Qualität dieses Menschenmaterials, das Heilige und Mörder aus Torheit hergeben kann, Melodien von trauriger Größe und besessener Liebe. Er sieht nicht die Güte des slavischen Menschen, dessen Roheit noch anständiger ist, als die gezähmte Bestialität des Westeuropäers, der sich in Perversionen Luft macht und das Gesetz umschleicht, mit dem höflichen Hut in der furchtsamen Hand. (JR, 10)
>
> And so, conversely, the Eastern Jew sees none of the advantages of his own homeland. He sees nothing of the boundless horizon,

> nothing of the quality of the people, in whom simplicity can produce holy men and murderers, melodies of melancholy, grandeur, and obsessive passion. He fails to see the goodness of the Slav people, whose coarseness remains more decent than the house-trained animality of the Western European, his secretive perversions, his cringing before the law, with his well-bred hat in his apprehensive hand. (JRE, 6)

Roth portrays Western culture as a decadent perversion of natural impulses; the superiority of East Europeans is that they stay true to their nature, that they are capable of extremes that are more "authentic" than those of their Western counterparts. Culture, in particular Western culture, is defined as a removal from the impulses that make us more human, with a humanity that is necessarily more "primitive" by Western standards. What is striking about the passage above is that Roth is speaking about non-Jews living in Eastern Europe rather than East European Jews. He complicates this picture of a more natural and authentic existence by contending that the reason East European Jews do not see the advantages of Eastern Europe is that they do not live in conditions that would allow them to do so. Constantly threatened by their Christian neighbors, not allowed to live in large cities or in the country, faced with few employment opportunities, the East European Jew lives a limited existence: "Die große Mehrzahl kennt den Boden nicht, der sie ernährt. Der Ostjude fürchtet sich in fremden Dörfern und in Wäldern. Er ist teils freiwillig teils gezwungen ein Abgesonderter" (JR, 10). ["The majority don't understand the soil that feeds them. The Eastern Jew feels apprehensive in unfamiliar villages and forests. He is a case apart, partly from choice, partly by force" (JRE, 7).] Roth connects this position as an outsider with a lack of connection to the land. More importantly, in this passage Roth hints at a theme that he will return to throughout the text—the outsider position of the East European Jews is both a strength and a weakness, both voluntary and involuntary, and this position depends on the separation East European Jews feel to their land. They may be unable to take advantage of Eastern Europe's superiority over Western Europe, but at the same time, they are able to avoid the need to identify with their surroundings. They are able to have an identity that remains uniquely their own. Here we see echoes of Simmel's stranger—distance allows for agency, for the possibility of an identity that is not tied to one's surroundings.

According to Roth, what these Jews fail to realize is that the West is no better. Furthermore, this dark existence is, according to Roth, preferable to the other ways of living in Eastern Europe. More specifically,

Roth asserts that living one's life as a persecuted religious Jew in Eastern Europe is better than living as a secular, assimilated Jew. Roth is highly critical of assimilated Jews in Eastern Europe: they have sacrificed their culture, religion, and language but still fail to achieve total equality and live in fear of being associated with their more obviously Jewish relatives. Then there are those who turn to Jewishness as a national identity. Roth describes the nationalists in the following manner:

> . . . indem sie ihr Judentum nicht nur nicht verleugnen, sondern sogar kräftig betonen und sich zu einer "jüdischen Nation" bekennen, über deren Bestand seit einigen Jahrzehnten kein Zweifel mehr ist und über deren "Berechtigung" unmöglich ein Streit entstehen kann, weil schon der Wille von einigen Millionen Menschen genügt, eine "Nation" zu bilden, selbst wenn sie früher nicht bestanden haben sollte. (JR, 12)

> . . . not only by not denying their Jewishness but by emphasizing it at every turn and proclaiming their allegiance to a "Jewish nation" whose existence has for several decades now been indisputable, and whose "right to exist" is similarly unarguable. The will of several million people is already enough to form a "nation," even if it has not existed before. (JRE, 9)

The use of quotation marks qualifies Roth's statements about the legitimacy of a Jewish nation; the end of the sentence completely undermines it. At best, Roth seems to begrudgingly acknowledge the support Jewish nationalism in its various forms has in Eastern Europe. He sees that the driving force behind this identification with a Jewish nation is, as with the assimilationists, the desire for equality and acceptance. Yet these Jews are also far removed from the traditional and religious ones: "Auch diese Juden leben nicht mehr im Ghetto, ja, nicht einmal mehr in der wahren und warmen Tradition—heimatlos, wie auch die Assimilierten und zuweilen heroisch, weil sie freiwillig Opfer für eine Idee sind—und sei es auch für eine nationale . . ." (JR, 13, ellipsis in original). ["These Jews no longer live in the ghetto either, nor even in their warm and true traditions. They are (homeless) as their assimilated brothers are, sometimes to the point of heroism, because they are willing victims of an idea—even if it's nothing better than the idea of a nation . . ."[28] (JRE, 9).] Roth makes a distinction between two concepts of homelessness in relation to national identity. One is the homelessness of assimilationists and nationalists, a loss of Jewish traditions and religions without a secure and fulfilling replacement. The other is a homelessness defined by the refusal to take on a national identity, one that allows Jews to create a sense of belonging that is dependent on their separation from the non-Jews around them—in other words, a sense of belonging and home that is rooted in a lack of national identity. According to Roth, only without a nation do Jews have a true home.

Yet this last group are the Jews who immigrate, in the hopes of finding a place where this lack of national identity is not the disadvantage it is in the East. They seek a cosmopolitanism that they associate with Western Europe:

> Die Emigranten also sind Menschen, die müde werden dieser kleinen und grausamen Kämpfe und die wissen, fühlen, oder nur ahnen, daß im Westen ganz andere Probleme lebendig werden, neben den nationalen, und daß die nationalen Streitigkeiten im Westen ein lärmendes Echo von gestern sind, und nur ein Schall von heute; daß im Westen ein europäischer Gedanke geboren ist, der übermorgen oder sehr spät und nicht ohne Leid zu einem Weltgedanken reifen wird. (JR, 13)

> The ones who emigrate are those who have wearied of the petty but unremitting struggle, and who either know or feel or merely guess that a different set of problems presents itself in the West; that the national squabbles there are just a hollow echo of yesterday's; that the West has a vision of Europe, which, maybe one day, not before time and not without suffering, will ripen into a vision of the world. (JRE, 10)

Roth does not directly refute this view of Western Europe, but in the context of the text as a whole, it would be consistent to attribute these ideas to the falsely held beliefs of East European Jews rather than a reality. Nevertheless, the lack of a direct contradiction to these ideas of a Western cosmopolitanism that has "overcome" notions of national identity, and the acknowledgment that even East European Jews recognize that this goal has not yet been achieved, does point to a hope that it may one day come true, even as the text emphasizes how unlikely this future is.

If cosmopolitanism is seen as a Western fantasy and potential future, nationalism is a Western invention and a current reality. In his discussion of the detrimental effects of Jews' adopting national identities, Roth conflates notions of nation and national identity with those of the West, modernity, and assimilation. He argues that without a nation East

European Jews are much more and that the adoption of a fatherland leads to their decline. Little is gained and too much is lost when Jews take on a national identity. According to Roth, all forms of nationalism, whether assimilationist or Zionist, are fundamentally Western concepts and only in the "Orient" is it possible to be free of such concepts (JR, 18). Roth describes this "Orient" as a place where one's fatherland is just the place where one has military duties, and although one is loyal to this country, one's identity is not bound to it. He gives the example of the Caucasian Armenians: "Die kaukasichen Armenier waren lange Zeit weder Russen, noch Armenier, sie waren eben Mohammedaner und Kaukasier und sie lieferten den russischen Zaren die treuesten Leibgarden" (JR, 18). ["The Armenians of the Caucasus were for a long time neither Russians nor Armenians; they were Muslims living in the Caucasus, and yet they furnished the czars of Russia with their most loyal bodyguards" (JRE, 15).] The use of a non-Jewish reference here reinforces the idea that the reason East European Jews are allowed to live without a national identity in the Western sense is that East Europeans in general do not have the same concepts of nation and national identity. The military motif occurs several times in the text; Roth is providing examples that contradict the idea that a lack of a national identity is the same as a lack of interest in the military or a disloyalty to the country, a stereotype common about Jews in Western Europe.[29] Roth says of Zionism: "Der moderne Zionismus entstand in Österreich, in Wien. Ein österreichischer Journalist hat ihn begründet. Kein anderer hätte ihn begründen können" (JR, 18–19). ["The cradle of modern Zionism was Austria, was Vienna. It was founded by an Austrian journalist. No one else could have founded it" (JRE, 15).] After the pointed reference to Theodor Herzl as an Austrian journalist, implying that he has no credentials that qualify him to be the "father" of Zionism, Roth argues that the reason Zionism in its contemporary form came to be is that the political situation in Austria made it impossible for one to have any rights if one did not belong to a nation. Thus Austrian Jews have given up their long-held identity of being people in exile in order to become a nation in exile, and this did not improve their standing, since they were not bestowed even the most basic human rights, much less the ones that would make them equal to other citizens of Austria. With this group identity comes loss without any compensatory gain. Their past is lost, and they have become part of a group that exists only for political power and fails to achieve that goal (JR, 19).

This Western concept of nation is, according to Roth, a move backward for East European Jews for two reasons—their identity is much more than a national identity, and furthermore, they have already been a nation before and have progressed beyond such a limiting identity: "Die Epoche der 'Nationalgeschichte' und 'Vaterlandskunde' haben die Juden schon hinter sich. Sie besetzten und besaßen Grenzen, eroberten Städte, krönten Könige, zahlten Steuern . . . Wollen sie es noch einmal? Beneiden sie die europäischen Staaten?" (JR, 20–21). ["The era of 'national history' and 'patriotic studies' lies way back in the Jewish past. Jews patrolled and defended their own borders; conquered cities; crowned kings; paid taxes . . . Do they want all that again? Can it be that they're *envious* of European states?" (JRE, 17–18).] Roth answers this question by arguing that this desire for a national identity has to do with basic human rights: "Sie wollen gewiß nicht nur ihre 'nationale Eigenart' bewahren. Sie wollen ihre Rechte auf Leben, Gesundheit, persönliche Freiheit, Rechte, die man ihnen in fast allen europäischen Ländern entzieht oder schmälert" (JR, 21). ["Certainly they want more than merely to safeguard their 'national characteristics.' They want their rights to life, health, and liberty, rights that in almost every European country they are denied outright or have only in curtailed form" (JRE, 18).] Roth once again argues that European discourses of legal rights make it impossible to insist on your rights outside the context of nations and national identities and that Jews are thus forced to fit themselves into these paradigms. The time for a Jewish national identity belongs in the distant past; the distance between the present and this past is emphasized by a lack of specific dates or events. As a result, the "present" is marked by its continuity and constancy; a Jewish identity independent of a national identity has existed from the end of this long-ago epoch until the present day. In his discussion of Palestine in the same paragraph, Roth emphasizes that these concepts of nation are Western and alien to what he considers an authentic Jewish identity:

> Leider sind die Chaluzim auch gezwungen, zu kämpfen, Soldaten zu sein und das Land gegen die Araber zu verteidigen. Und damit ist das europäische Beispiel nach Palästina übertragen. Leider ist der junge Chaluz nicht nur ein Heimkehrer in das Land seiner Väter und ein Proletarier mit dem gerechten Sinn eines arbeitenden Menschen; sondern er ist auch ein "Kulturträger." Er ist ebenso Jude, wie Europäer. (JR, 21)

> Unfortunately the *halutzim* are also obliged to take up arms, to be soldiers, and to protect the land against the Arabs. Thus the European example has been carried into Palestine. Unfortunately, the young *halutz* is not only a returnee to the land of his forefathers

> and a proletarian with the righteous outlook of a workingman; he is also a disseminator of culture. He is as much a European as he is a Jew. (JRE, 18)

Jews in Palestine are forced into the role of colonizers, of creating a nation in the European model, and thus they are not just Jews, but also Europeans, a fact that negatively impacts their relationship with the others in Palestine, namely the Arabs. Furthermore, being European means a loss of agency and of an independent Jewish identity; in the act of creating their own country, Jews become more enmeshed in and dependent on European conceptions of identity and nation. Roth says of the Jews in Palestine:

> Der jüdische Statthalter von Palästina ist ohne Zweifel ein Engländer. Und wahrscheinlich mehr Engländer, als Jude. Die Juden sind Objekt oder ahnungslose Vollstrecker europäischer Politik. Sie werden benutzt, oder mißbraucht. Jedenfalls wird es ihnen schwer gelingen, eine Nation mit einer ganz neuen, uneuropäischen Physiognomie zu werden. Das europäische Kainszeichen bleibt. (JR, 22)

> The Jewish governor of Palestine is beyond question an Englishman. He's probably even an Englishman first and Jew second. The Jews are either victims or helpless tools of European politics. They are exploited or abused. At any rate it will be difficult for them to become a nation with a completely new, un-European physiognomy. The European mark of Cain won't wash off. (JRE, 19)

Whereas on the page before, Roth puts the word "Jew" before that of "European" in his description of the Jews in Palestine—implying that although the Jews there cannot escape the European influence, they are still Jews first and foremost—here the order is reversed and the outlook even bleaker. Although Roth acknowledges the validity of a Jewish nation, he sees it as a tragic necessity created by European politics. And rather than at least creating the possibility of an independent Jewish people, this endeavor forces Jews into the position of pawns, unable to determine their own fates. Roth even refers to Cain's mark, an interesting choice since the story of Cain is often referred to as a possible source for the story of the Wandering Jew, a figure evoked by the title of Roth's text. With this biblical reference, Roth foregrounds the punitive aspects of the wandering of both figures—Cain and the Wandering Jew are forced into exile—further emphasizing the lack of control Zionists have over their own lives. Within the logic of this critique, the more positive discourse of wandering is possible only if Jews can extricate themselves from national identity altogether.

Döblin too sees nationalism and an authentic Jewish identity as mutually exclusive. Although Döblin's first encounters with the Hasidim cause him to flee in horror, he "discovers" later in his travels the true "Kern" of the Jewish among them, and its source is religion. He writes:

> Ich kann mich nicht enthalten zu denken, wie ich hinausgehe: Welch imposantes Volk, das jüdische. Ich habe es nicht gekannt, glaubte, das, was ich in Deutschland sah, die betriebsamen Leute wären die Juden, . . . die zahllosen unsicheren unglücklichen feinen Menschen. Ich sehe jetzt: das sind abgerissene Exemplare, degenierende, weit weg vom Kern des Volkes, das hier lebt und sich erhält. Und was ist das für ein Kern, der solche Menschen produziert wie den hinflutenden reichen Baal-schem, die finstere Flamme des Gaon von Wilno. Was ging in diesen scheinbar kulturarmen Ostlandschaften vor. Wie fließt alles um das Geistige. Welche ungeheure Wichtigkeit mißt man dem Geistigen, Religiösen zu. Nicht eine kleine Volksschicht, eine ganze Masse geistig gebunden. In diesem Religiös-Geistigen ist das Volk so zentriert wie kaum ein anderes in seinem. (AD, 137)

> I can't help thinking as I go out: What an impressive [people] Jews are. I didn't know this [people]; I believed what I saw in Germany, I believed that the Jews are the industrious people . . . the countless insecure unhappy refined people. Now I see that those are isolated examples, degenerating, remote from the core of the [people] that lives here and maintains itself. And what an extraordinary core is this, producing such people as the rich, inundating Baal-Shem, the dark flame of the Gaon of Wilno. What events occurred in these seemingly uncultured Eastern areas. How everything flows around the spiritual! What tremendous importance is placed on spirituality, on religion! Not a minor stratum, an entire mass of people—spiritually united. Few other [people] are as centered in religion and spirituality as this one. (ADE, 102)[30]

Döblin connects two competing eighteenth-century Jewish religious movements by giving them a common origin. Although in previous paragraphs Döblin has explored the differences between these two movements, here he foregrounds their similarities. They are evidence of the important role that religion and spirituality play in Jewish identity and are part of the same Jewish essence. The Hasidim and Mitnagdim are linked to a past that provides a linear story of progress with an unchanging constant—spirituality.[31] The Jews he encounters are therefore the remnants of this glorious past who still contain these qualities that are gone forever in the West. As is clear in other examples, this "Kern" is endangered by the intrusion of Western culture into Eastern Europe; Döblin is extremely critical of assimilated Jews in Poland. According to Döblin, this Jewish world needs to stay separate in order to maintain the qualities that make it authentic and real. The temporal space the East European Jews occupy plays an important role in this separation. They have a history, but what makes the East European Jewish culture strong is its static nature. This relationship between identity and dynamism differs starkly from Döblin's portrayal of non-Jewish Poland. For Döblin this Polish history is about dramatic change, a change that is central to an emerging Polish identity. Ties to a geographic location play an important role in this relationship between change, history, and identity. In contrast, the Jews are a "Volk, das den Tempel in sich trägt" [people who carry the temple within themselves] (AD, 138). It is important not only that the Jews have a special relationship to their religion, but also that this relationship makes their identity mobile—they carry it with them. Thus they are not tied to a geographical space. In the case of the Jews, Döblin makes the distinction between "Volk" and "Nation." The difference, according to Döblin, is that "Volk" is about connections to other people, in this case through religion. "Nation," on the other hand, is about the political reality of a nation-state, and this concept of nation-state is tied to geography and the contestation of borders. Döblin states that concepts of the nation-state are destructive to the existence of community:

> Nationales Bewußtsein, nationale Bewußtlosigkeit. Es gibt aber noch Religionen, die fragen nicht nach "Nation," "Staat" und haben eine andere Gemeinschaft. Wie blind sie werden, wie schlimm sie übertreiben und sich abgrenzen, diese Völker, die alle nach denselben westlichen Gütern jagen. Es gibt noch andere Gemeinschaften als die nationale . . . Man soll nicht verschleiern: die Nationen sind durch vieles zerklüftet, und was sie zerklüftet, sind andere wichtige Gemeinschaften . . . Man liebt ein Volk und ein Land um seiner Werte willen. Der Staatspatriotismus, den westliche und östliche Regierungen von ihren Massen, ihren Untertanen verlangen, ist Barbarei. Die Staaten von heute sind Zufalls-, kaum Zweckmäßigkeitsgebilde. (AD, 199)

> National consciousness, national unconsciousness. However, religions still exist that do not ask about "nation," about "state," and they have a different kind of community. How blind they become,

> how terribly they exaggerate and cut themselves off, these [peoples], all of the chasing after the same Western goods. National communities are not the only kind . . . One shouldn't hide the facts: nations are torn apart by a lot of things, and these things are other important communities . . . One loves a [people] and a country for the sake of their values. State patriotism, which Western and Eastern European governments demand from their masses, their subjects, is barbarity. Today's states are random entities, hardly expedient ones. (ADE, 151)

The narrator makes the case for a community free of notions of nation and state. In this passage the two—nation and state—appear to be interchangeable concepts. Often nation and state are separated from one another in that the former is the coming together of a people (Volk) whereas the latter is a political entity, tied together by a government and laws. Here the two are conflated and the concept of Volk is tied not to nation, but rather to religion. The narrator claims that religions allow for the possibility of a community. Although he does not identify these religions by name, it is clear from the rest of the text that he primarily means Judaism. According to the narrator, a community defined by nation or state is one in which love for one's people and one's land is replaced by a forced patriotism that creates a ruling government and its underlings. It is interesting to note how strong the sense of community (Gemeinschaft) remains in this passage: instead of moving away from notions of community, the narrator attempts to redefine it, to search for a meaning of community that is independent of nation. Döblin argues for the possibility that a group of people without a nation can be a community. It is nationalism, he argues, that prevents this kind of belonging to one another. Furthermore, nationalism hinders interactions between various groups of people because it forces divisions between them: one example he gives is the inability of Poles, Ukrainians, and Jews to coexist. Döblin thus implies that Judaism proves community can exist without a nation, and that this nationless existence should be used as a model for the people of Poland.

According to Döblin, it is only the lack of nation-state that allows Jews to have this special position: "Wenn man jetzt die Geschichte rückwärts schraubte und ihnen wirklich Zion gäbe? Und es drängt darauf hin . . . Die Neuzeit, die Wirtschaftsnot drängt die Juden aus der Abschließung. Die Rückwärtsbewegung, sie ist im Gange. Die Tragödie der Erfüllung ist im Gange" (AD, 138). ["What if history were turned backward and the Jews were really given Zion? And this is becoming an urgent issue . . . The modern age, economic necessities, are driving the Jews out of their seclusion. The backward movement is rolling. The tragedy of fulfillment is rolling" (ADE, 102).] Here Döblin brings together several different notions of history and nation. The Jews are held outside the discourse of national identity by the timelessness of their religious life; the Poles are modern because they have a progressive history that moves them forward. If the Jews obtained such a history, however, it would be a move backward; the only possibilities for the Jews are either a non-national and ahistorical space or a nation that would mean having a history that precludes the possibility of timelessness.

Central to Döblin's definition of Jewish identity is his distinction between a people (Volk) and a nation (Nation/Staat). Yet it is difficult to make this distinction because the two have a complicated relationship, one that requires another look at the relationship between Gemeinschaft and Gesellschaft. As Joseph Vogl outlines in his introduction to *Gemeinschaften: Positionen zu einer Philosophie des Politischen,* this dichotomy between "nation" and "people" is a common one, but one that harbors an intrinsic paradox, for one should exclude the possibility of the other. The concept of a people is based on a notion of common origins and Gemeinschaft; that of a nation on a notion of individuals who come together under a contract. Yet the rhetoric of nation-building is that a people comes together to build a nation. This paradox is a manifestation of the paradox at the center of the Gemeinschaft/Gesellschaft dialectic as it has been understood: it is implied that society is produced through a noncommunicated contract, through a shared commonality; yet this commonality, which would normally be associated with community, precludes the possibility of belonging together as a people, because if that were the case, the contract would be unnecessary.

Vogl explains the relationship between Gemeinschaft and Gesellschaft as follows: "Jeder handelt so, als ob er der andere seiner selbst wäre; was der eine denkt, hat der andere schon gedacht, und die Voraussetzung für die gemeinsame verträgliche Übereinkunft ist daher eine Art Nicht-Kommunikation" ["Everyone acts as if he were the other of himself; what the one thinks the other one has already thought, so the prerequisite for a communal contractual accord is thus a kind of non-communication"].[32] Vogl goes on to state the result of this noncommunicated contract:

> Das Gemeinsame ist Separation, die Separation aber die Auslöschung der Differenz—in diesem Zirkel betreibt die liberale Deduktion der Herrschaft eine zentrifugale Ausstoßung sozialer Erfahrung und illustriert damit das Dilemma, daß gerade die Gleichheit jede Gemeinschaft ausschließen muß: Es gibt kein Prinzip einer

> Gemeinschaft von Gleichen, das zugleich ein Prinzip gesellschaftlicher Organisation darstellen könnte . . .[33]

> The communal is separation; however, the separation is the extinction of difference—in this circle the leadership's liberal deduction conducts a centrifugal expulsion of social experience and thus illustrates the dilemma that it is precisely sameness/equality that makes every community impossible: There is no principle of a community based on similarity/equality that could simultaneously constitute a principle of societal organization . . .

According to Vogl, the idea of a people does not come before a nation; rather, it is created through the nation's constitution. Paradoxically, this act denies the possibility of the existence of a people in the way that it is traditionally conceptualized, namely as something that creates a nation rather than being created by it.[34]

In Döblin's text this notion of a people as something that exists independently from nation can be seen, for example, in the section about community/Volk without nation. In this context, a people is the attractive alternative to nation, a belonging that comes from within rather than being imposed from without. The text can be read as an affirmation of the way most saw notions of Gemeinschaft and Gesellschaft, Volk and Nation, during the Weimar Republic and, I would contend, up to the present day. Yet Döblin's use of the word "Tempelvolk" provides a way to complicate Vogl's reading of the creation of a people through nation, by introducing the question of the role of religion for a people. According to Döblin, what makes Jews a people is their lack of nation and their adherence to their religious traditions. One could argue that this negation serves the same purpose as the constitution of nation and that the Jewish lack of nation remains in the confines of the Nation/Volk discourse. In other words, it is only because everyone else belongs to a nation that the Jewish lack of one becomes a topic. Yet what about the role of religion in the conceptionalization of the Jewish people? Does the common religion allow for a people without a nation, a Gemeinschaft without Gesellschaft?

These questions are addressed in the works of the historian Simon Dubnow. For Dubnow the question of the relationship between nation, state, people, and religion comes down to the question of history. Born in Russia in 1860, Dubnow moved to Berlin in 1922. He was a historian of Jews and was most famous for his exploration of diaspora nationalism, or the notion that Jews, although they lacked a nation, still had a national identity. His ten-volume *Weltgeschichte des jüdischen Volkes von den Uranfängen bis zur Gegenwart* appeared in German in the 1920s. In his *Die jüdische Geschichte: Ein geschichtsphilosophischer Versuch* (first edition in German in 1897 and an expanded one in 1921) Dubnow addresses the following question: what is a Jewish history? The subtext of that question is: can Jews have a history? For Dubnow there are historical and unhistorical peoples, also known as "geistige Typen" [intellectual types] and "zoologische Typen" [zoological types]. Of the historical type there are three categories, each successive one more developed than the next: ancient Asian, ancient Greek/Roman, and new European/American. Ancient Asia was "an der Schwelle der Geschichte" [on the cusp of history] and was replaced by the Greeks and Romans, who brought their people further along and then were replaced by the Europeans and Americans. After each people was replaced, they disappeared from the historical narrative.[35] Dubnow claims that the Jews are the only people with a continuous history throughout all these phases, thus making them the most historical people.[36]

Dubnow addresses the issue of history and nation by making a distinction between nation and state. Jewish history is divided into two phases: in the first half Jews lived as a nation with land, in other words, as a state. The second half begins in 70 A.D. with the fall of the Jewish state at the hands of the Roman Empire. This phase is marked by the loss of all things normally associated with a nation—territory, army, political power—but according to Dubnow, Jews are at this point still a nation. The Jewish nation is unique in that it is based on religious beliefs, traditions, and intellectual pursuits. Dubnow emphasizes that this introverted focus on the "Geistesgebiete" [intellectual fields] was not only necessary, but also has always been a part of Jewish identity, even when Jews had a state. This natural inward nature is what connects Jews throughout the ages and allows for the possibility of a continuous Jewish history. Dubnow also describes the position of the Jews in terms of Gemeinschaft and Gesellschaft: Gemeinschaft is what they have among each other, while Gesellschaft describes one's external existence, primarily Jewish experiences in the non-Jewish world.

With the shift from state to nation came the shift from a universal religion to a national and exclusive one. One day people will recognize the Jewish god as theirs, writes Dubnow, but until that time, the religion belongs to the Jews. Their religion and the traditions and practices that stem from it are what keep Jews separate from others, what make them a nation, but Jews are also the preservers of this possibility for everyone. History progresses for Jews, but there is also a constancy. The Jewish nation is a "geistige Nation" both in the sense of spiritual pursuits and in the sense of intellectual ones. And according to Dubnow, the Jewish spirit is immortal, and the Jewish nation has always existed and will continue to, since its role in history is far from finished. History and timelessness are not mutually exclusive here. Instead, Dubnow offers an alternative model of history, including its relationship to religion, to those proposed by Döblin and Roth.

This question of Jewish history is implicitly addressed in Döblin's and Roth's writings by the way they focus on the ahistorical aspects of Jewish identity. In these texts, Jews cannot have a nation. As in Dubnow's model, their identity is based on religion, but in their texts the Jews do not have a history that progresses. Instead, East European Jews are often portrayed in these texts in a manner that emphasizes the universal and timeless aspects of Jewish identity. Dubnow describes a stateless nation among nation-states, a nation whose trajectory may be different from the others but nonetheless has a linear history like everyone else's. Yet Jews have a continuity other peoples do not have, and this is due to the central role religion plays for them. Although religion in Dubnow's text is a source of continuity and hints at the eternal, Jews continue to progress and live in history. Döblin and Roth view Judaism and its traditions as something old, almost prehistorical. For them becoming part of history means giving up this identity, becoming assimilated and corrupted. In these texts, Jews cannot have a history and cannot be a nation, and the only way to be authentically Jewish is to exist outside of time. This becomes particularly apparent in the writings about the Hasidim. Roth's and Döblin's narrators travel back in time when they visit the Hasidim, but this past/present is a static one and is thus simultaneously historical and ahistorical, or outside of history.

In all three of the texts, Jews are championed as a guiding light for those around them. For Dubnow, Jews occupy this unique position because they have been part of history longer than any other people; they have a continuous, unmatched history. For Döblin and Roth, East European Jews have been left behind by history. They belong to the past, and in them West European Jews can catch a glimpse of their former and more authentic selves. East European Jews are situated in a semi-isolated and static past, and this elevates them to their status as an example for others. Dubnow's text, in its focus on Jewish historicity, highlights the central role that ahistoricity plays in Döblin's and Roth's portrayals of East European Jews. Unlike Dubnow, Döblin and Roth equate history with assimilation and a loss of identity within a Jewish context; for them history can only mean the Western history of the dominant culture at the expense of all other narratives.

The Stranger, the Traveler, and the Wanderer

Tied to questions about Jewish history and nationality is the concept of mobility, in particular a mobility based on a lack of nation and history. This diaspora existence fundamentally defines the Jew as an outsider from elsewhere, but he is bound to other Jews through religion and religious traditions. As travel texts, *Reise in Polen* and *Juden auf Wanderschaft* also approach their subjects from a position of mobility, of a traveler whose authority is rooted in discourses of modernity and the urban stranger. These texts navigate the intersecting and at times conflicting concepts of mobility and the outsider through three figures—the stranger, the traveler, and the wanderer. In this context, it is important to take a brief look at the classic example of the forced stranger/wanderer in the German Jewish context—Ahasver.

Originally a Christian motif, the Wandering Jew has been part of the German imagination since the Middle Ages. The legend's origins are not clear, but there are some predecessors, including the Italian legend of Johannes Buttadaeus and the Christian Oriental legend of Cartaphilus. The story was popularized in Germany in the 1602 chapbook *Kurtze Beschreibung und Erzehlung von einem Juden / mit Namen Ahaßverus.*[37] The author is unknown, and he tells of meeting Paul von Eitzen, who studied with Martin Luther and later became Schlesvig's bishop. According to the author, von Eitzen recounts having met the Wandering Jew. Since he died four years before the pamphlet appeared, he cannot confirm the story, but the memory of him is alive, adding to the account's authenticity.[38] In the text, Paul von Eitzen remembers having met Ahasver in 1542 in the church in Hamburg where Ahasver told him his tale. Ahasver, a shoemaker, meets Christ as he is carrying the cross to Golgotha. Christ asks Ahasver if he can rest in front of Ahasver's home. Ahasver refuses to help, calling Jesus a heretic. Jesus then curses him to a life of eternal wandering, and Ahasver will not be able to rest until the Second Coming.[39] In this version of the story, several elements are introduced to the legend that did not appear in the Italian or Christian Oriental ones: Ahasver's name, his profession, his Jewishness, and the concept of eternal wandering as punishment.[40]

From the Middle Ages onward Ahasver has epitomized the plight of Jews: always the stranger and always wandering, Jews have been ostracized and scapegoated and have suffered in brutal pogroms. The legend served as a justification for their fate: the Jews, like their forefather Ahasver, had brought their condition on themselves. In 1694 Ahasver is referred to as *Ewiger Jude,* Eternal Jew, for the first time.[41] While in the German tradition Ahasver is often referred to as *Ewiger Jude,* in the

French tradition he is *juif errant,* Wandering Jew. As Alfred Bodenheimer points out, these two names do not point to a different interpretation of the legend. Instead, they highlight two crucial aspects of Ahasver that are inextricably linked—eternity and restlessness.[42]

The nineteenth and twentieth centuries mark a turning point in the relationship between the figure of Ahasver and German Jewish identity. In his book *Wandernde Schatten: Ahasver, Moses und die Authentizität der jüdischen Moderne,* Alfred Bodenheimer explores the interactions between the figures of Ahasver and Moses during this time period. Ostensibly Bodenheimer seeks traces of the Moses story in artistic and literary representations of Ahasver to show the shifts that occur when Jewish artists reappropriate the figure. I would argue, however, that what Bodenheimer is actually doing is using the figure of Moses as a lens through which to see the changes in German Jewish identity in the late nineteenth century and interpret them. His look at Moses is less a mapping of the historical development and more a use of the Moses motif as an interpretive tool. Although I do not agree with Bodenheimer's linear trajectory of the Moses motif, I find that in his interpretation of various appearances of the motif he provides some valuable insights into the figure of Ahasver and his role in discourses of German Jewish identity.

Ahasver represents restlessness, and German Jewish authors and artists of the time considered the notion that restlessness may not, as had been seen in previous centuries, be a punishment forced on Ahasver and implicitly on all Jews. Instead, they theorized, mobility may be an integral and positive part of Jewish identity. In this context, the figure of Moses is often used to propose that the Promised Land is not a place, but an ideal that should not be reached since Moses led his people to freedom but was not able to set foot in the Promised Land himself. This criticism of Zionism explores the notion that the diasporic nature of Jews is not merely a result of political and historical realities but, rather, essential to Jewishness. In fact, Bodenheimer claims that Jewish authenticity during this time period is dependent on the absence of a homeland and that the founding of the state of Israel is the source of an authenticity crisis in discourses of Jewish identity today.[43] In many ways the figures of Ahasver and Moses are diametrically opposed—Ahasver is a legend, imposed by others, and a figure of darkness and pain; Moses is a historical figure who led the Jews to freedom, a figure of light and hope. Both, however, are wanderers who never reach their goals—Ahasver is not allowed to die, and Moses does not enter the Jewish homeland.[44]

Bodenheimer's focus is West European modernity and West European Jewish identity, primarily within the German Jewish context. Eastern

Europe and East European Jews lie outside the scope of his work. He does mention briefly the importance of the East European Jew as a symbol of the suffering all Jews endure, but does not develop this idea. I feel that a closer examination of the role East European Jews played in the West European Jewish negotiation with dominant categories of identification will expand on and enrich the work Bodenheimer began. I will therefore weave a continuation of my reading of Döblin's and Roth's texts into my exploration of Bodenheimer's ideas.

Ahasver's transformation parallels transformations in German Jewish identity. For example, in the nineteenth century the legend's ties to "christlichen Heilvorstellungen" [Christian notions of salvation] weaken and Ahasver is transformed into a secular symbol of the Jewish people within the Jewish community. Yet this appropriation of the figure is incomplete: although it represents a positive interpretation of diaspora and homelessness, it is also a negotiation with the Christian views of Jews, in which Ahasver is a figure of darkness. One can see this phenomenon in the frequently occurring portrayal of Ahasver as a shadow figure, more specifically as a darkness that cannot be integrated. I use the word "negotiation" here rather than "internalization" because the latter term creates too passive a relationship between Jewish writers and the dominant culture. There are indeed instances in which the figure of Ahasver is used to project the dominant culture's negative perceptions of Jewish qualities onto a subgroup of Jews to both reinforce and distance oneself from these qualities, as in the Sander Gilman model of "Jewish self-hatred."[45] But I agree with Paul Reitter that this model is too limiting and does not allow for discursive shifts, for German Jewish contributions to these shifts, or for a multiplicity of meanings.[46]

In the move to make Ahasver into a figure of positive identification for Jews, authenticity plays a central role. Bodenheimer states that the source of this authenticity is a "verdeckte Transzendenz" [concealed transcendence].[47] He maintains that in the late nineteenth and early twentieth centuries, secularized and assimilated Jews saw themselves as no different from their non-Jewish counterparts yet were still marked by the others as not belonging; this stigmatization played a crucial role in Jewish identity discourses. Because the alternative was total acceptance of dominant discourses of Jewish identity, which would mean Jews remaining second-class citizens, assimilated Jews sought to find a way to gain agency in the identity formation process. One way was to conflate Ahasver and Moses and, through this conflation, reach the understanding that restless homelessness is not a punishment forced on Jews but an advantage Jews have and a positive and integral part of Jewish identity. Bodenheimer argues that this move is not a rejection of assimilation; rather, it should be seen as a "Versuch, der heteronomen Zuschreibung eine zusätzliche, autonome Komponente zu verleihen" [attempt to lend the contingent attribution an additional autonomous component].[48]

Roth's title, *Juden auf Wanderschaft,* an allusion to the Wandering Jew, is also a reinterpretation of the figure. Because it uses the plural, the Wandering Jew is no longer a lone individual condemned to a life of wandering and not-belonging. Instead, he is now part of a community of wanderers, and wandering is a positive attribute that brings Jews together and defines them. This theme is reinforced throughout the text in Roth's insistence that the Hasidim and their mysticism can exist only if Jews maintain their separation from Western secular values and refuse a national identity. Like Roth, Döblin explores the position of the wanderer and the position's relation to Jewish identity. Although Döblin's interpretation of wandering and Jews brings us to a world of individuals given maximum freedom and maximum ability to define themselves, this separation from others also allows these individuals to be aware of the truths of Judaism and live as authentic Jews.

Any reinterpretation of the Wandering Jew is necessarily in dialogue with the preceding interpretations. Bodenheimer explains the relationship of this more positive image of Jews in relation to older ones:

> Der Jude wird hier zum Gegenentwurf, der die Realität der rastlosen Moderne zugleich dechiffriert und antreibt, er verkörpert gewissermaßen jenen Glauben in einen Fortschritt, der letztlich nur durch den utopischen bzw. messianischen und damit wiederum transzendenten Charakter des finalen Ziels erreicht werden kann. Damit gewinnt der Jude der Moderne in der Identifikation mit Ahasver und Moses seinen historischen Ort als ausdrücklichen geografischen Nicht-Ort zurück.[49]

> Here the Jew becomes the alternative that simultaneously deciphers and drives the reality of restless modernity. To some extent he embodies that very belief in progress that can only be achieved through the utopian or rather messianic and thereby once again transcendent character of the final goal. For this reason the Jew of modernity re-attains in his identification with Ahasver and Moses his historical place as an explictly geographical non-place.

Here Bodenheimer mentions the relationship between discourses of modernity and Jewish identity. Jews simultaneously uphold and deconstruct notions of restless modernity; they represent the positive aspects of an unrooted life, yet this mobility stems from a notion of utopian and messianic transcendence that is denied in secular modernity. The Promised Land becomes a "geographical non-place," and this transformation points to the need for such a space even as it is denied physical reality. The transcendence is concealed (*verdeckt*) because it depends on a sense of home that cannot exist. Yet it is this home that is simultaneously there and not-there which legitimates wandering as an integral aspect of the authenticity at the center of Jewish identity: although identity and authenticity are not the same thing, identity is dependent on authenticity, and authenticity in turn is dependent on a notion of transcendence that legitimates mobility and rootlessness.

This "verdeckte Transzendenz" leads to a universal but also specifically Jewish homelessness, and this combination of the specific and the universal also marks the position of Jews in society. Bodenheimer quotes Rudolf Kayser: "Das also ist die Mission der Juden: selbst staatenlos die Erde zur Menschenheimat zu machen, durch Ethos die Menschenbrüder zu erlösen" [This is then the mission of the Jews: to make the earth into a home for all while maintaining their statelessness, to free their fellow men through ethos].[50] In his reading of Kayser's position, Bodenheimer writes: "Daß hier in einer territorial orientierten Richtung des Judentums ein Übel gesehen wird, das qualitativ demjenigen Übel gleicht, vor dem es einst geflüchtet war . . . Moses wird zum Schutzpatron einer territorialen Heimatlosigkeit" [That a Judaism driven by a territorial orientation is seen as an evil, one that qualitatively resembles the evil that it once fled from . . . Moses becomes the patron saint of a territorial homelessness]."[51] Unlike Lukács's "transcendental homelessness,"[52] Bodenheimer's term makes explicit the need to have a space that one can call home, even though it becomes home only because it has been lost. Home then becomes a physical space that is partially transformed into a symbolic one, but it is crucial that the space be a combination of the two, just as it is crucial to our understanding of the figure of the Wandering Jew that he be both a Christian figure representing Jews as a punished people and a modern figure of mobility and freedom.

Attempts to add agency without completely rejecting the imposed categories are manifest throughout Döblin's and Roth's portrayals of East European Jews. Döblin and Roth do not attempt to refute negative assertions and depictions of "Ostjuden." Instead, they work within them to find positive aspects and reinterpret commonly held assumptions. Döblin and Roth still describe East European Jews as rootless and removed from others, but these attributes are praised as being a source of authenticity.

They argue that East European Jews should serve as a model for a nationless people; Döblin and Roth assert that nations and nationalism only lead to war and hatred and wasted lives.

Moreover, in their texts both Döblin and Roth blur the distinctions between traveler and wanderer while simultaneously highlighting them. By arguing that East European Jewish itinerancy is the source of their identity and a model that should be emulated, Roth and Döblin remove some of the oppressive quality of the Ostjuden's lack of home and national identity. Although the poverty and difficult living conditions of the Ostjuden cannot be envied, there is still much that should be admired. Nationless existence should be embraced, thus lending the wanderer some of the agency and privilege of the traveler. This move, however, is undermined in several ways. For example, although the East European Jews are wanderers in the sense that they are without nation and strong ties to the land, they lack the ability to move as they please. They are still wanderers who primarily move when forced to by their living conditions; they move to Western Europe and America to seek a better life. Another is that Döblin and Roth create a palpable distance between themselves and the Ostjuden they describe. Despite their admiration of the Ostjuden, Roth and Döblin are clearly not part of the world they describe and make no attempt to be a part of it. They may have found a space that has not been spoiled by modernity, but its existence only emphasizes that such authenticity has been lost elsewhere and that, once lost, it cannot be regained. Given the temporal distance they create, they are as removed from this world as Kracauer is from the authentic reality of premodernity.

In *Reise in Polen,* Döblin and the Hasidim represent different aspects of the relationship between mobility and an outsider position—Döblin is the modern traveler/stranger whose mobility is, for the most part, a position of privilege. He chooses to travel to Poland and always has the possibility of returning home. The Polish Hasidim represent the eternal aspects of Jewish identity. They are also wanderers in the sense that they do not belong to a particular nation or specific geographical space, but they lack the freedom of movement that Döblin has. If they were to actually move, as many East European Jews did, to Western Europe, they would lose their unchanging and eternal Jewish identity. Thus their mobility, or lack thereof, has a significant impact on both Döblin's and the Hasidim's relationship to real geographical spaces.

The text ends with Döblin's return to Germany; in Danzig (now Gdańsk) he negotiates the connection he feels to Poland and the distance that his privileged position as a traveler necessitates. In Warsaw for the last time before taking the train to Danzig, he writes:

> Ich bin wehmütig, dankbar. Alles gerät ins Blitzen. Gern war ich hier, gefesselt bin ich; was ist das für ein Menschenschlag, Gemisch von Menschen; welche brodelnde Lebendigkeit, starken Reize. Hätte mich gern tiefer in alles hineinbewegt: aber blieb mit Taubheit und Stummheit geschlagen. Nun ade. Es gibt dieses Land. Ich weiß es herzlich. (AD, 335)

> I feel wistful, grateful. Everything flashes. I enjoyed being here, I'm [captivated]; what kind of human breed is this, human mixture; what seething life, powerful stimuli. I would have loved to get deeper into everything; but I remained deaf and dumb. And now, farewell. This land exists. I realize it from the bottom of my heart.[53] (ADE, 256)

With two short phrases linked together with a comma—"Gern war ich hier, gefesselt bin ich"—Döblin expresses his conflicted feelings about his trip. He enjoyed (past tense) his stay but now feels (present tense) "gefesselt"—a word that like its translation, "captivated," connotes both fascination and a sense of being trapped. One interpretation of this sentence is that Döblin is locked into place by his fascination with the people and all that he sees; his admiration for Poland and its peoples has grown with time, and now he not only enjoys the sights—they mesmerize him. Yet the phrase also expresses some of the conflicted feelings of the traveler: he was happy to have gone where he has, but now he has been here long enough and cannot move freely as a traveler; it is time to go home. The last four sentences of this passage also convey the conflict between the connection he feels to his new surroundings and his desire to leave them. His wish to have been more deeply involved in the world he has encountered is moderated by the subsequent farewell and the statement that now he knows the land exists. These sentences obliquely define the traveler's boundaries: he must leave because he does not belong, but he leaves with a knowledge of a place that could only have been gained through the experience of travel.

On the way back to Germany, Döblin's displacement is more specific than the vague disembodiment that marks the beginning of his travels. When he arrives in Danzig, Döblin's sense of not belonging is acute:

> Hier hängen in dem Schaufenster des Photographen solide wohlgenährte Gesichter . . . Der—Herzenstod! Was fällt mir das Wort ein, ich bin doch kein Lyriker. Hartnäckig das Wort: Herzenstod! Stumpfheit, Ausdruckslosigkeit auf den Gesichtern des Photographen. Und nicht nur in seinem Kasten; er hat sie gut getroffen . . .

> Es ist etwas Vegetatives, Leeres. Ich muß die Augen niederschlagen, will nicht hinsehen. Warum nicht? Ich schäme mich, ich fühle mich furchtbar verlassen.
>
> Und dies, liebes Herz, erwartet dich weiter in Deutschland. Hier hast du Sauberkeit, Ordnung, Wohlstand. Hier bist du zu Haus. Es wird—nicht alles so sein. Im ersten Augenblick schlägt es nur so auf dich ein. (AD, 338–39)

> Here, respectable well-nourished faces hang in the photographer's window . . . This is—*Herzenstod,* the death of the heart! Why does this word haunt me now—I'm no poet. It haunts me doggedly: death of the heart! Dullness, blankness on the faces of the sitters. And not just in the photographer's vitrine; he caught them expertly . . . It's something vegetative, empty. I have to lower my eyes, I don't want to look. Why not? I'm embarrassed, I feel terribly abandoned.
>
> And this, dear heart, also awaits you in Germany. Here you have cleanliness, order, prosperity. Here you're at home. Not everything—will be like this. It only crashes down on you during the first moment. (ADE, 259–60, italics in original)

The city gives him a taste of what is waiting for him in Germany—the "cleanliness, order and wealth" cause Döblin to lose his footing. For this brief moment, he is no longer a traveler, but a wanderer, at home nowhere. It is no coincidence that it is in this situation that he meditates on the relationship between nation-state and individual. Döblin adopts the position of the wanderer, of a person who no longer feels connected to a home, in order to explore the position of a rootless individual without ties to a particular land. It is interesting to note that Danzig was in the interwar period a free city that belonged to neither Germany nor Poland. Furthermore, it was geographically situated in Poland, but the majority of its citizens identified themselves as German. Thus the location in which Döblin explores the possibilities of a nationless existence is one in which nationality was a contested issue. Yet the emphasis on the temporary nature of Döblin's position as wanderer highlights the differences between him and the East European Jews. Although he did not choose to feel this displacement, he knows it will pass and so can treat it as a way of opening up his perspective rather than as a plight he must endure. He embraces the position of the wanderer not as one of punishment, but as one of privilege. This position as a wanderer is one that Döblin can adopt and then discard; the East European Jews he encountered do not have this choice.

The text ends with a turn toward nature and individuality as a way to escape the questions of nation, religion, and identity that have confronted him during his travels. Döblin speaks with himself:

> Du bist am Meer; die Reise durch das fremde Land ist zu Ende.
>
> Dies hier, was ich sehe, erscheint mir am stärksten, die unermeßliche Natur. Immer wieder sie. Ich brauche mich nicht zu korrigieren. Ein Stück von ihr liegt vor mir; das Meer, der flüssige Garten voller Tiere und Pflanzen; der Wind behaucht es.
>
> Und das andere, das zweite Stärkste? Die—Seele. Der Geist, der Wille des Menschen . . .
>
> Es gibt eine gottgewollte Unabhängigkeit. Beim Einzelmenschen. Bei jedem einzelnen. Den Kopf zwischen den Schultern trägt jeder für sich. (AD, 344)

> You're by the sea; the journey through the strange land is over.
>
> What I view here strikes me as the mightiest thing: immense nature. Always nature. I don't have to correct myself. A piece of nature lies before me: the ocean, the liquid garden full of plants and animals; the wind breathes upon it.
>
> And the other, the second strongest thing? The—soul. The human spirit, the human will . . .
>
> There is an independence ordained by God. In the individual. In every individual. Each man carries his own head between his shoulders. (ADE, 264)

Döblin has arrived. It is not entering Germany, however, that makes him feel that his travels have come to an end; instead, it is being on the ocean. His description of his surroundings is devoid of any specific markers; he could be in any country, on any coast. By looking out onto the ocean, Döblin turns his back on the people who make him feel displaced in his "home." His new "home" is one that necessitates shedding nationalism, and religion is spoken of only on the abstract level of the spirit, the soul, the will. Döblin's temporary homelessness enables him to find a new sense of belonging. But this belonging is fleeting; the last words of the text call for a radical individualism—one in which each person is an "Einzelmensch." This individual is stripped of nationality, and God exists only as the source of one's individuality.

Encountering the Hasidim allows Döblin to explore questions of nationality and religion and their relationship to Jewish identity. And at the end of the text, he moves into a geographically nonspecific space in which markers of idiosyncrasy are missing—"the ocean" and "the wind" are present, but Döblin mentions no specific animals or sites that could remind readers where they are. Abstract concepts such as nature, the will, and the spirit reign here. Like the Hasidic spaces, this one has a sense of timelessness; the landmarks and concepts do not change, do not belong to a specific time. In this nonspecific space, Döblin's viewpoint is also abstract and universalized. Yet it is important that this space exists in reality. Without his travels, without a concrete point from which he abstracts, Döblin could not as effectively make his argument against the construct of nation-states. Döblin arrives at this abstract individuality through his travels. He performs this position in his role as the traveler and at the end of the text encourages the reader to take on this position that combines traveling and wandering. It is voluntary, like traveling, but with the notion that a concrete home connected to nations either does not exist or cannot be reached and that this lack of nationality is what shapes one's identity.

Reise in Polen creates a tension between notions of modern mobility and Jewish identity through specific conceptualizations of space. The ideals Döblin expresses at the end of the text undermine his praise of East European Jews; he seeks a dynamic individualism that is the very opposite of the static group identity of the Hasidim. He forgoes the specificity of an authentic Jewish existence for the nonspecific space in which radical individuality is possible. This space Döblin finds at the end is a physical space that he partially transforms into a symbolic one. And he can only reach this space—in both its physical and its symbolic aspects—through this journey into Poland and his exploration of Jews in their "native" environment. In his explorations of a Jewish "home," Döblin travels with the intended West European reader to an Eastern Europe that is simultaneously an unattainable idealization and a physical reality. And in the end he reaches a space, albeit temporary, in which he can redefine himself and become a radical individual through the loss of specificity. How tenuous and fragile such a space can be, and the constraints put upon this search for individual agency by historical realities, will be demonstrated in an exploration of the life and works of Hugo Bettauer.

Chapter 3

✦

The Stranger, the Jew, and the City

Hugo Bettauer's work provides us with a look at how discourses of urban modernity appeared in texts that were meant for a more general public. Like Kracauer, Benjamin, and others, Bettauer presented a reading of modernity that saw alienation and the inability to connect to others as a universal modern condition. The difference is that Bettauer was concerned with the individual less as an abstract entity, and more as the man or woman he encountered on the street. He used everyday language and drew on current events so as to reach as many people as he could. Bettauer thought it important that the "average" man or woman reading his work see him- or herself reflected in it and feel that Bettauer was writing about him or her. Yet at the same time, throughout his novels and also in his journalistic writings, Bettauer utilized the position of the stranger in order to provide this mirror, a stranger who is distanced from others and possesses the ability to see more clearly than they do. The position of the stranger allowed him to connect to others, but his authority was based on abilities that set him apart.

Bettauer was born in 1872 in Baden, Austria.[1] Information about his family and childhood is scant. In 1890 he left the Jewish faith and in the same year became a member of the Protestant Church, and remained so until his death. He also joined the military that year, but his service lasted only five months. Unsuited for military discipline and corporal punishment, he deserted and moved to Zurich. At twenty-four he came into a sizable inheritance, which he lost through bad investments. After his mother's death he traveled to the United States and became an American citizen, but, unable to find work, he went to Berlin in 1899. There he was the editor for the *Berliner Morgenpost* and used the paper to attack corruption, mismanagement, and protectionism. During his tenure he was sued numerous times for defamation, and in the course of two years was found guilty twelve times and even served time in jail. After he wrote articles uncovering the crimes of one of the wealthiest Berlin citizens as well as the director of the Berlin Hoftheater, he was forced to leave his position at the paper and was expelled from Berlin by the government. After stays in Munich and Hamburg, he went back to New York and worked as a reporter for three New York papers for German immigrants: *Die deutsche Zeitung, Die New Yorker Staatszeitung,* and *Das New Yorker Morgenjournal.* In 1910 he returned to Vienna. He worked on several papers as editor and was a prolific author—from 1920 to 1924 he wrote three to five books a year.

As evident even in a brief overview of Bettauer's career, his writing incited controversy long before the scandal surrounding his journal *Er und Sie: Wochenschrift für Lebenskultur und Erotik* and his murder. Nevertheless, Bettauer has been defined by these two events. His death at the hands of a dentist with National Socialist affiliations and the antisemitic rhetoric of the media attacks against him surrounding the *Er und Sie* controversy have led to a portrayal of Bettauer as a tragic victim of antisemitism whose death is seen as a warning of what is to come. It is thus no surprise that the focus of almost all recent scholarship on Bettauer is his *Die Stadt ohne Juden: Ein Roman von übermorgen;* the novel's plot and Bettauer's biography mutually reinforce an interpretation that foregrounds the themes of antisemitism and victimhood and what is read as their inevitable trajectory.[2] Yet a closer look at his work and its reception demonstrates the role individual agency plays in navigating the discourses of urban modernity and German Jewish identity. I argue that the majority of Bettauer's writings and of his role in Viennese culture did not focus on specifically Jewish topics and that this absence is itself significant.[3] Furthermore, a consideration of *Die Stadt ohne Juden* within the context of his other works provides us with a more complicated portrayal of Jewish identity. A look at the novel and the film version of *Die Stadt ohne Juden* shows the tensions between a Jewish identity created by others and the ones that an individual creates for himself. These tensions also play a central role in the reception of Bettauer's work and his own biography, in part explaining the impulse in his other writings to create a narrative position that is decidedly non-Jewish in the face of these limitations.

Bettauer's novels and journalistic writings often focus on the rights of the individual to choose how he or she wants to live. A leitmotif is that bourgeois notions of morality are used to repress individuals and limit their choices, particularly in terms of sex and sexuality. Bettauer addresses specific examples of this problem—abortion, premarital sex, homosexuality—but, like the writers discussed in previous sections, uses universal themes to legitimize the validity of his arguments. Like Georg Simmel, Bettauer also utilizes the specific as representations of larger social truths;

on a broader level his work is defined by its focus on individual agency in all aspects of one's life. Within this context, his novel *Die Stadt ohne Juden* is a continuation of this theme. The relationship between Jewish identity and antisemitism is one in which the possibility of individual agency plays a vital role—antisemitic sentiments and politics are further examples of how society represses the individual.

There is a disconnect between the intentionally universal themes of the majority of his writings and the narrow focus of much of its reception. The novel stirred controversy, one that primarily fit into the philosemitism/antisemitism binary. That is to say, much of the debate about the novel was in deciding whether it portrayed Jews in a positive or a negative light. Even before his murder, but more pronouncedly afterward, the novel was not seen in the context of his other writings; the connection between questions of Jewish identity and more universal questions of individual rights was for the most part ignored. As Bettauer had done throughout his career, he struck a nerve by presenting what he saw as society's most pressing problems through the medium of popular literature. In this particular case, the nuances of his portrayal were lost in a public debate about Jewish identity that left little room for complexity and ambiguity. That the legacy of this rigid focus is evident in recent Bettauer scholarship points to the need to reexamine some of the underlying assumptions that inform our reading of these texts and our understanding of Bettauer's public persona.

Although Bettauer never identified himself as a Jewish writer and his writings rarely addressed Jewish topics, attacks on his person often relied on antisemitic rhetoric. Yet like Döblin and Roth, Bettauer does not thematize his own Jewish background in his writings. As is particularly evident in his journal *Er und Sie,* Bettauer took on the role of the objective outsider, a role that relied on abstract qualities that set him apart from others and his surroundings so that he could see objectively. He is a chronicler of urban life, not Jewish life. In his struggle to present himself to the public in a manner of his own choosing, we see an enactment of the difficult relationship between the figure of the urban stranger and that of the assimilated West European Jew. He defines himself as the former in order to escape the limitations of the latter, but such a position is only partially successful, as it must be accepted by others. His work often includes references to current events and debates, but in a way that emphasizes the universal. What most Bettauer reception does is force his work into a historical context that limits not only our understanding of his work, but also our understanding of the historical context itself, by presenting a closed system supported by rigid binaries.

Hugo Bettauer, his work, and its reception serve as an example of how cultural and historical context limit the ability of the outsider/stranger to determine his own position. Bettauer serves as a representative of the Jewish intellectual who identifies himself as a cosmopolitan urbanite, an outsider who maintains his position by not identifying too specifically with any one particular category of identification, particularly any overtly Jewish identity. Yet as can be seen through a close reading of his work and by looking at its reception, such a position is only partially possible. The abstract nature of Simmel's stranger and the necessity thereof become clear when we see the failure of Bettauer's characters and Bettauer himself to be recognized as urban individuals rather than as Jews.

Redefining the Historical Context

Scholarship on German and Austrian Jewish topics of the early twentieth century is inevitably influenced by our knowledge of what is to follow. Whether we view Weimar culture as part of a continuous tradition that contains within it the roots of National Socialism, or a moment of unprecedented freedom and creativity cut short in 1933, we cannot forget about the Third Reich and the Holocaust. This lens not only impacts how we interpret texts produced in the interwar period; it also influences which texts we choose to read. In recent years there has been renewed interest in Bettauer's novel *Die Stadt ohne Juden,* an interest sparked in large part by the rediscovery and restoration of the film version in the 1990s. The film and the novel have been read as tragically prophetic warnings about National Socialism—the novel was published in 1922 and the film two years later, and both portray a city that decides to solve its economic crisis by expelling all the Jews. The plot of both the film and the novel is as follows: A city is suffering an economic depression. The citizens are out on the street protesting the high unemployment rates and the ever-decreasing value of their currency. Some right-wing politicians, under the leadership of the chancellor, decide to scapegoat the Jews and pass a law to force them all out of the land. The land suffers even more economic troubles as well as a loss of culture with the exodus of the Jews. The protagonist is Leo Strakosch, an assimilated Jew in love with a Christian, who comes back to the city in the disguise of Henry Dufresne, a Parisian. Through several clever maneuvers, he manages to help the parliament overturn the law and allow Jews to live in the land once more. The reading of the texts as prophetic of antisemitic violence is influenced by the murder of Bettauer at the hands of a dental assistant with Nazi affiliations.[4]

Our readings of these texts and of Bettauer's life create a cause-and-effect explanation for Bettauer's death—he was the victim of those antisemitic elements of Viennese culture that he so astutely wrote about.

Murray Hall's *Der Fall Bettauer* presents a well-researched overview of Hugo Bettauer and his work, but the ultimate focus of his book is Bettauer's role as a victim of antisemitism.[5] In his introduction, Hall explains the origins of the controversy surrounding Bettauer and his writings: "Denn Bettauer war Jude. Und viele, die für christliche Sitte und Anstand, deutsche Zucht und Ordnung zu kämpfen vorgaben, wollten in Wirklichkeit bloß den Juden Bettauer und—wenn möglich—auch alle übrigen beseitigen." [Because Bettauer was a Jew. And many who claimed to be for Christian morals and decency, who purported to fight for German discipline and order, actually wanted nothing more than to eliminate the Jew Bettauer, and if possible all other Jews as well.][6] Hall argues that the attacks against Bettauer were primarily antisemitic in nature and implies that since Bettauer was primarily seen as a Jew in the eyes of these Christian attackers, he also represents Viennese Jews in general. Thus Bettauer is defined not only as a Jew first and foremost, but also as a Jewish victim of antisemitism. Similarly, in his book *Vienna and the Jews, 1867–1938,* Steven Beller describes *Die Stadt ohne Juden* as a "cutting, but all too perceptive, description of what Vienna would be without the Jews . . . Bettauer envisaged what would happen if the antisemitic government of Austria were to expel all the Jews."[7] For Beller, what is most interesting about the novel is its perceptiveness, both in terms of the context in which Bettauer wrote it and in his ability to predict the future. In the same sentence in which Beller points out that "Bettauer was making a polemical point rather than a serious prophecy," he also mentions that "there are remarkable similarities between what Bettauer foresaw and what the present day city is like."[8] For Beller, Bettauer and his novel are inextricably linked to discourses of antisemitism. Scott Spector's 2006 essay "Modernism Without Jews: A Counter-Historical Argument,"[9] which I will discuss in greater detail below, also focuses on the question of antisemitism. It is an irrefutable fact that antisemitism played a crucial role in *Die Stadt ohne Juden*'s historical context. Yet, as can be seen in these examples, this focus lends itself to a reading of Bettauer's work that privileges the question of historical accuracy and makes it difficult to look at the novel as a work of fiction or to consider the text in relation to other notions of Jewish identity.

Although Bettauer's contemporaries were not influenced by knowledge of the Holocaust, they were preoccupied with the question of accuracy as well. Many contemporary critics seemed to be of the opinion that although the book had little artistic merit, it struck a chord with its readers. As one reviewer for a Jewish Viennese journal called *Die Wahrheit* writes: "In diesem Buche wird, wie gewiß allen bekannt . . . in nicht ganz origineller, dafür umso witziger Weise ausgeführt, wie Wien verdorfen würde, wenn es seine lieben Juden nicht hätte. Und was hier en miniature an die Wand gemalt wird, hat sich tatsächlich in Spanien vollzogen." [As everyone knows, this book describes in a not very original but all the more witty manner how Vienna would become a provincial village if it did not have its beloved Jews. And what here is painted on the wall in miniature actually occurred in Spain.][10] The reviewer attests to the accuracy of the novel on two levels. The first is that the novel correctly predicts what would happen if the Jews were to leave Vienna. The second is that the starting premise of the book—that the Jews could be driven out of the city—is possible because it has happened elsewhere; Spain's history proves that the hypothetical situation portrayed in Bettauer's novel is not as far-fetched as some would like to believe.

The book also provoked strong reactions from antisemites who saw it as dangerous Jewish/anti-German propaganda. As Alfred Rosenberg, later an influential member of the National Socialist party, writes in "Der Fall Bettauer," about the novel:

> Dieser bewußt jüdischen Rassenpropaganda ist ein ganzer Roman Bettauers gewidmet, betitelt "Die Stadt ohne Juden." Gemeint ist Wien, das eine Austreibung der Juden vornimmt; aber da Handel, Kunst und Wissenschaft ohne Hebräer zugrunde gehen, werden die Juden demütig wieder zurückgebeten. Es wird bloß die Kleinigkeit vergessen, daß weder der Stefansdom, noch die Paläste, Theater und Museen Wiens, über die Hebräer heute schalten und walten, von Juden erbaut worden sind.[11]
>
> A whole novel from Bettauer, titled "The City Without Jews," is dedicated to this deliberate Jewish race propaganda. The city in question, Vienna, undertakes an expulsion of the Jews; but since trade, the arts and the sciences collapse without the Hebrews, the Jews are humbly asked to come back. It merely overlooks the trifling fact that neither St. Stephen's Cathedral, nor the palaces, theaters and museums of Vienna, over which the Hebrews today preside, were built by Jews.

As in the review in *Die Wahrheit,* what is at stake is the historical veracity of the novel. One can read this article as an example of the fear Bettauer's novel exposed about the majority culture's potential loss of control of the portrayal of Viennese Jews and their roles in the city. The lengths to which Rosenberg goes to disprove the idea that Jews are responsible for the economic, artistic, and scientific success of Vienna show that for Rosenberg, the potential threat of the novel is its being seen as an accurate portrayal. That these comments are in a footnote rather than in the main body of the text can be read as an attempt to minimize the threat, to confine it to an aside. Since one of the main sources of Rosenberg's ire is that others do not address Bettauer's Jewishness, it is all the more notable that *Die Stadt ohne Juden* receives so little attention in the article.[12]

It is clear that there is a debate centering on the novel's ability to tell the "truth" about Jews. In both of these reviews, there is no question about the possibility of accurately portraying Jews; instead these articles address whether or not this particular portrayal is the correct one. There is a struggle for agency over the categories, but no questioning of the validity of the categories as such. The relationship these reviews have to questions of accuracy places them in the larger context of German Jewish identity discourses of the time. The anxiety and ambivalence toward portrayals of German Jews are a result of the limited malleability of the discourses that define them. One can interpret a quality or characteristic as favorable or unfavorable, create exceptions or show that the quality itself is an exception, but one cannot operate outside the categories these discourses create. Another reason for this preoccupation with the accuracy of *Die Stadt ohne Juden* may have to do with the texts themselves. Particularly in the case of the novel, it is difficult for the reader to discern a definitive stance about Jewish identity, or more specifically about Jewish life in Vienna. Although the novel is written in an easily accessible style, the portrayals of the figures and their situations are less straightforward than one might expect. Thus the reviews of the novel provide it with certainties that are not to be found in the novel itself. In other words, the prevalent theme of historical accuracy in the novel's reception points both to the inflexibility of discourses of German Jewish identity and to their potential fluidity. What gets lost in an approach to Bettauer's work that relies on debating the novel's accuracy is the fact that the novel is a creative work rather than a historical representation. That is to say, the discourses about modernity, the stranger, and German Jewish identity that appear in the novel have a relation to the world outside the novel, but at the same time, these discourses and their relationship to one another are created through the text. They are not fixed ideas, but an ongoing debate.

In his essay "Modernism Without Jews," Scott Spector addresses the relationship between Jews and German modernism with regard to questions of history and historicity. Spector argues that any attempt to establish a body of work or a group of writers as representative of the "Jewish Modern" presupposes a concrete definition of the term and that this approach ignores just how many different ideas are covered by these two words. Rather than take a historical approach that attempts to establish the relationship between Jews and modernism in terms of historical facts, Spector proposes to look at the history of the discourse, one that itself is "not singular, prescriptive, or consistent, but may perhaps better be characterized by its operation rather than by its contents. If this is the case, then our question cannot be what is or was Jewish modernism, but what work does and did the figure 'Jewish modernism' do for its users."[13] Spector's reading of the Paul de Man essay "Literary History and Literary Modernity" offers a suggestion as to how to ask this question and what role history plays in this approach: "But de Man's claim in this essay we have been discussing was precisely not that history should be ignored, in the name of aesthetic autonomy; rather, he asserted that intense scrutiny to the work on its own terms would constitute historical work."[14]

I agree with Spector's assessment that looking at questions of modernity in relation to concrete definitions and historical facts precludes an understanding of the concept that allows for a multiplicity of meanings, often in conflict with one another. Yet I find that his readings of Bettauer's *Die Stadt ohne Juden* and of Bettauer as a representative of the "Jewish modern" fall back on the accuracy/inaccuracy binary, one that Spector urges his readers to move away from. To be fair, Spector does not claim that Bettauer's text depicts the historical reality of a Jewish conspiracy of modernity, but he does argue that Bettauer's text "seems not to be able to help but compulsively name and confirm every tenet of anti-modernist antisemitism."[15] For Spector, *Die Stadt ohne Juden* provides proof that the conceptualization of modernity as a Jewish conspiracy permeates both promodernist and antimodernist stances, as well as the accompanying philosemitic and antisemitic rhetoric. Furthermore, Spector maintains that Bettauer's reception at both extremes demonstrates a preoccupation with the "Jewishness" of German modernity. In comparing Murray Hall's work *Der Fall Bettauer* with Alfred Rosenberg's article of the same name for the antisemitic *Der Weltkampf*, Spector writes:

> The articulation and interpretation of these strands of meaning is an objective shared to a remarkable extent by the two "Bettauer case" texts, one Nazi and one German studies. Both concern themselves with the network of "new" mass culture texts, including pulp novellas, popular sex education, erotica, scandal, and sensation.

> For both critics, this was a modernity infused and obsessed with Jewishness.[16]

Spector treats Bettauer and his work as confirmation of this obsession: *Die Stadt ohne Juden* contributes to the discourses solely in that it depicts ideas that already exist. Thus Bettauer's work is interesting only in that it shows us how someone who was a proponent of modern media and ideas could write a text that fit so well with antimodernist and antisemitic rhetoric. Furthermore, Spector conflates reception of the novel with the novel itself, and together they serve as evidence of a particular discourse of modernity. To look at Bettauer's body of work in this light is to leave it, and in particular *Die Stadt ohne Juden,* confined to the role of affirming the existence of a discourse, a discourse still locked within a philosemitism/antisemitism binary, even as it is shared by the two. What I propose is that we need to look at Bettauer's works as creative texts that not only depict a discourse, but also are involved in creating it, engaging with it, and perhaps even complicating it. By taking this approach and looking at *Die Stadt ohne Juden* in relation to Bettauer's other writings, particularly the periodical *Er und Sie,* we see the interactions of various discourses of the urban, modernity, and German Jewish identity. Most importantly, this approach allows us to explore the notion of individual agency and its limits in relation to these discourses.

Die Stadt ohne Juden: The Novel

Vienna is a central character in the novel, and, as is evident starting from the opening sentence, the story is mapped onto the city's geography: "Von der Universität bis zur Bellaria umlagerte das schöne, ruhige und vornehme Parlamentsgebäude eine einzige Menschenmauer" [From the university up to Bellaria, the beautiful, peaceful and distinguished Parliament building is surrounded by a single human wall] (SJ, 1). Two buildings and a street corner are mentioned before we even encounter any people. Significantly, the people are not individuals walking down the street, or even an unruly mass, but rather a "human wall." The people are part of the architecture of the city and are as permanent and crucial to the city as the other landmarks mentioned. The beginning of the second sentence emphasizes the inextricable relationship between the city of Vienna and its people: "Ganz Wien schien sich an diesem Junitag um die zehnte Vormittagsstunde versammelt zu haben" [All Vienna seemed to have assembled on this June day around ten in the morning] (SJ, 1).

In the first sentence the people are part of the architecture, and now they are the city. The novel conflates the city with its inhabitants, and throughout the novel one cannot be imagined without the other. Who is a part of the city's human architecture can, however, change. The narrator first lists those who are there, emphasizing the diversity of the group—young, old, working class, bourgeois, healthy, and infirm. Then we learn the reason that they have gathered together: "Und immer wieder fand sich ein Begeisterter, der plötzlich an den Kreis um ihn herum eine Ansprache hielt und immer wieder brauste der Ruf auf: 'Hinaus mit den Juden!' " [And time and time again a zealot suddenly addressed the circle around him and time and time again the cry erupted: 'Out with the Jews!'] (SJ, 1). The narrator remarks that what is unusual about this particular situation is not the behavior of the people, but the absence of Jews. The novel begins with a vision of unity at the expense of one group. The stereotypes used to describe the absent Jews ("Leute mit gebogener Nase oder besonders schwarzem Haar" [people with crooked noses or particularly black hair] [SJ, 1]) are mitigated by the fact that these clear and easy distinctions between Jews and the rest of the Viennese population will be disrupted shortly in the novel. This undermining of the stereotypes opens up the possibility that this physical description of the Jews is not the narrator's opinion, but rather that of the masses. The lightly mocking tone and exaggerated details that pervade the novel also provide the narrator with a position that leaves a distance between the stereotypes he utilizes and his own views. This ambiguity is not necessarily subversive, but it does unsettle or question some of the categories of identification presented to the reader. Similarly, the city of Vienna represents Austria as a whole in the novel, but Bettauer does not forget those who oppose this relationship. Although the novel mocks the nonurban citizens of Austria and their concept of culture (or rather their lack thereof), the references to them serve as reminders of a common urban bias among the city's inhabitants, the coding of Vienna as Jewish, and the complicated relationship between Viennese, Austrian, and Jewish identies.[17]

The figure of the outsider is present in the novel even before the protagonist Leo Strakosch is introduced. Before Dr. Schwertfeger's public announcement of the Jews' banishment, Holborn, a British reporter, asks the other reporters to explain to him what the current situation is. Although the British reporter is a useful literary device for quick exposition, he also complicates the idea of an objective outsider in his interactions with the other reporters. One of the Jewish reporters begins to tell Holborn of the situation, only to be immediately interrupted by a Christian reporter with the words: "Sie verzeihen, aber diese Aufklärung wird besser von uns ausgehen" [Pardon me, but it is better if this explanation comes from us] (SJ, 5). A description of the manner in which this sentence is delivered immediately follows: "Tonfall drohend, das 'uns' bedeutungsvoll unterstrichen" [Tone threatening, the 'us' insinuatingly underscored] (SJ, 5). The aggressive manner with which the Christian reporter asserts himself highlights the combative relationship between the Christian and Jewish reporters, with the approval of the British reporter serving as proof of one side's superiority over the other. Implied is the idea that since the foreigner is not a part of the political happenings in Vienna, he can be persuaded to see the "truth." One must only make the more convincing argument. The British reporter does not, however, attempt to find out what the Jewish reporter has to say, belying the notion that the foreigner is seeking to consider both sides before reaching an objective conclusion. One side wins by silencing the other. As a result the figure of Holborn undermines the notion of the disinterested outsider. How little we should trust Holborn is emphasized in his reaction to the Christian reporter's words: "Holborn nickte, obwohl er keine Ahnung hatte" [Holborn nodded, although he understood nothing] (SJ, 6). These exchanges provide a warning of the dangers of idealizing the stranger and complicate our view of later events. Holborn, who does not appear in the film, provides an interesting lens through which to view Leo.

Although the division into a Jewish and a Christian side of the journalist's loge is new, the narrator is quick to point out that the tensions between the two groups were not: "Sonst mischten sich die jüdischen und christlichen Journalisten fröhlich durcheinander, im Berufskreis war man nicht Parteigänger, sondern nur der Herr Kollege, und da die jüdischen Journalisten gewöhnlich mehr Neuigkeiten wußten und sie besser verwerten konnten, standen die antisemitischen zu ihnen in einem starken Abhängigkeitsverhältnis" [Normally the Jewish and Christian journalists mingled happily with one another; in the profession one was not a partisan, but rather just a colleague and since the Jewish journalists usually had the latest scoop and could better exploit it, the antisemites were strongly dependent on them] (SJ, 3–4). Collegiality only exists out of necessity, and as always with the characters in this novel, self-interest is the force that dictates their actions. This description simultaneously debunks the idea that the Vienna of the novel was harmonious before the new law and points out that when one is convinced of some personal advantage from a relationship, political differences can be set aside, if not forgotten. Thus the novel shows us the discourses of Jewish identity that exist and also demonstrates how individuals ignore, manipulate, or utilize them for their personal gain without significantly changing the discourses themselves, in much the way that Certeau describes in his *Practice of Everyday Life*. Even the hero of the novel, Leo Strakosch, is not motivated by lofty goals such as justice or equality for Jews. Instead he is dedicated to reuniting with his love, Lotte, and the only way to do this is to overturn the law and be allowed to return to Vienna as a Jew.

Another example of the discrepancies between professed beliefs and actions is Antonius Schneuzel and his family. Schneuzel, an antisemite, goes home to celebrate the imminent expulsion of the Jews and is surprised to find his family less than enthusiastic about the new law. He has forgotten that his son-in-law is Jewish, even if his son-in-law has not. Thus Alois Corroni and his two children, Schneuzel's grandchildren, are banned from Austria, and the same fate awaits his own daughter if she does not divorce her husband. Nor are these the only members of the household affected. The cook Pepi announces that she is going to go to Palestine with her fiancé, the butcher Isidor. The fact that an antisemite of such important standing in the community (he is introduced in the novel as "Nationalrat, Gemeinderat, Armenrat und Gewerberat" [member of the national council, the municipal council, the council for the poor and the trade council]) could fail to realize the impact the new law would have on his personal life could be seen as an example of how pervasive the "invisible" Jewish presence is. I would, however, argue that an alternative reading, one consistent with the rest of the novel, is that Schneuzel's antisemitism is pointed at Jews in the abstract, but has little impact on his daily interactions with them. It is not that he did not know that Corroni was a Jew who had converted to Christianity when his daughter married him; Schneuzel knew but then forgot it. This ability to hold on to an antisemitic political stance, while making everyday life choices that would seem to be in direct opposition to it, demonstrates how these beliefs often fail to serve as a reliable indicator of one's actions on a personal level.[18] Later on in the novel, as more people who had originally greeted the law with enthusiasm begin to change their minds, the recurrent theme is that they should not have expelled all of the Jews; the "useful" ones should have been allowed to stay. This opinion allows one to maintain one's core beliefs and still act differently; by distinguishing between "desirable" and "undesirable" Jews, one can argue that the law was not wrong but that its scope was too broad. That these distinctions as a way of categorizing Jews already existed in discourses of Jewish identity only makes it easier for the antisemites to adopt them and use them as they see fit. It is no coincidence that Leo uses this line of argument as well; the most effective way to help people change their actions is to provide them with a solution that at least allows for the appearance of keeping their core beliefs intact.

Throughout the novel, the narrator seems to take one position and then quickly turns it on its head, leaving the reader uncertain of the narrator's opinion. One example of this move deals with the theme that Spector finds to be the central topic of the novel—the Jewish conspiracy of modernity. We are introduced to the figure of Josef Kallop, the right-hand man of Mayor Karl Maria Laberl. Although his grandfather was Jewish and the name "Kallop" was originally "Pollak," Kallop is considered Christian, since both his grandfather and his father married Christians. It is Kallop who convinces Laberl that he should distance himself from Chancellor Schwertfeger and take the position that the new law went too far and should be at least partially repealed. Kallop gives Laberl the words he should say; it is clear that Kallop is the one pulling the strings. When he finds out his actions have been successful, he reacts as follows: "Und nachdem er sich vergewissert, daß weder ein Kollege noch ein Amtsdiener im Zimmer war, sagte er laut und vernehmlich: 'Maseltoff!' und klopfte dreimal unter den Tisch" [And after he made certain that no colleagues or clerks were in the room, he said loudly and clearly: 'Mazel tov!' and knocked under the table three times] (SJ, 168–69). The not-so-subtle connections between Kallop's political savvy and his Jewishness culminate in this depiction of Kallop as a Jewish mastermind who manipulates others to serve his own means. Immediately following this moment of self-congratulation that seems to cement Kallop's role as a member of the Jewish conspiracy, we learn that his motivations are, like everyone else's, about personal gain:

> Wobei zu bemerken ist, daß Herr Kallop eine üppige, zwar schon zweimal geschiedene, aber dafür mit zahlreichen Millionen gesegnete Jüdin verehrte, die in Prag im Exil lebte. Und er wünschte nichts sehnlicher, als ihre und ihrer Millionen Rückkehr ins teure Vaterland, schon deshalb, weil er mit seinem Gehalt als Präsidialchef unmöglich die Teuerung länger aushalten konnte und außerdem falsch in polnischer Mark spekuliert hatte. (SJ, 169)
>
> It should be noted that Mr. Kallop adored a voluptuous Jewess, indeed twice divorced yet blessed with abundant millions, who lived in Prague in exile. And there was nothing he wished more ardently than the return of her and her millions to the dear fatherland, if for no other reason than that it was impossible to endure the inflation much longer on his salary as head of the executive committee and besides he had speculated poorly in Polish currency.

While these reasons do not put Kallop in a positive light, they do put him on even footing with the Christians around him. His current financial distress is in part due to his inability to speculate in the money markets; he does not have this "Jewish" ability and thus, like other Christians in the novel, loses a great deal of money. And though it is true that his desire to have his beloved return to Vienna seems to be in no small part driven by pecuniary interests, these interests drive home the fact that Kallop is not trying to further some grand plan of Jewish dominance. He acts purely for his personal interests and supports the politics that will allow him to realize his desires. The fact that in this novel greed is associated with Christians at least as often as with Jews supports this reading. When Chancellor Schwertfeger learns that the state did not profit as much as it should have from the expulsion of the Jews because Christians helped Jews smuggle their assets out of the country for a profit, he says to his deputy Fronz: "'Ob Jud' oder Christ—habgierig und selbstsüchtig sind sie alle!" [Whether Jew or Christian—they are all greedy and selfish!] (SJ, 43). Fronz's reaction acknowledges how damaging it would be to Schwertfeger's political credibility if his viewpoint on the universality of human greed were known: "Das dürften die Judenblätter nicht erfahren, dachte Fronz" [The Jewish papers can't find out about this, thought Fronz] (SJ, 43). The fact that Schwertfeger shares his views in private, rather than in a public forum, gives credence to the interpretation that these sentiments he shares with his trusted colleague are to be given more weight than the content of his public speeches. As such, these private words both cause the reader to question Schwertfeger's public persona and open up the possibility that his private opinions are more complex than those of his polemical political speeches.

As for Leo, we get few glimpses of such private conversations, making it even more difficult to ascertain his personal opinions. The fact that for the majority of the novel Leo is always someone else means that the reader never hears Leo's opinions about Jews or politics directly; instead they come from one of his many personas when he reenters the city, and they are often filtered through someone else. Even the few times we hear about what Leo himself thinks, it is from Lotte in her letters to Leo, thus the sentiments are Lotte's interpretation of his words. In his role as the "Society of True Christians" he uses the rhetoric of "good Jews versus bad Jews": "Wir sehnen uns nicht nach den jüdischen Bankiers. Aber die intelligenten, klugen, wertvollen Juden, müssen wir mit offenen Armen aufnehmen, wenn wir nicht rettungslos verelenden wollen!" [We do not desire the Jewish bankers. But we should greet the intelligent, clever and valuable Jews with open arms, if we do not want to sink hopelessly into poverty!] (SJ, 146–47). With the use of such rhetoric, Leo makes the reader aware of the various discourses that shape public opinion about Jews, but he carefully avoids letting us see his own opinions. This absence makes him a more effective protagonist. The novel's refusal to take a firm stance on these questions of Jewish identity also makes it, if potentially more troubling, also more thought provoking. In addition, this fluid position allows the novel to satirize and mock the entire range of discourses about Jewish identity, to at least put them on a more even footing with each other.

Leo occupies the position of the stranger, both as an assimilated Jew in the beginning of the novel and in his guise as a Parisian artist. His original outsider position informs his new role; he has the ability to see the others from a distance and use their prejudices and desires to further his own plans. Through the introduction of Holborn, however, this outsider objectivity has already been made suspect. In this light we see that Leo simultaneously is an outsider and also plays one; the notion of outsider objectivity is both reinforced and brought into question. With the help of a French friend's papers, Leo Strakosch comes to Vienna as Henry Dufresne. Often when Leo speaks as the Parisian Henry to others to convince them of his opinions on the current problems in Vienna, he emphasizes his foreignness to give his words more weight. When he speaks in front of a group of protestors gathered in city hall, he makes it clear that he is speaking as an outsider:

> Er tat, als würde er die deutsche Sprache nur unvollkommen beherrschen, betonte immer wieder, daß er als Franzose eigentlich nicht befugt sei, sich in die Angelegenheit Oesterreichs zu mischen, aber von Wohlwollen für diese unvergleichlich schöne und liebreizende Stadt, der schönsten nach oder mit Paris, erfüllt, doch nicht umhin könne, seiner Meinung Ausdruck zu geben. (SJ, 160–61)
>
> He acted as if he had only partial command of the German language, emphasized repeatedly that as a Frenchman he was actually not entitled to get involved in Austria's affairs, but admitted that, filled with goodwill for this incomparably beautiful and enchanting city whose beauty was only surpassed or equaled by Paris, he could not refrain from voicing his opinion.

Leo is a foreigner in the subjunctive; his ability to effect change depends on the fact that he plays a stranger, knows the Viennese well enough to understand how they perceive him, and uses this knowledge to his advantage. At the same time, the reason he can so successfully play the Parisian is that he was a stranger in his own home. Yet his Jewishness is also what necessitates Leo's taking on the role of a Parisian; banished for being an "undesirable" outsider, Leo must take on the role of a more acceptable outsider. That he does not take on the role of a Christian Austrian though he is perfectly capable of doing so attests to the special advantages of the outsider position, just as the necessity for playing a role points to the potential powerlessness of such a position when it is not accepted by the dominant society.[19]

The novel foregrounds how much the stranger relies on others in order to occupy a privileged position. We are introduced to Leo Strakosch's new identity by his entrance into the Hotel Bristol. Our first glimpse of Henry Dufresne is through the eyes of the hotel manager, someone trained to quickly assess a person by his or her appearance: "Der Hoteldirektor musterte mit geübtem Blick den schweren Lederkoffer und das Handgepäck und dann erst den Fremden, dem ein kleines Knebelbärtchen im Verein mit dem aufgezwirbelten und in Wien sehr unmodernen Schnurrbart einen exotischen Anstrich verlieh. Südfranzose!" [With a practiced eye the hotel manager examined the heavy leather valise and the hand luggage, and only then did he look at the stranger whose small goatee in conjunction with the waxed and, in Vienna very unfashionable, mustache gave him an exotic flair. Southern Frenchman!] (SJ, 91). The manager's assessment provides confirmation of Leo's ability to convincingly play the role of the French artist and also reminds the reader that Leo can move about the city freely only if others believe he is Henry Dufresne. The fact that his facial hair is what "betrays" his identity also underscores how superficial and arbitrary many of the criteria are by which we categorize others; the novel's plot, however, ensures that the reader does not forget the serious consequences these categories can have on people.

Die Stadt ohne Juden: The Film

The reception of the Hans Karl Breslauer's 1924 film version of Bettauer's *Die Stadt ohne Juden* is undeniably linked to the reception of the novel—the release dates were only two years apart—and the film anticipated this connection with some of the plot and artistic choices it made. In its attempt to remove itself from the historical context in which the novel is embedded, the film foregrounds the relationship between the historically specific and ahistorically universal that is a theme in many of the texts we have explored. Aware of the controversy surrounding the novel,

Breslauer and Ida Jenbach, the screenwriters for the film, took steps to remove elements of the narrative they thought to be too incendiary.[20] It is commonly thought that this is why the film plays in "Utopia" instead of Vienna, as it does in the novel. Significant portions of the film were filmed on location in Vienna, but with an emphasis on choosing sites that would make it difficult to easily recognize the city. The shots of Vienna were still recognizable to those who knew Vienna well, but for the most part they successfully masked the location of the film.[21] Despite these changes to subdue the film's political and social critique, or perhaps because of them, the film was not nearly as well received as the novel. The popularity of the book also meant that the audience already connected the story with Vienna. The reviews show that the common opinion of the film was that it had little artistic merit but, unlike the book, did not have the compensatory ability to successfully portray society. The critic Fritz Rosenfeld in the Viennese *Arbeiter-Zeitung* writes of the film: "Der antisemitelnde, gegen den Antisemitismus gerichtete Film ist auch rein filmmäßig miserabel. Die abgedroschenste Karikerei wird herangezogen, die geschmacklosesten Mätzchen sind gut genug, um Lachen zu erzeugen" [The quasi-antisemitic film against antisemitism is a failure even if just seen as a film. The most hackneyed caricatures are drawn, the most tasteless gimmicks are enough to produce laughter].[22] Rather than show a complicated society and a realistic interpretation of what would happen should the Jews be banished, the film only shows crude caricatures meant to elicit easy laughs.[23] In the same review, Rosenfeld also points to the film's failure to erase geographical specificities for the sake of the story's universal appeal:

> Die Straßenbilder sind aus Wien, die Gesamtansicht ist nicht Wien, die Antisemiten sind echte christlichsoziale Wiener Spießer und die Soldaten sind russische Kosaken. Soll angedeutet werden, daß das Problem nicht nur für Wien gilt, so kann man nicht gut zahllose Kleinigkeiten anbringen, die wieder nur dem Wiener verständlich sind. Von ausgesuchter Stumpfsinnigkeit sind die Witze der Ausschriften, für die Dr. Robert Weil verantwortlich zeichnet. Hält er "Angesichtskarte" statt "Ansichtskarte" und "Biskuit und Bruder" statt "Zwieback und Bruder" tatsächlich für sehr lustig?[24]
>
> The images of the streets are from Vienna, the overall portrayal is not Vienna, the antisemites are true Christian-Socialist Viennese bourgeoisie and the soldiers are Russian Cossacks. If it is to be implied that the problem is not specific to Vienna, then one cannot bring in countless trivia that are only understandable for the

> Viennese. The wittiness of the signs, which are attributed to Dr. Robert Weil, is particularly obtuse. Does he actually find "Angesichtskarte" instead of "Ansichtskarte" and "Biskuit und Bruder" instead of "Zwieback und Bruder" funny?

Rosenfeld maintains that the film is pulled in two directions: one uses a non-culturally-specific approach that is supposed to demonstrate the universality of antisemitism, and the other makes references to a specific location and time, references that are understandable only to a small and specific audience. According to Rosenfeld, the film fails to connect to the universal audience as well as the culturally and historically specific one. The film is thus inaccurate on both levels, and Rosenfeld claims that these inaccuracies are the film's downfall.

When the film premiered in Berlin, two years after its release in Vienna, the reviews were equally critical:

> Man versucht, für die Rassenversöhnung dadurch einzutreten, daß man mit kleinlichen Mätzchen und einer wahren Flut von Taktlosigkeiten für die Juden eintritt. Der Endeffekt ist das genaue Gegenteil von dem, was man beabsichtigt . . . Die Juden bleiben häßliche Karikaturen und ihren Gegnern geht es genau so.[25]

> It attempts to advocate for racial reconciliation by advocating for the Jews through small gimmicks and a veritable flood of tactlessness. The end result is exactly the opposite of what was intended . . . The Jews remain ugly caricatures and the same applies to their opponents.

Contemporary critics seemed to believe that instead of accurately showing the political and cultural situation of the times, the film was merely a set of grotesque caricatures, unable to evoke any sense of compassion or identification on the part of the audience. Since most felt that the novel's success was its accuracy, the film, left without this vital component, was apparently doomed to fail.[26] The film's attempt to appeal to a wider audience by erasing some of its specificity was met with criticism for this lack; the film failed to create a connection to its audience.

Another important difference between the novel and the film is the absence of Orthodox Jews in Bettauer's novel. The novel focuses more on the wide range of positions and identities occupied by established assimilated Jews in Vienna. In the film we see allusions to these distinctions in the comparison between Corroni[27] and Strakosch and in the appearance of Kraus (a character similar to Pinkus in the novel) and his fluid Christian/Jewish identity. What the film adds is the appearance of Orthodox Jews who because of their lifestyle and appearance do not move as easily within society as do the assimilated Jews. The appearance of the Orthodox Jews hints at the tension between various German Jewish identities, a theme less explored in the novel.[28] Beatrix Hoffmann-Holter makes a connection between the portrayal of Jews in the film and the position of East European Jewish refugees in Vienna after World War I. About the mass exodus on foot in the third act of the film she observes: "Es entsteht der Eindruck, dass nur Alte, Kranke, Frauen und Kinder von der Exekutierung des Ausweisungsgesetzes betroffen sind" [One is given the impression that only the elderly, the sick, women, and children were affected by the execution of the expulsion law].[29] The images of these poor Jews conform to popular images of "Ostjuden" as religiously observant, old-fashioned in their clothing, and generally strange and removed from the rest of the "Western" world. As Hoffmann-Holster points out, those targeted by antisemitic laws during World War I and the interwar period were usually Jewish war refugees who fled to Austria from Galicia and Bukovina. Hoffmann-Holter claims that the film gives us a glimpse of Jewish refugees from Eastern Europe as they no longer existed by the time the novel was published.[30] I would argue, however, that the film is not only giving us a glimpse of the lives of Jewish refugees during this earlier time; it is also showing the audience the images they have of the "Ostjuden" in the time of the film and the book. The film hints at the tension between various German Jewish identities and also indicates the significant presence of this view of Jews as "exotic foreigners" in the German imagination. The addition of the Orthodox Jews foregrounds the themes of distance and proximity as they relate to German Jews and their relationship to the majority culture and also demonstrates the power of the majority culture to label a diverse population under the homogenizing rubric "Jew."

In the film, there is a conflation of Orthodox Jews and "Ostjuden." After World War I about 20 percent of the Viennese Jewish population were Orthodox Jews. Among the Orthodox Jews there were several subgroups, including Hasidim, traditionalists, modernists, and Zionists.[31] In the film, the ones who are marked as Orthodox Jews are traditionalists and Hasidim. In contrast to the assimilated Jews, they are set apart from the rest of Utopia's inhabitants, including the assimilated Jews, by their clothing and open displays of religious worship and Jewish traditions. The film even went so far as to use "authentic" East European Jews as actors; in an article about the filming of *Die Stadt ohne Juden,* comments were made about these "Ostjuden": "Bemerkenswert ist es, daß es im Interesse der Echtheit auch eine Anzahl von Ostjuden zur Darstellung kleinerer Rollen herangezogen wurden, die sich während der bisherigen Atelieraufnahmen wider Erwarten ganz ausgezeichnet bewährten" [It is noteworthy that in the interest of authenticity a number of East European Jews were brought in for smaller roles, who, counter to expectations, have proven to be excellent in the studio filming so far].[32] The choice to use "real" East European Jews is driven by concerns for historical accuracy. The flawed logic of this decision is that if these people exist in the "real" world, then the depiction of Jews in the film is accurate. At first glance, the inclusion of these nonactors may seem counterintuitive when one considers the filmmakers' attempts to make the film less controversial than the book by removing historical specificity. But I would argue that by focusing on Jews who are strange and different, and by emphasizing that these exotic Jews really exist, the film attempts to shift the focus from the assimilated Jews who are integrated into Viennese society to these outsiders who are easily recognizable and separated from mainstream society.

I interpret these images of the poor and sick marching out of "Utopia" as a commentary on the laws and whom they are supposed to affect. After the parliament scene in which the law is made public, we see the masses outside and then the Orthodox/"Ostjuden" family from earlier in the film. The son walks into the room and laments that they are to be thrown out like dogs. The father lies in bed, too weak to sit up. What we see in this scene is the image of those who are "supposed" to be affected by the law—"Ostjuden" who are not productive members of society. When the law was passed, both Christians and the assimilated Jews who supported the law had this image of the outsider "Ostjuden" in mind and saw them as the ones who would be affected by the banishment. With the inclusion of these images of the "Ostjuden," the film reassures its audience by confirming that these outsider Jews exist, that they rather than the assimilated Jews are the target, even as the plot of the film contradicts such assumptions. In the novel, however, "unproductive" Jews exist within the realm of political rhetoric, with the implication that what is important is the role they play in the popular imagination, not an actual debate about who is productive and therefore worthy of living in Vienna. The film makes the scapegoats real, and thus the film loses some of the ambiguity present in the novel.

Hoffmann-Holster also mentions other stereotypes of "Ostjuden," some of which make more of an appearance in the novel than in the film. For example, there are the ostentatiously wealthy, whose number was greatly exaggerated. Along with this image was the notion that Jews became wealthy through inflating prices to their great advantage—the image of

Jews as "Wucherer" [racketeers]. Throughout the novel there are hints of the assimilated Jews' disdain for the recent immigrants or "Ostjuden" and their desire to exclude these Jews from the category to which they belong. In these displays of prejudice, the image of the "Wucherer" is often present. The film focuses more on the poor recent refugees, perhaps to take the focus away from this stereotype of the Ostjude as a greedy profiteer. In doing so, however, the film introduces another stereotype—that of the Ostjude as a poor, isolated, and old-fashioned Jew who cannot or will not assimilate.

Kraus/Pinkus is an example of how the novel and the film complicate stereotypes in a way that belies the notion that they are thoughtlessly racist caricatures. I would not go so far as to say that these portrayals of certain "types" of Jews necessarily undermine the stereotypes, but they do point to some of the inconsistencies in the categories that separate Jews and Christians. In the novel, the name of the publisher character is Pinkus. In a meeting of various artists and writers at a villa,[33] he is outed as an "Urchrist"—only his grandfather was a Jew—and the response is laughter, since he is "in Art und Äußerem ganz entschieden ein Duplikat [s]eines Großvaters" [in mannerism and appearance without contest a duplicate of his grandfather] (SJ, 35). In and of itself this little scene is a stab at the impossibility of identifying who is a Jew and who is not, even among Jews. The scenes directly preceding and following emphasize this point. An actor who has been praised by the media as the "Verkörperer des christlichen Schönheitsideales" [embodiment of the Christian ideal of beauty] has a Jewish father and must leave; this revelation is also greeted with laughter. But the chapter ends on a dark note. A poet whom we meet earlier in the chapter and who somewhat melodramatically proclaims that his art can only be produced in Vienna is brought into the room after he has shot himself by the lake. The actor and Pinkus are opposites, one the Aryan Jew and the other the Jewish Aryan. They are also similar in the humor with which they present their situations and the seemingly light-hearted manner with which they face their fates. It is implied that neither one of them will suffer too greatly as a consequence of the new law. The young poet, however, lends a sense of gravity to the situation; he cannot imagine his life other than it has been, and the prospect of exile is so great that he chooses death. Although the tragedy of his death is somewhat diminished by his youth and inflexible idealism, the act nevertheless shows the dark reality underneath the other characters' somewhat flippant banter.

This villa scene is not included in the film, and the only character from this scene who appears in the film is Pinkus, as Kraus, a not-so-subtly-named journalist. The loss of the other characters lessens the ambiguity of Jewish identity and diminishes the sharpness of the critique. Nevertheless, his appearance in the film points to the arbitrary nature of these categories of identification and the lack of an essential Jewish identity. As Schwertfeger gives his speech about the new law banishing the Jews, Kraus sits in the journalists' loge. The Christian and Jewish sections of the loge are divided physically by a low barrier. After Schwertfeger declares that the grandchildren of converted Jews are to be considered Christians, Kraus hops over the barrier to join his fellow Christians. In an intertitle he announces: "Ich bin ein waschechter Goi" [I am a dyed-in-the-wool goy]. The use of the term "goy" underscores how Kraus's behavior and cultural references do not change, despite his new identity. As such, this joke, although somewhat crude, illustrates how the others unquestioningly accept the new categories of identification as truth. Although Kraus makes clear and unsubtle references to his identification with a Jewish identity, he is now accepted as a Christian because the law has defined him as one.

Leo Strakosch as Simmel's Stranger

The film can be seen as a concrete example of the more abstract discourses of thinkers such as Helmuth Plessner, Georg Simmel, and Siegfried Kracauer. In particular, Simmel's concept of the stranger resonates with the portrayal of the protagonist Leo Strakosch. In both the film and Simmel's essay, there is an exploration of the complicated relationship between notions of the stranger as a potential wanderer and the stranger as a potential forced exile within the context of German Jewish identity. The texts show that the figure of the stranger is not either one or the other, but ambivalently both, and that the two aspects are interdependent. The film is about the abstract stranger and the impossibility thereof, or how ahistoricity does not provide an escape from historical reality.[34]

When the film and essay are read together, the historical context of Simmel's stranger becomes clearer. In the first section of the book I read Simmel's essay in relation to other early twentieth-century thinkers. There I examined the move within the text toward an ahistorical framework in which to discuss an idealized stranger. Here I will take a closer look at one of the historical contexts that have been decontextualized in the essay.[35] Both texts, one implicitly and the other more explicitly, privilege a specific outsider position, namely that of the assimilated Jew. He is the ultimate insider/outsider—close enough to the others that he can blend in, but enough of a stranger that he can move about freely. He can see others as they cannot see themselves and is both a part of the community and apart from it. Seen in relation to discourses of German Jewish identity, Simmel's conception of the stranger takes on new nuances: it is not only important that the stranger has a unique combination of proximity and distance in his relationship to the others of the communities; it is also significant that only a certain kind of stranger can occupy such a position. Not all strangers can, even if they are all allowed to live within a community.

As we saw earlier, Simmel argues that one needs to look at the stranger as part of his new community, but Simmel creates this perspective at the expense of ignoring the community from which the stranger came. In fact, this move to separate the stranger from any sense of community or history is central to Simmel's conceptualization of the stranger. In terms of thinking about German Jewish identity, this move is particularly interesting, as one can read it as a rejection of the categories used in other definitions of the stranger/Jew. Instead of placing the categories of the dominant culture at the center of his argument, either to refute them or to agree with them, Simmel rejects their use altogether. Instead he claims that the stranger, although a part of the community, is not subject to its categorizations: he decides for himself who he is and how he is to act.

What becomes clear when we juxtapose Simmel's text with Breslauer's film is that the stranger's ability to define himself comes not only from being set apart from others, but also from belonging to the community in which he now finds himself. He needs to move within the community with ease, to be enough a part of it that he is not ostracized as being too different. Yet he must also maintain enough difference that he can occupy the privileged position of the outsider. In the film, this balancing act is performed by the protagonist Leo Strakosch, an assimilated Jew.

The film comments on the roles of Jews in society within this paradigm of distance and proximity through the juxtaposition of various tableaus of family life. In an early scene there is first a shot of Lotte, the hero's love interest, being consoled by her father after finding out about the city's plans to banish all the Jews. This is immediately followed by a portrayal of an Orthodox Jew who has a long beard, wears a caftan, and is rocking back and forth, reading from a prayer book. His daughter is sitting on the bed, and the wife walks into the room and pulls the daughter onto her lap. Then the film cuts to the home of Volbert,[36] one of the antisemites in Parliament, first with a shot of their cook and her Jewish love interest, then showing Volbert playing with his granddaughter. The Linders'[37] bourgeois living room and Volbert's study emphasize the poverty of the Jewish family. These differences are made even more prominent by the dark lighting used for the Jewish home and by the curtains hanging unevenly from the cords that divide one section of the dwelling from the other, in stark contrast to the sense of permanence given by the heavy furniture and multitude of paintings and other decorative items in the other two homes. The curtains remind the viewer of the Jews' transitory nature; the stability of a permanent home is denied them. Through the similarity in the lighting and set-design of the shots, it is implied that the Linders and the Volberts have more in common with each other—despite diametrically opposed politics—than with Orthodox Jews. These shots are an enactment of Simmelian distance: the Orthodox Jews are too strange, too distant, to be a part of the rest of the community. This distance also plays out on a diegetic level in the film: we are never told the names of the Orthodox Jews—these scenes lack intertitles explaining who these people are, their relation to one another, their personal stories.[38] There is also the issue of class difference: the Volberts and Linders belong to the bourgeoisie, while it is clear that the Orthodox Jews are poor.

Directly following this scene in the Volbert home is a portrayal of Orthodox Jews in prayer. Here we see a tight shot of three Jews sitting on a bench, rocking back and forth much like the Jew with his family. There is an intertitle of the Jews' prayers, followed by a very high shot of two men in the middle of a synagogue, then a cut to the entire synagogue showing more people spread throughout the space. This scene implies that Orthodox Jews have a community only through religion; the synagogue is what connects the groups of two and three. Entrance into this community means lack of admittance into mainstream society; these Jews are contained in the space of the synagogue. One can read this scene in the following manner: the Orthodox Jew and his family are not a part of the world of the Linders and the Volberts. They can only be understood in the context of other traditional Jews and are defined solely by their religion and customs.

The few intertitles that do appear further emphasize the alienation of the Orthodox Jews from the rest of society. For example, in one scene there is a crowd of Jews on the street, all with long beards and hats, huddled around a newspaper, discussing their imminent banishment. They share one paper, passing it around among themselves, a sign of their poverty. One of them says to the others: "Mit uns könnten sie doch eine Ausnahme machen" ["They could surely make an exception for us"]. Here we see echoes of Rathenau—the Jews are not outraged by the banishment; they merely want to be exceptions to the rule. Yet it is precisely these Jews for whom there will be no exception: when Bernart,[39] a member of the Großdeutschen Partei and a rabid antisemite, has nightmares about the Jews, he dreams of Jews with long beards and caftans who bear a striking similarity to those in the street scene. Later on, when Leo tricks Bernart into missing the vote to allow Jews back into the city, he hovers over Bernart's bed to change the time on his watch. This reference to Bernart's dream comments on the misguided opinion that Bernart has of Orthodox Jews. They do not pose a threat because they are too removed from society; it is people like Leo who have the power to impact Bernart's world.

Yet even with something as straightforward as the role of Orthodox Jews in society, the film allows for nuances and complications. Linder holds Lotte in his lap just as the Jewish mother does, comforting her in the same way. This similarity gives us the sense that the two families have something in common, particularly in contrast to the idyllic scenes at the Volberts' home. It is also ironic that the one content household we see is that of an antisemite with his half-Jewish granddaughter as well as his cook and her Jewish love interest. As we will see later on in the film, this happy family will have as much to lose as the two others, despite seeming at this moment to be unaffected by the new laws Volbert helps implement.

Before I move on to an examination of Leo's role in this society, I would like to look at the other extreme—that of being too close—in the figure of Alois Carroni, a converted Jew. As in the novel, he has changed his name and his religion, married into a Christian household, and left his Jewish identity behind. In the film we see Carroni at the Volberts' home as the entire family berates Volbert for supporting a law that will ruin his family. Carroni is fully integrated into the shots; whenever he appears, there are other members of the household in the shot, showing how much a part of society he is. He sits behind and to the right of Volbert as the others share their opinions of the new law. Their body language is quite similar, and through these similarities we see that Carroni empathizes with Volbert; instead of joining in the criticism, he implicitly takes Volbert's side.[40] This gesture emphasizes Carroni's helplessness, which results from his inability to remove himself from the societal norms and rules. As we will see, this lack of distance appears frequently in the film's plot.

The film situates Leo Strakosch as being part of society, but not quite of it. We see Leo walking with Lotte, his fiancée, and her father, Councilman Linder. They walk together, and her father assures Leo (through an intertitle) that no matter what, they will stay loyal to one another. Then he shakes hands with Leo and enters through the gate; Lotte follows her father, leaving Leo to close the gate behind them. He holds on to the gate for a moment, while facing away from it. This scene marks Leo's place in society: he moves easily within it, but he always remains something of an outsider. He has contact with society, as is demonstrated in the shaking of hands with Linder and the kissing of Lotte, but he is also aware of the borders represented by the gate. He faces away from the gate, not toward the Linders' home, showing his potential mobility—both voluntary and forced.

The stories of Leo and Carroni parallel each other, emphasizing the differences in their reactions to the situation at hand. When Carroni gets on the train to leave Utopia, he is surrounded by his daughter, wife, and father-in-law, emphasizing the close-knit environment that he is forced to leave. His daughter jumps into his arms several times, representing the difficulty with which the others let him leave. There are many others surrounding them in similar situations, both leaving on the train and saying goodbye to those who are. Though Leo's goodbye to Lotte and her father is similar to Carroni's farewell to his family, Leo is on the last train out of Utopia, and it seems that he is the only one boarding the train. Carroni is leaving his family and the society they are all a part of; Leo—never having been a full member of that society—is only saying goodbye to his loved ones. He closes the train's door, evoking the gate scene; but this time instead of facing away from the Linders, he faces toward them, marking the forced nature of this departure.

Carroni chooses to move to Hamburg, Leo to Paris. Although the film is supposed to be located in Utopia, it is clear that it is at the very least a German-speaking society, if not Austria. Carroni's choice expresses his desire to be in a society similar to the one he has left. He also writes his wife a letter to tell her that the best possible solution for her would be a divorce so that she can remain in Utopia. He is too much a part of the society that created the law to see a way around it. Leo's identity is not as tied to Utopia, therefore he chooses Paris. His flexibility is also evident in his reaction to Linder's request that he end his letter contact with Lotte because of the distress it causes her. He writes a response to Linder stating that he is ending the correspondence, but returns to Utopia in the disguise of a Parisian artist. He is removed enough from the society to find a way to manipulate it to his own ends.

Regardless of the "type" of Jew one is in the film, all are defined as "Jew" by law and subsequently banished from Utopia. Simmel acknowledges that the tension created by a stranger in the community often leads to an emphasis on the characteristics that make a stranger different. This emphasis, however, often leads the community to place the stranger—whether he is a stranger by citizenship, race, or otherwise—into categories that deny him his individuality. According to Simmel, one can be a true stranger only when one does not belong to any other category of identification. By placing a stranger into a community of strangers, one makes assumptions about that person and his behavior, in part dictating his actions through their expectations. The stranger is thus robbed of his agency and freedom because he is locked into a category projected onto him.

Simmel's anxiety about the stranger's loss of power is his anxiety about history's interference with his ideal stranger. The portrayal of Utopia in the film can be seen in the same light: the film attempts to avoid conveying a sense of location and history, but it also points to the impossibility of doing so, since Vienna is still recognizable in the plot and some of the location shots. These two texts negotiate the connections between a historical moment and a purposefully noncontextualized ahistorical stranger. History, in the form of categorizations by the dominant community, is not, however, just a hindrance to the stranger's agency. In some ways, it can also be seen as the source of it. In Simmel's text there are assumptions made about the community in which the stranger lives. It is fairly homogenous; otherwise the stranger would not be recognizable as such. And its members easily fit into given categories, reacting in ways predictable to an outsider. The character Leo tricks is Bernart, a stereotypical antisemite, not Volbert. Although Bernart's excessive drinking is the ostensible reason for this choice, I would argue that the implicit one is that Volbert, with his more than half-Jewish household, does not easily fit into predictable categories and is therefore much more difficult to manipulate. By having two members of the Großdeutschen Partei in its narrative, the film shows just how predictable Bernart is, especially in relation to the much more complicated Volbert.[41]

Leo also depends on given categories for his other transformations—during the film he is also "the true Christian" who secretly posters the city with messages about the usefulness of the Jews from the "Society of True Christians." In these messages, he plays the ultimate insider, encouraging his "fellow" Christians to see the value of the Jews and allow them back into the land. Politically, he is a "friend" to the liberals as well as to the conservatives. At the end of the film, we also see that his deceptions are allowed because of his role as the "Jewish trickster." As Kraus tells him when Leo relates the story to him, "So etwas kann wirklich nur einem Unsrigen einfallen, seien'S mir net bös!" ["Only one of us could come up with something like that, no offense!"]. The recognition of being "one of us"—that is, a Jew—by Kraus, who through the course of the film is a Jew, a Jewish-looking Christian, and apparently at the end of the film again a Jew, only foregrounds the fluidity of these categories of identity.

The risk of being systematically categorized and ostracized for one's perceived differences is a constant one in the stranger's life. Yet as Simmel argues, and as one can see in the figure of Leo, there is an enormous potential freedom and agency in playing the stranger. I use the word "playing" deliberately here, for Leo easily plays the role of the Parisian, "the true Christian," as well as the "Jewish trickster." As I mentioned earlier, Bernart fails to see Leo as a transgressive threat, instead focusing on the traditional Jews who are not allowed this flexibility of identity. Leo breaks down the categories of identity with the ease in which he shifts from one to the other, but he simultaneously reinforces society's need for categories by constantly creating new ones for himself. He cannot attain Simmel's ideal; he cannot just be a stranger, in control of his own identity. Instead, he must take on identities that are easily recognized by others, and although he does not necessarily act in the ways that are expected of him, he is effective only because of his ability to predict how other people will perceive him.

Leo is both a transgressive threat and the upholder of social stability; his goal is to return Utopia to the society it was before. He uses the categories provided by the dominant society, but the ease with which he moves from one to another undermines the notion that they are somehow inherently "real" and thereby permanent. Leo's fluid identity also points to the potential breakdown of other categories. To return to the statement of one of the traditional Jews in the film that they should be considered an exception: what happens when the group most obviously targeted by this exclusionary law refuses to be included in the category provided? On one level the statement only reinforces the internalization of the categories, because the Orthodox Jews do not question the necessity of banishing the Jews; they only wish to be made an exception. On another level, the rejection of the category of that "kind" of Jew by the ones most clearly marked as such shows that these categories also depend on one's recognition of belonging to the category. This scene reminds the viewer that being an Orthodox Jew and a patriot are not mutually exclusive identities and that there are Orthodox Jews, like the ones portrayed in film, who see themselves both as devout Jews and as Austrian patriots. Ultimately the discrepancy between how the Orthodox Jews see themselves and how the others see them in the film is too great, and the viewpoint that they are too strange and too distant is the one that dominates. They cannot be strangers in the Simmelian sense because they are too restricted by the perceptions of others. But the very fact that they question these perceptions and do not hold them to be self-evident points to the possibility for change.

Through Leo's actions, the film shows how the stranger is both the potential wanderer and the potential forced exile; it also points the way to the radical breakdown of these categories for all, not by rejecting the categories but by showing their instability. Yet it simultaneously shows that such a breakdown would lead to the loss of the stranger's mobility and agency. Leo is a stranger who can manipulate the codes and categories to his own ends, but only if he upholds the social norms of a society that can potentially take his agency away. Leo cannot be a stranger in Simmel's sense, because historical and cultural contexts obstruct such an abstract freedom. Here we see the historical necessity for the ahistorical realm in which Simmel's concept of the stranger exists.

Béla Balázs on Bettauer

The impact that the relationship between historical context and the abstract figure of the stranger had on the public persona of Bettauer and the reception of his work is perhaps best illustrated by his short-lived periodical *Er und Sie: Wochenschrift für Lebenskultur und Erotik*. In the five weekly issues, which appeared from February 14 to March 13, 1924, Bettauer positioned himself as a nonjudgmental giver of advice, someone who could help others navigate the confusing and often lonely circumstances of urban life. As such, Bettauer and his writings fit into another category of Jewish identity, that of the assimilated, secular, cosmopolitan Jew. This position is one that relies on a universalization of modern alienation, so as to make the outsider someone who can speak for others. At the same time, it is also rooted in a specific historical and cultural context, and it is no coincidence that so many of the writers concerned with questions of modernity and urban alienation, such as Georg Simmel, Siegfried Kracauer, and Walter Benjamin, were of Jewish ancestry. In this regard we might also see Bettauer as another kind of victim, to the extent that the attacks on him and his work demonstrate the rejection of a notion of universal stranger that includes Jews. I argue that in Bettauer's writings we can see an insistence on the possibility of agency within the modern city and on the ability of an individual to decide how to live his or her life, and that this insistence has in part to do with his Jewish identity. Bettauer is both a victim and a privileged stranger. These discourses are not in opposition to one another; rather, they interact to create a more complicated position. On a broader level this position is about the relationship between discourses of urban modernity and those of Jewish identity in interwar Germany and Austria, a relationship that both creates and limits the possibility of individual freedom.

The attacks on Bettauer and *Er und Sie* created and reinforced notions of Jewish sexual depravity, Jewish sensationalist journalism, and Jewish cosmopolitan morality, but an examination of his work reveals that he avoided linking questions of sexuality and morality to notions of Jewishness and did little to encourage his identification as a Jewish public figure.[42] Instead, a dominant theme in his writings is a universalization of discourses of sexuality. He popularized scientific discourses that clearly emphasized sexuality's human aspect rather than its links to a particular ethnicity or subgroup. This disconnect between the topics that Bettauer wrote about and the attacks on his writings highlights a central theme in his work, namely that of individual agency. In his writings about sexuality, he educates the public to facilitate an atmosphere of acceptance and challenges notions of morality that unnecessarily restrict an individual and the life he or she wishes to lead.

Béla Balázs's article about Bettauer, published in the weekly *Die Bühne* in 1925, illustrates both the difficulty and the necessity of lifting Bettauer out of the narrow confines of these categories of Jewishness. Such difficulties are evident even in the editor's introduction to the article. It includes a long detailed list of the accomplishments of "Hugo Ignotus," Balázs's pseudonym,[43] to add weight to the following statement: "Selbst die Hochachtung vor diesem wirklich edlen Literaten konnte die Zeitungen nicht bestimmen, seine Stellungnahme zu Bettauer zu veröffentlichen" [Even the high esteem in which this truly noble literary figure is held could not persuade the papers to publish his commentary on Bettauer] (BB, 20). Balázs had actually written the article six months before its publication in *Die Bühne,* as a defense of Bettauer in the wake of the scandal caused by *Er und Sie*. Even though Balázs had no knowledge of Bettauer's murder while writing his article, it is clear that *Die Bühne*'s decision to publish his piece is motivated by the sensationalism surrounding this event:

> Die Schilderung der Figur des Schriftstellers, der heute als Opfer eines verruchten Attentats zwischen Leben und Tod schwebt, ist indes so packend, daß wir es uns nicht versagen können, den Artikel jetzt, da er uns zukommt, ohne Änderung zu veröffentlichen. Es erscheint uns überflüssig, angesichts dieser Schilderung mehr über Bettauer und das Attentat zu sagen. (BB, 20)

> The depiction of the author, who today hovers between life and death, the victim of a wicked assassination attempt, is meanwhile so enthralling that we could not fail to publish the article now, since we have it, without changes. It seems to us to be unnecessary, in light of this portrayal, to say more about Bettauer and the assassination attempt.

The paper does not explain why the article was turned down by Viennese newspapers, although most likely it was fear of being seen as sympathizing with a controversial figure. But once Bettauer becomes a victim of a sensationalist crime, he becomes an object of interest. The paper takes the position that Balázs's portrait of Bettauer will speak for itself, that it is unnecessary to go into the details of the murder. Yet the two sentences devoted to denying the need to mention it emphasize the event's importance in the printing of the article. They also support the interpretation that what prevents the paper from going into the details of the attack on Bettauer is not the paper's sense of decency and decorum, but the fact that the event and all its details are common knowledge thanks to the multitude of Viennese papers that have covered it. The claim that Balázs's portrait of Bettauer eliminates the necessity of discussing the event is also somewhat ambiguous. One reading is that the article's sympathetic depiction of Bettauer makes clear the paper's position on the murder attempt as an attack on an undeserving victim. Another is that the article provides insights into how Bettauer and his contributions could incite such violence. In any case, the introduction foregrounds the historical context from which the article cannot escape, even as Balázs's article tries to redefine it as a way of reinterpreting and understanding Bettauer.

Much of the article focuses on explaining Bettauer's enormous popularity. Balázs describes Bettauer as follows:

> Eine liebenswürdige, bescheidene, gar nicht vordringliche Schriftstellerfigur, die ihre fabelhafte Popularität mit Geschmack trägt, und als Entgelt für sie die sittlich-öffentliche Pflicht empfindet, mit einer jeden Zeile, sei diese nachdenklich oder erzählend, für Freiheit und Aufklärung und gegen Scheinheiligkeit und Grausamkeit namentlich in Sachen der Liebe loszuziehen, wozu sich selbst im gütigen und duldsamen Ländchen Österreich Grund und Gelegenheit bietet. (BB, 20)

> An amiable, modest, not at all pushy literary figure, who wears his phenomenal popularity with good taste, and finds that as remuneration for this popularity it is his moral and public duty, with every line that he writes, whether it be contemplative or telling a story, to advocate for freedom and enlightenment and against hypocrisy and cruelty specifically in regards to love. Even in the benevolent and tolerant land of Austria there is reason and opportunity for this stance.

According to Balázs, one of Bettauer's defining characteristics is his sense of duty to the public. He argues that Bettauer is motivated by a need to educate his readership, thus detracting from critics who claim that Bettauer's work is cheap and tawdry sensationalism.[44] And central to Bettauer's ability to reach the people are his writing style and the topics he chooses. His style is "eine an den Zeitungen aufgezogene charakteristische Gesprächsprache, die für die Syntax wenig übrig hat, doch mit Sicherheit verständlich macht, wovon die Rede ist" [a characteristically spoken language cultivated by the papers, a language that has little use for syntax but certainly makes it clear what is meant] (BB, 20). The use of such language ensures that clarity is privileged over a style that draws attention to the author's command of the written word. Balázs's description of Bettauer's style brings together Bettauer's use of newspaper language and everyday speech. Balázs describes a language that is rooted in the spoken vernacular as mediated through newspapers. It is familiar to the masses, but also contains a sense of objectivity and authority. The topics that Bettauer chooses are also familiar to the masses—since they are drawn from current events reported on in newspapers—but are distilled in such a way as to enlighten his readers: "So verwebt Bettauer die Massengeschehnisse des Gestern zu einem Massentraum für das nächste Morgenblatt und packt damit die Leute sinnlicher, als er es mit irgendeiner Psychologie könnte" [Thus Bettauer weaves the events of yesterday into a collective dream for the next issue of the morning paper and affects the people in a more gripping manner than some kind of psychology could] (BB, 20). This accessibility through language and content is important so that Bettauer's writings can reach his primary audience—"die kleinen Leute" or "den kleinen Mann." Yet as Balázs emphasizes, Bettauer does not merely report what has happened, nor does he merely titillate his audience with salacious innuendo. Instead, what makes Bettauer's writings effective is the combination of his intellect, his chosen topics, and his approach to them:

> Der kleine Mann findet sich, seine Interessiertheiten, seine Art, zu sehen und zu empfinden, bei Bettauer wieder, die literarisch und intellektuell höchstgradig aufgeklärt und furchtlos kampfentschlossen anmutend dem kleinen Mann zum beseligenden Selbstgefühl verhilft: "Was muß ich doch für ein intelligentes und erhabenes Wesen sein, daß ich an diesem intelligenten und erhabenen Schriftsteller so meine rechte Freude habe!" (BB, 21)

> The little man recognizes his interests, his way of seeing and feeling, in Bettauer, who, literarily and intellectually enlightened and

> appearing to be fearlessly combative, helps the little man achieve a blissful self-confidence: "What an intelligent and superior being I must be, that I derive so much joy from this intelligent and superior author!"

Balázs counters accusations that Bettauer's writing is worthless, and popular only because of its "low" appeal by contending that Bettauer's popularity depends on being perceived by his readership as intelligent and well educated. Bettauer as a public figure occupies the same position as his writing—accessible but also apart and thus able to provide insights that change the way the readers look at themselves.

The antisemitic tone of some of the attacks on Bettauer during the *Er und Sie* scandal does prompt Balázs to address the question of Bettauer's "Jewishness." But he takes care first to enumerate Bettauer's many accomplishments and his unique sensibility; only at the end of the article does he turn to this topic. Balázs defends Bettauer against attacks based on his Jewish nature in two ways. First, he maintains that this whole notion of Jewish writing and the idea that Bettauer's work is distinguished by its Jewishness occur only because he happens to be writing in a part of the world in which there is a large Jewish population that, unlike in France, is recognizable to the general public as a separate group. Second, he offers a different definition of what qualities are Jewish. The following sentence combines these two elements of his argument:

> In Rom und in Paris, wo die Juden im übrigen Volke verschwinden, sind Zeitungsschreiber und Kaffeehäuser nicht anders wie in Wien, Prag oder Budapest, und greift das Jüdische des Juden als Massenwirkung durch, so gewiß nicht mit semitischen Eigenschaften, die es nicht gibt, sondern mit der städtisch und vom religiös herkömmlichen Lernzwang bedingten Intellektualität, mit der es dem Provinzler, den es in die innere Stadt zieht, begeistert. (BB, 21)

> In Rome and in Paris, where the Jews disappear into the rest of the population, journalists and coffee houses are not any different than in Vienna, Prague or Budapest, and if the Jewishness of the Jews has any influence on the masses, this is not because of their semitic characteristics, which do not exist. Instead this influence comes from an intellect resulting from a compulsion to learn with roots in the city and in religion, an intellect that excites those from the provinces and draws them into the city.

Balázs refutes the idea that there is such a thing as "Semitic qualities," but in the same sentence he maintains that what is Jewish about Bettauer and others like him is a certain intellectual nature that is rooted in both urban and religious traditions. Religion in this case is important not as a set of beliefs that sets one apart from others, but as part of a long tradition of placing importance on education and learning. This secularization of Judaism is connected to the city and the work of these Jewish intellectuals and serves to introduce others, namely those from the provinces, to urban life. Thus Balázs not only implies that this kind of Jewishness is an integral part of the city; he also suggests that it is responsible for the image that cities project to the rest of the world. The only thing Jewish about Bettauer is his intellectualism, but the difference is mitigated by the object of this intellect's focus—bringing the city to others and attracting people to the city.

In a curious turn, Balázs ends the article by stating that Bettauer is not the first controversial Jewish journalist in Vienna—Moritz Saphir was in Vienna "zwei Menschenalter" [two generations] before Bettauer. Balázs compares the two: "Doch Saphir war ein frecher und zudringlicher Kerl, Bettauer hingegen ist ein netter, gütiger, edeldenkender Junge" [Yet Saphir was an insolent and intrusive guy; Bettauer, however, is a nice, gracious and noble-minded youth] (BB, 21). It appears that he introduces Saphir as a reminder to the readers that Vienna has a long tradition of Jewish journalists, that Bettauer is not a new Jewish threat. The implication is that Vienna survived Saphir's popularity and writings and that Bettauer is even less dangerous because he possesses qualities of character that Saphir did not. Foregrounded is the fact that Bettauer is harmless. Yet Balázs makes this point by comparing him to another Jewish journalist who, it is implied, was not as harmless. By juxtaposing the two figures and connecting Bettauer in the reader's imagination to a less exemplary Jewish journalist, Balázs somewhat undermines his defense of Bettauer.

The article makes a convincing argument for Bettauer's importance to Viennese popular culture and the need to evaluate what it means to consider him a Jewish journalist. At the same time, it demonstrates the difficulties of such an endeavor and the need to confront the categories that one wishes to redefine. What follows attempts to negotiate this precarious balancing act in an exploration of Bettauer's contributions to the discourses of intimacy, social interactions, and urban life in his literary and journalistic work. It focuses on how Bettauer's endeavors to educate others about sexuality and urban life can be read as an attempt to create an environment in which one can choose one's own identity. In Bettauer's case this freedom is associated with a cosmopolitan and secular position, one that works both within and against discourses of Jewish identity.

Bettauer's novels share many themes and concerns and explore larger historical events and their impact on personal lives with an approach that focuses on bringing these connections to the reader's attention. The most frequent themes are a brutalization of morality resulting from a character's experiences in World War I and the effect of inflation on social stability. The novels often feature a central character who is charming but determined to live a life of secure luxury, regardless of the cost to others. His actions, which can include lying, stealing, and even killing, are justified by both the world in which he lived during the war and the one in which he now finds himself. What makes the protagonist sympathetic to the reader, apart from these qualifications and justifications, is that he is not completely morally bankrupt. He is aware that his actions have consequences, and he chooses victims who are truly reprehensible—injustice for the unjust, but for personal gain.

Another common feature of Bettauer's novels is that these social factors also affect the personal relationships of the characters. The novels abound with contentious marriages in which the unhappy party cannot leave because he or she cannot bear to imagine the ensuing life of poverty and deprivation. If there is a lesson to be learned from Bettauer's novels, it is the impossibility of separating personal, romantic relationships from the larger social issues of financial instability and the ramifications of the war. The novels are in a broader sense about the impact of social conditions on morality.[45] Yet another facet they share is a certain pedagogical impulse that Balázs also recognized—the relative nature of morality is explored in order to teach lessons about individual agency and responsibility for our actions. There is a constant conflict between the notion that society and experience make us what we are and the belief that individuals make their own fate. The popularity of these novels shows that this theme struck a nerve. For example, *Kampf um Wien,* which first appeared in the Viennese newspaper *Der Tag* between 1922 and 1923, was in such demand that the paper's publisher also printed it as a book. *Die freudlose Gasse* shared the same fate, and in less than a year thirty thousand copies were sold.[46] In addition, many of the novels were made into films shortly after the books were published.[47]

Private Concerns in the Public Sphere

These topics were explored in Bettauer's journalistic work as well, often in a more interactive and direct manner. In 1924, with the help of Viennese author Rudolf Olden, Bettauer founded the weekly newspaper

Er und Sie: Wochenschrift für Lebenskultur und Erotik. In the first issue (which appeared, appropriately, on Valentine's Day), he laid out the publication's focus—the "erotic revolution." He sees it as impossible to ignore this revolution if one is even minimally aware of one's surroundings; the only choice is whether to greet it with joy or horror (ES, 14.2.1924, 1–2). According to Bettauer, public life, as it pertains to questions of sexuality, is built on hypocrisy, lies, and deception because of the false importance placed on marriage. The root of the problem is that all erotic desires are supposed to be confined to marriage. It is the woman who is the victim in this social order—without a husband she is doomed to become an "abscheuliches und verdorrtes Wesen" [abhorrent and withered being] or to be accused of being a prostitute. On the surface, capitalist industrialization has improved women's social and financial independence. In reality, the restrictions women face in their sexual lives are no different from before; they only appear to have changed. Yet there is hope: Bettauer mentions that the people, especially the youth, have begun to question this fundamental principle of marriage and are striving to free themselves from these social constraints on their happiness (ES, 14.2.1924, 2).

The mission of the paper was to support this revolution. The articles covered topics central to this cause, such as sexual freedom, morality, abortion, prostitution, and questions of gender and sexual preference. The underlying theme was always choice, or rather the impact a lack of choice has on an individual's life. The paper also answered readers' questions about love, sex, and relationships. *Er und Sie* was quite popular, which can be seen in the ever-increasing number of personal ads in each subsequent issue and in the fact that by the second issue, *Er und Sie* had already sold sixty thousand papers and most likely reached a readership of about two hundred thousand.[48] In the fourth issue of the paper, there was a notice explaining that the price for ads had to be raised because given the number of copies that were selling, the cost of printing the ads was actually higher than the paper's revenue from them (ES, 6.3.1924, 3). The number of imitators also attests to the paper's success; some examples include *Wir Zwei, Ich und Du, Adam und Eva, Wir Beide,* and *Das Rendezvous.*[49]

The introductory article of the paper navigates notions of truth, social constructions, and morality. Here as in many of the subsequent articles, Bettauer challenges the notion of absolute morality by showing us how morality is contingent on social institutions and norms. Instead of being a code of conduct based on irrefutable truths, this morality, as can be seen in the example of marriage and sexuality, is a social construct that encourages hypocrisy and unnecessarily punishes people for pursuing personal happiness. Yet Bettauer does not dismiss the notion that such truth is possible. He sees the erotic revolution's goal as that of removing the shackles of harmful notions of morality, not to replace them with another social construct, but to be free from them. This freedom is based on a belief in the objective truth of science. Within this context, erotic desires cannot be morally reprehensible because they exist everywhere in the living world and can be quantified and analyzed. Bettauer points to the existence of the erotic in the animal and plant worlds and argues that this force is not something that must be overcome in the human world but is, rather, that which connects all of us. Bettauer's use of nature imagery illustrates this point:

> Die erotische Revolution, die freie glücklichere Menschen schaffen soll. Denn es ist nun einmal so und kein Mucker kann es ändern, daß alles, was ist, auf Erotik beruht, alles, was schön, gut, lieblich auf Erden, untrennbar mit Erotik verknüpft ist. Die Blume auf der Wiese, der Schmetterling, der sich über ihr schauckelt, das Singen der Vögel, das Zirpen der Grille; das Rauschen der Bäume und das Reifen der Früchte—erotisches Symbol, erotischer Zweck, erotisches Wollen. (ES, 14.2.1924, 2)

> The erotic revolution that should create free and happier people. It's just the way it is and no grumbler can change it: everything that exists is based on the erotic, and everything that is beautiful, good, and lovely on earth is inextricably bound to the erotic. The flower on the meadow, the butterfly that sways above it, the singing of the birds, the chirping of the cricket, the rustling of the trees and the ripening of the fruits—erotic symbol, erotic purpose, erotic desire.

Restrictions on and expressions of erotic desires may be socially constructed, but the desire itself is not. Bettauer connects this constant to images of nature that are removed from a sense of time and also from man-made interventions and institutions, thus emphasizing its permanence and invariability. The implicit argument is that we should live in a more "natural" state in which our desires are allowed to exist and be acted upon because they are an integral part of ourselves.

As a whole, the newspaper celebrates urban life, but here we see an urge to escape the city, where social norms create an "unnatural" state that is harmful to individuals and their interactions with one another. Scientific discourses are also used to legitimate the notion that sexual desire is a constant and irrefutable part of our existence and should be treated as such, further emphasizing the notion of a truth independent of societal influence. *Er und Sie* includes articles written by medical doctors, whose professions are prominently displayed in the header: for example, "Seltsame Liebesfälle. Von einem Nervenarzt" [Strange Love Cases. From a Neurologist]. These doctors serve as guides into the inner workings of our psyches and bodies, speaking with authority about impotence, masturbation, frigidity, and other topics. For the most part, they use language that can be understood by the lay reader, but they are careful to emphasize the scientific basis for their viewpoints with the use of tools such as statistics and medical terminology. In other sections of the newspaper, particularly one called "Erotica aus aller Welt" [Erotica from Around the World], prominent figures in sexual research such as Richard Freiherr von Krafft-Ebing and Magnus Hirschfeld are mentioned. These references serve not only to legitimate the information and viewpoints of these articles, but also as a platform to popularize and disseminate the belief that these intimate topics belong in the public sphere. They are not lewd, pornographic, or dangerous; rather, they are aspects of our biological and psychological makeups. It would be disingenuous to suppose that titillating topics and stories were not utilized to increase readership, yet throughout the newspaper there is a strong drive to educate the public. The use of scientific discourses challenges ideas of morality that lead to oppressive laws and societal pressures by replacing a truth contingent on societal and cultural norms with one based on scientific facts. As can be seen in the content of these articles, there is an underlying belief that the triumph of science over social conventions leads to greater personal freedom and individuality.

This focus on individuality can also be seen in the paper's role as a public forum for individuals to express themselves, seek advice, and find like-minded others, all under the protective cloak of anonymity. In *Grenzen der Gemeinschaft: Eine Kritik des sozialen Radikalismus,* Helmuth Plessner argues that anonymity and individuality do not work in opposition. Instead the anonymity we achieve through the public "masks" that we wear protects us and allows our individuality to grow and develop. We cannot expose our true selves to everyone every day; it would leave us vulnerable and unable to sustain our individuality. *Er und Sie* made private concerns public in a way that also protected the identity of the individuals by not exposing their identities. Two areas of particular interest are the personal ads and the advice column. The ads demonstrate the wide variety of personalities and needs of the readership and, extrapolating from there, the Viennese population at large. Some were looking for marriage prospects, others for a dancing companion, still others for a rich, unhappy married woman. The readers' letters also discussed topics that ranged from the various causes of impotence to the relationship between social mobility, self-confidence, and one's ability to find a mate.

The phenomena of personal ads and advice columns were by no means new in the 1920s. Personal ads have existed in West European cultures for more than three hundred years. The first one advertising for a spouse in England appeared in the periodical *Collection for the Improvement of Husbandry and Trade* on July 19, 1695.[50] Because of doubts about both the accuracy of the information in the ads and the sincerity of the person's desire for marriage, personal ads did not become widespread in England until about one hundred years later. In Germany the first such ad appeared on July 8, 1738, and they became more widespread by the end of the eighteenth century.[51] In both countries, the emphasis was on marriage, and the language was often very specific about the desired financial situation of the prospective spouse, in keeping with norms of marriage at the time. As notions of marriage changed and more emphasis was placed on compatibility and love, the personal ads changed as well. But it was not until the twentieth century that personal ads were also used for seeking companionship, instead of almost exclusively for marriage.[52] Writing letters to be published in newspapers also has a long tradition in Germany. By the end of the eighteenth century they were an established part of newspapers. They piqued the readers' interest, thus increasing newspaper sales. The letters allowed the readers to share their opinions with others in a public forum and to have the sense that they were participating in discussions as they unfolded.[53]

The ads and advice column of *Er und Sie* are enlightening as well as entertaining, but what sets the paper apart are the discussions about the sections themselves, the purposes they serve, and advice for how to use the opportunities such forums provide in an effective manner. In the first issue of the paper, a how-to guide is provided in the personal ads section, appropriately named "Menschen die einander suchen" [People Seeking One Another] (ES, 14.2.1924, 9–10). The article begins by stating that personal ads are a viable solution for lonely individuals looking for a spouse, something the author of the article has witnessed firsthand.[54] What follows is "eine kleine Untersuchung" [a small investigation] of the four possible ways to meet a potential spouse: (1) one meets someone by chance and falls instantly in love; (2) one comes to know the other person because he or she belongs to the same social circle, and the two develop feelings for one another; (3) the two meet through a third party; and (4) the personal ad. The author[55] gives his critique of the first three methods: It is difficult to find someone with whom one immediately falls in love, and it is also difficult to distinguish love from sexual attraction when one relies on first impressions. Meeting someone through one's social circle requires a great deal of leisure time as well as a large social circle. And having someone else involved in the search for a spouse necessarily includes that person in the relationship, since they are now personally invested in its success. The advantages of the personal ad are many, but according to Bettauer, the most significant of these is the personal ad's impersonal nature: "Gerade das Nüchterne, Unpersönliche dieses Vorganges macht ihn sauber und einwandfrei" [It is precisely the sober and impersonal nature of this process that makes it orderly and irreproachable] (ES, 14.2.1924, 9). Because of its anonymity, the advertiser can vet a number of possibilities with a minimum risk of embarrassment and hurt feelings for all parties. Here, as is the case throughout *Er und Sie,* we see the complicated relationship between private and public, intimate and anonymous, as it relates to personal interactions and questions of choice in an urban environment.

The article proceeds to demonstrate the correct and incorrect ways to place a personal ad. It is not the ads' impersonal nature that creates their ill repute: rather, it is that "die meisten Menschen schon bei ihrer Abfassung plump und geschmacklos sind" [most people are crude and tasteless even in their formulations] (ES, 14.2.1924, 9). An example of this kind of ad is then given: "Mädchen, brav, wenn auch arm, wünscht sich mit wohlhabendem, charaktervollem Mann zu verheiraten. Anträge unter 'Märchenglück' usw" [Girl, good though poor, seeks a wealthy man full of character to marry. Applications to 'fairy-tale happiness' etc] (ES, 14.2.1924, 9). The article critiques the unrealistic expectations of the advertisement's writer, whose only positive attribute seems to be that she is "brav" yet who still expects to find a rich man with character. (Bettauer surmises that the girl is most likely unattractive, since there is no mention of her appearance.) The article suggests that the girl would have more success with the following ad: "Mädchen ohne Geld, aber tüchtige Hausfrau, wünscht sich mit bescheidenem Mann, eventuell Witwer mit kleinen Kindern, zu verheiraten. Anträge unter 'Sehnsucht nach Häuslichkeit' " [Girl without money, but a capable homemaker, seeks a modest man, possibly a widower with small children, to marry. Applications to 'Longing for Domesticity'] (ES, 14.2.1924, 9). According to Bettauer, naive hopes must be replaced with realistic goals in order for the personal ad to be effective. Following this critique of the content is an observation about the style of many personal ads. The ideal personal ad should be "kurz und bündig" [short and succinct], using only as many words as absolutely necessary to get the point across. An exemplary ad is provided:

"Bankbeamtin, 23 Jahre, blond, schlank, mittelgroß, hübsch, musikalisch, sucht die Bekanntschaft eines gebildeten Mannes zwischen dreißig und fünfunddreißig, dessen Einkommen nicht unter fünf Millionen monatlich ist. Anträge unter 'Wohnung vorhanden'" [Female bank clerk, 23 years old, blond, slender, average height, pretty, musical, seeks the acquaintance of an educated man between thirty and thirty-five whose income is no less than five million a month. Applications to 'Apartment Available'] (ES, 14.2.1924, 9). According to Bettauer, there is not a superfluous word in this ad, and it gives a clear view of its author. It allows us insight into the woman's character, but because of the medium of the personal ad, there is no personal contact with each reader, and thus no risk to the woman even though she has exposed herself.

As Simmel describes in "Die Großstädte und Geistesleben," the dense population of the city necessitates a certain psychological distance from others to counteract the physical proximity. It is impossible to have close and intimate relationships with all those around, so a certain aloofness is critical to avoid overstimulation of the nerves. Simmel, although somewhat ambivalent about the consequences of this distance, finds attractive the resulting possibility of defining oneself as an individual. As Bettauer explains the advantages of the personal ad, he evokes the benefits of such a stance. Rather than lament the more calculating and impersonal manner of interaction in the city, he praises the personal ad's embodiment of these characteristics. The anonymity and distance between people in the city actually increases the chance of finding a compatible mate by allowing logic and rationality to inform one's search. Thus the city offers more self-determination rather than less. Yet there are limits to this freedom. Although the format of the personal ad has changed little since its inception—short, with a clearly stated goal[56]—it takes on new meanings in this modern urban environment in that it shares certain qualities with personal interactions between individuals in the city as Simmel describes them. Just as the personal ad has limited resources with which to make an impression on others, people in the city, according to Simmel, are overwhelmed with stimuli and need ways to stand out from the rest, to be easily identifiable. There is, however, the risk that by cultivating such differences, one does not develop fully as an individual. In similar ways, the personal ad allows the writer to reveal distinguishing qualities and particular needs and desires. The anonymity frees the writer of certain social niceties and inhibitions. But the tools one has within this format are somewhat limited and exaggerate both similarities and differences without much room for nuance. These limitations can be seen in the number of personal ads that are similar to one another—for example, the adjective "fesch" [jaunty/

fetching] is used quite often to convey a youthful and playful nature. Many also claim that they are "kein Alltagsmensch" [not an average person], and the fact that the same formulation is used frequently to convey that one is not like everyone else points to the difficulties of standing out with a limited number of words and with the intent of attracting a reasonable number of respondents. Those advertisements that make a lasting impression do so at the expense of potentially reducing the number of respondents, as illustrated in this ad from the fourth issue: "20jähriger sucht exzeptionelles Erlebnis mit nur verheirateter vermögender Dame, Type 1924, auf nur rein idealer Basis. Zuschriften unter 'Mamas Liebling 1123' a.d. Exp" [20-year-old seeks exceptional experience with married wealthy lady only, model 1924, on a purely ideal basis. Replies to 'Mama's Darling 1123' addressed to the dispatch] (ES, 6.3.1924, 15).

While the article emphasizes the advantages of urban life, the existence and content of the personal ads and readers' letters point to the disadvantages—namely, potential loneliness and a lack of personal interactions. Bettauer writes in the first issue:

> Es ist ein eigenartiges Problem der Großstadt, daß in ihr Tausende von Menschen einsam umhergehen, die einander suchen und nicht finden können. Wenn unsere Rubrik "Menschen, die einander suchen," in der die Einsamen, die einen Gefährten haben wollen, ihren Wunsch vorbringen können, dazu führt, daß hier und da ein halbwegs harmonischer Bund geschlossen wird, so hat sie ihre Aufgabe erfüllt. (ES, 14.2.1924, 10)

> It is a problem unique to the big city that in it thousands of people wander around lonely, seeking and unable to find one another. If our column "People Seeking One Another," in which the lonely can present their wishes for a companion, leads now and then to a halfway harmonious union, then it has served its purpose.

This is an example of how the city is the source both of the problem and of a possible solution. The city might make it difficult to find a partner, but the anonymity that creates these difficulties also makes it possible for personal ads to function with a certain impersonal efficiency. Urban life results in the need for this public forum, but also provides the tools and circumstances necessary for creating a space in which one can openly discuss intimate concerns.

The advice column also operates in this public forum of intimacy. In the first issue's introduction to the advice column called "Probleme des

Lebens" the editors write: "Es ist das Bedürfnis dafür vorhanden, daß Menschen sich mit jemand aussprechen, den sie nicht persönlich kennen, zu dem sie aber Vertrauen haben. Die, die sie kennen, sind oft auch gerade deshalb nicht zu einer intimen Aussprache geeignet" [The need already exists for people to speak with someone whom they do not personally know, but trust. The people they know well are often for that very reason not suited for an intimate discussion] (ES, 14.2.1924, 12). In contrast to the particularly urban problem of searching for a partner, *Er und Sie* presents the difficulties of talking about personal and intimate problems as a universal one—at times one cannot turn to friends and family because they are too involved in one's life and might very well be part of what one needs to discuss. The solution the paper offers, however, is a uniquely urban one because it relies on the anonymity the city provides.

This anonymity extends in both directions—the person or persons responding to the letters also remain nameless. Unlike in the introduction to personal ads, which is written in the first person and whose tone and content lead the reader to believe the writer is most likely Bettauer, the introduction to the advice column carefully distances itself from Bettauer. He is referred to in the third person, and the article is attributed to the "Redaktion." In contrast, the article on personal ads was not attributed to anyone. These choices create an additional sense of distance and anonymity—rather than being answered by a public figure, someone with a distinct persona and idiosyncrasies, these letters are answered by someone the readers do not know at all, thus increasing the sense of objectivity. (As will be addressed shortly, this distinction between the advice giver and Bettauer was not always successful.) In the advice columns, the qualities of anonymity and objectivity are foregrounded to allow the columnist to occupy the position of mediator and educator.

This sense of objectivity is crucial to the paper's ability to give credibility to the letter writer's current predicament. Having a letter published in the paper validates an individual's problem on at least two levels. First, the disinterested editors saw the problem as important enough to warrant a response. Second, they saw it as one with which other readers would identify. The individual becomes the "voice" of a problem shared by others, and by helping the letter writer, the paper can also help others. For example, one reader writes that her boyfriend of six years refuses to discuss the possibility of marriage and also has made no indication that he is sexually interested in her. Yet when she suggests that they break off their relationship, he threatens to hurt himself. The advice offered in the third issue is as follows:

> Wir können Ihnen nur raten, sich mit Ihrem Freund gründlich auszusprechen. Es scheint, daß bei ihm die typische Sexualangst vorliegt, die Angst vor dem entscheidenden Schritt, sei es, weil er krank ist oder weil er fürchtet, zu versagen. Eine offene Aussprache ist unter allen Umständen notwendig. (ES, 28.2.1924, 13)
>
> We can only advise you to have a thorough discussion with your boyfriend. It seems that he is exhibiting typical sexual anxiety, anxiety about the decisive step, perhaps because he is sick or because he is afraid of failure. In any case an open discussion is necessary.

By emphasizing the need for communication between the reader and her boyfriend, the paper validates the severity of the problem and the need for resolution. At the same time, by using the word "typical" the paper also lets the reader know that her problem is not uncommon, reassuring both her and readers with similar problems that their circumstances are not highly unusual and that there is hope for a solution.

In the second issue, the advice column and personal ads come together as a reader writes to the paper about her previous unsuccessful experience with personal ads. In her letter, she describes her disappointment in detail; the men she met through her ad were either terribly unattractive, interested only in sex, or arrogant fools. The stated purpose of the letter is to warn others about the inefficacy of personal ads, but more space and effort are used to describe the letter-writer's frustration, her person, and how she would define a suitable mate. She is, in essence, both asking for advice and placing a personal ad herself. The answer she receives is also a combination of the two. It begins as follows: "Wenn Sie uns geschrieben hätten, wie der Text Ihrer Annonce gelautet hat, würden wir Ihnen unschwer beweisen, daß er unzweckmäßig war" [If in your letter you had provided us with the text of your announcement, we would be able to prove without difficulty that it was unsuitable] (ES, 21.2.1924, 11). The problem, then, lies in the manner and content of her personal ad. In order to avoid arousing the interest of "ungebildete[n], minderwertige[n] Männer[n]" [uncultured, inferior men], the letter-writer must be far more specific about the qualities she seeks—the preferred occupation, age, and education of the man are the absolute minimum of information the ad should provide. As further proof of the paper's belief that personal ads can be effective, the columnist asks the writer to send her address so that he can forward any letters of interest that come to the paper regarding her, thereby turning her letter into a personal ad. The reply ends with an emphasis on anonymity. The columnist assures the letter-writer that the paper is the only party that will have access to her personal information; the paper will serve as an intermediary between two parties who will have no direct contact with one another unless the letter-writer so chooses.

This letter is not the only one to combine the genres of advice letter and personal ad. Both the publication of such letters and the editorial response to them point to the potential limitations of the personal ad in the pursuit of personal connections. In this letter, as in a similar one printed in a subsequent issue, the writer is no longer limited to a few words to describe his or her person. As a result, a more detailed and complex portrait is possible. And even as the editors promote the use of personal ads as a solution to the loneliness experienced by the writers, they acknowledge the effectiveness of a longer and more personal portrayal by publishing the letters and also by requesting that the letter writers send the newspaper contact information so that interested parties can reach them. The newspaper thus recognizes the potential of a less rigid format, and implicitly hints at the restrictions of the personal ad. What does not change, however, is the emphasis on anonymity; the advice letter may be less structured, but it also offers the freedom to express one's desires without exposing oneself completely.

The paper positions itself as the disinterested stranger. This position resonates with contemporary discourses of the privileged outsider such as Walter Benjamin's flâneur, who is separate from his surroundings and thus has a unique ability to understand them. Of course, unlike these figures, the paper chooses to utilize this position in order to bring others together, to build a community that has as a necessary precondition a city full of alienated individuals. In the first advice column the paper outlines its position:

> Ohne äußerste Diskretion wäre ja das Ganze wertlos . . . So oft ja sieht ein Fremder klarer, gerade weil er fremd ist. Aber es muß natürlich ein moderner Mensch sein, der die Verhältnisse des heutigen Lebens kennt . . . "Probleme des Lebens" werden hier unparteiisch, vorurteilslos, mit kühlem Kopf, aber mit warmen Herzen diskutiert werden. (ES, 14.2.1924, 12)

> Without the utmost discretion the whole thing would be worthless . . . Often a stranger sees more clearly, precisely because he is a stranger. Naturally he must however be a modern person who understands the circumstances of life today . . . "Life Problems" will be discussed here impartially, without prejudice, with a cool head but with a warm heart.

The statement begins with the position of the outsider, the stranger who can see more clearly because he is not involved. But at the same time, this stranger needs to understand the lives of the readers; "modern person" becomes code for "one of us." This balancing act continues in the insistence on a "cool head" but a "warm heart." The paper tries to create a position that has it both ways—disinterested efficiency, but also genuine concern—for a readership that is simultaneously isolated and believes in the possibility of and need for connecting with others.

The Short Life of *Er und Sie*

The paper put out only five issues before Bettauer discontinued it, largely because of the scandal the paper had caused and the ensuing trial.[57] *Er und Sie* attracted the attention of the police department, child protective services, Vienna's socialist mayor Karl Seitz, and the chancellor Dr. Ignaz Seipel, a Roman Catholic priest and member of the Christian Democrat Party. In the trial, Bettauer and Rudoph Olden[58] were accused of impugning public decency and morality, and particular attention was given to the personal ads and the accusation that Bettauer and Olden brokered illicit and immoral acts for profit through these ads.[59] Both argued that they were not responsible for the personal ads—that the ads were overseen by employees who had specific instructions not to include any that were indecent or offensive. Bettauer stepped down as editor on March 13, 1924, before the trial even began, effectively ending the newspaper, as he was its driving force. The *Neues Wiener Journal* printed a statement from Bettauer explaining his position. In it Bettauer once again emphasizes what he sees as the central mission of the paper, a public forum for the intimate problems of daily life:

> Der konzentrische Angriff, der von allen Seiten gegen die von mir gegründete Wochenschrift "Er und Sie" gerichtet wird, beweist mir, daß meine Absichten mißverstanden wurden. Ich war überzeugt davon, daß eine offene und freie Erörterung heikler Lebensprobleme notwendig sei und die Sittlichkeit viel mehr fördern als schädigen würde.[60]

> The concentric attack from all sides against "Er und Sie," the weekly paper that I founded, has proven to me that my intentions were misunderstood. I was convinced that an open and free discussion of sensitive life problems was necessary and that it would support rather than harm morality.

Both Bettauer and Olden were found not guilty. The personal attacks continued nonetheless, but this did not stop Bettauer. Although he had stepped down from *Er und Sie,* he began a new publication called *Bettauers Wochenschrift* two months later, also before the trial began. This paper's focus was broader, but most of the articles are indistinguishable in content and style from those of its predecessor.

According to Murray Hall, antisemitism was the motivating factor in the trial against *Er und Sie.* He claims that Bettauer would have been left alone were it not for his Jewish ancestry. More plausibly, Guntram Geser claims that the scandal surrounding the paper concerned primarily Bettauer's open attacks on public figures and policies with which he disagreed.[61] Yet while antisemitism was not the main motivation for the attacks on Bettauer, the attacks themselves extensively used antisemitic rhetoric, and the inexcusable defense of Otto Rothstock, Bettauer's murderer, by right-wing newspapers was undeniably antisemitic in nature. A look at the larger context and at the paper itself supports Geser's interpretation. The topics of censorship and pornography played a large role in Austrian politics of the time, and the paper became a target of these debates. The "Sittenpolizei" [vice police, literally "morality police"] were extremely active, and false accusations were not unusual. Bettauer was a vocal critic of these actions and used his role as a public voice to decry intrusions into the private sphere. He supported the notion that topics such as abortion and homosexuality are personal and individual choices, that public policy should not be used to regulate them. His position is somewhat complicated by the fact that he finds it justifiable for someone to be arrested for public displays of homosexuality if, as he writes in the second issue, "die Heterosexuellen, auch Normale genannt, die sich in überwältigender Mehrheit befinden, in ihrem ästhetischen Empfinden verletzt, belästigt, angeekelt werden" [the heterosexuals, also called the normal ones, who are in the overwhelmingly majority, have their aesthetic sensibility injured, are disturbed, are sickened] (ES, 21.2.1924, 1). At the same time, in his passionate arguments against §129, he uses his own boyhood experiences to show the fluidity of sexual orientation. In the fifth issue, he writes as an explanation:

> Wie absurd, unwissenschaftlich und verbrecherisch aber ein solches Gesetz ist, will ich an einer kleinen Geschichte aus dem eigenen Jugendleben erweisen, an einer Geschichte, die in ihrer Art so deutlich und beweiskräftig ist, daß sie restlos auch von allen Laien verstanden werden wird. (ES, 13.3.1924, 1)

> I will prove just how absurd, unscientific and criminal such a law is with a short story from my own youth, a story whose nature is so clear and conclusive that all laypeople without exception will understand it.

Here Bettauer explicitly outlines the approach he uses throughout the newspaper: to put questions of morality and sexuality into terms that the larger public can understand, but with the assurance that they are supported by academic and scientific findings. His use of "unwissenschaftlich" in his description of the law underscores this point.

Bettauer tells a story of how he fell in love with another boy at the age of fourteen. It was only through a confluence of coincidences—the boy rebuffed him, and a beautiful blond girl showed interest in him—that he became interested in girls. But Bettauer asks himself: what if the boy had responded to his attentions?

> Es gibt nur eine Antwort auf diese Frage: Die erotischen Elemente in mir, die zum gleichen Geschlecht drängten, hätten sich entwickelt auf Kosten jener Triebe, die man normal nennt und zum anderen Geschlecht drängen! Mit einem Wort: Ich wäre homosexuell geworden! Wäre ich nun schlechter oder besser? Hätte ein brutales Gesetz das Recht, Triebe, die die Natur selbst in mich versenkt, mit Gefängnis zu bedrohen, hätten die Menschen das Recht, mich für minderwertig anzusehen und mit Steinen zu bewerfen? (ES, 21.2.1924, 2)

> There is only one answer to this question: The erotic elements in me that pushed me toward the same sex would have developed at the cost of those drives that one calls normal and that push one toward the opposite sex! In other words: I would have become a homosexual! Would I have been worse or better? Would a brutal law have the right to threaten me with jail for the drives that nature itself had sunk into me, would people have the right to consider me inferior and throw stones at me?

The argument that Bettauer presents here is that his age and innocence prove that these urges he experienced were natural. Furthermore, they were not desires that could be controlled: it was not his willpower or his sense of morality that influenced the outcome, but a series of arbitrary circumstances. Bettauer maintains that the law punishes people for something that is out of their control and is a natural part of who they are.

The newspaper takes a similar approach with the question of abortion rights. In the column "Erinnerungen einer Hebamme von ihr selbst erzählt" ["Memoirs of a Midwife Told in Her Own Words"] a midwife tells how her work convinced her of the importance of offering easily accessible abortions for those who need them. As in the case of homosexuality, the condemnation of abortion does not change behavior; it has a purely punitive function. And as the midwife's stories demonstrate, it is often social conditions outside one's control that lead to the necessity for an abortion. These women face social ostracism, shame, and worse if they do not have the abortion, and the same plus health risks if they do. The midwife's personal experiences with women in need show the impact of this political debate and the criminalization of abortion on these women's lives. The question is one not of morality but of quality of life for these women. Through her stories, the midwife argues that denying women access to safe and legal abortions creates unnecessary suffering for all concerned.

In its approach to these contested political topics, *Er und Sie* provides a public forum to discuss issues of privacy and private lives. The more personal aspects of these issues—emotions, particular circumstances, and so on—are emphasized, but primarily in order to show how "ordinary" people are affected. These individuals represent many others (a fact emphasized repeatedly in the midwife columns) and serve as points of identification for the readers: "If people like me are affected, then I could be as well." Interestingly, this move to personalize public debates also serves to argue for the need for a private sphere. The articles demonstrate that these issues reach into the most intimate and private aspects of an individual's life and that laws should not venture into this terrain but, rather, should allow people to make their own choices.

Er und Sie positioned itself as an anonymous public forum for intimate issues. The articles in the paper provide a fascinating study on the impact of various discourses of sexuality, modernity, and the city on daily life. Throughout the paper, the advantages of an efficient, objective urban environment are emphasized, even as the paper addresses the difficulties and problems that such an environment can produce. Yet the paper's commercial success does not lie with this promise of discreet anonymity. Instead, it depends on the cult of one public figure—Hugo Bettauer. *Er und Sie* ends when he leaves, and *Bettauers Wochenschrift* ends after his death.[62] And whereas some who write in search of advice address their letters to this anonymous public forum, others write directly to Bettauer. In one such letter in the third issue, a reader writes: "Ich kenne und schätze Sie als Verteidiger bei jedem Unrecht, das den Frauen geschieht" [I know and value you as a defender against every wrong that happens to women] (ES, 28.2.1924, 13). Another writes: "Warum ich Sie um Rat frage, werden Sie sich denken. Sehr einfach, weil ich ihre Art zu denken aus zahlreichen Ihrer Schriften kenne" [You will be wondering why I am asking you for advice. Quite simply because I am familiar with how you think from a number of your writings] (ES, 28.2.1924, 14). The anonymity of these advice seekers is protected, but they are not seeking answers from "the editors"—even though each answer begins with "Antwort der Redaktion." They are writing to someone whom they feel they know well.

This cult of personality depends, however, on the same conditions that allow *Er und Sie* to be a public forum. A large group of readers felt they knew Bettauer through his writings, but because of the sheer number of people involved, this kind of relationship relies on a particular combination of private and public spheres. As the letters indicate, these readers have an intimate relationship mediated through a public sphere. And those who chose to drop by his office hours to interact with him face-to-face were still for the most part interacting with a public figure rather than a private individual. These observations do not, however, diminish Bettauer's personal accomplishments. Although he interacted with his readers as a public persona, this persona still relied on the private individual who made specific choices about how to shape these relationships. He took on many roles—friend, adviser, intellectual, social critic, and storyteller—but always in the service of helping his readers understand and navigate daily life in the city. This ultimately was his significant contribution to Viennese popular culture, a contribution that depended on a complicated negotiation of public and private, universal and specific, to create a personable public figure who championed the rights of the individual.

Conclusion

> In vain, great-hearted Kublai, shall I attempt to describe Zaira, city of high bastions. I could tell you how many steps make up the streets rising like stairways, and the degree of the arcades' curves and what kind of zinc scales cover the roofs; but I already know this would be the same as telling you nothing. The city does not consist of this, but of relationships between the measurements of its space and the events of its past . . . The city, however, does not tell its past, but contains it like the lines of a hand, written in the corners of the streets, the gratings of the windows, the banisters of the steps, the antennae of the lightning rods, the poles of the flags, every segment marked in turn with scratches, indentations, scrolls.
>
> —Italo Calvino, *Invisible Cities*

> Cities also believe they are the work of the mind or of chance, but neither the one nor the other suffices to hold up their walls. You take delight not in the city's seven or seventy wonders, but in the answer it gives to a question of yours.
>
> —Italo Calvino, *Invisible Cities*

In these fantastical conversations between Kublai Khan and Marco Polo, the author Italo Calvino explores the relationship between the imagination, memory, physical spaces, and experience in the creation of cities. A city's narrative is written into the buildings, the streets, into all the concrete manifestations of the city. Yet the relationship between the experiences that have occurred in these physical spaces and the memories of them is ambiguous and constantly changing. The city does not speak for itself, but the narrative we give it is not completely in our control. A city needs a sense of cohesion, of purpose, but we are only partially responsible for it—we can ask the question, but it is the city that provides the answer. Marco Polo gives these cities names, but they remain invisible and unknowable; the descriptions are about the impossibility of "reading" a city, and our need to do just that so the city can exist. The title of the novel *Invisible Cities,* as well as the chapter headings, all refer to the city in the plural. The book is not about a singular city but rather about our concept of cities, or urban spaces; the plural emphasizes the abstract nature of these cities.

Similarly, the cities that have appeared throughout this book—Paris, Warsaw, Vienna, Utopia, and the nameless, abstract city as well—are also products of a negotiation between the abstract and the specific, of the possibilities and limitations of the individual to create not just the space of the city, but also one's place in it. All of these texts emphasize the fact that a city is constituted of experiences, and of our attempts to understand these experiences and through this understanding create and define the city. The various outsiders in these urban spaces—the stranger, the flâneur, the detective, the traveler, the assimilated Jew—search for ways to understand the city and their place in it. On the surface, the various texts I have brought together may seem more diverse than similar—cultural theory, travel writings, a popular novel, and a weekly newspaper that promotes sexual freedom. What these claims about urban modernity and alienation, searches for an authentic Jewish existence far removed from Western culture, and attempts to help others navigate life in the city have in common is that these texts are firmly situated within debates about modernity, German Jewish identity, and urban life. They can be read as attempts to create and legitimize a specific historical position—an outsider/minority position within German society—by establishing modernity as a universal condition.

Yet, as I have emphasized throughout the book, what makes the universal fascinating is its specificity. This book explores the common discourses that root these texts in a particular culture and historical moment, but at the same time, through careful attention to the texts as sites of production, I have also sought to reclaim some of the agency of the texts themselves. In doing so, I propose a shift in the way we see the relationship between history and German Jews: a shift toward seeing German Jews and their writings not as depictions of moments and experiences, but as active participants and creators of that history and its narratives. In various ways, the writers, narrators, and characters in these texts seek to find their place in history through language, to define their role in and contributions to society as individuals, by escaping history. The ahistorical is an unachievable goal, but in their search for something universal and absolute, these figures attempt to gain control over the specific and ephemeral, and neither they nor the cities they occupy would exist without these attempts. The fact that each of these endeavors is unique to a specific figure and, more importantly, to a specific text points out, as Calvino does in his novel, that each person with his own specific personal history, as well as with a more broadly shared cultural and social history, tries to reach the universal in ways that are simultaneously historically determined and unique.

NOTES

Introduction

1. For an overview of conceptualizations of the flâneur in the writings of Charles Baudelaire, Jean-Paul Sartre, Robert Musil, and Walter Benjamin see Keith Tester's introduction in Keith Tester, ed., *The Flâneur* (New York: Routledge, 1994).

2. Although it falls outside the scope of this book, there has been important work done on questions of gender and modernity, particularly in regard to the figure of the flâneur. See Janet Wolff, *Feminine Sentences: Essays on Women and Culture* (Berkeley: University of California Press, 1990); Anke Gleber, *The Art of Taking a Walk: Flanerie, Literature, and Film in Weimar Culture* (Princeton, N.J.: Princeton University Press, 1999); Deborah L. Parsons, *Streetwalking the Metropolis: Women, the City, and Modernity* (Oxford: Oxford University Press, 2000); and Aruna D'Souza and Tom McDonough, eds., *The Invisible Flâneuse? Gender, Public Space, and Visual Culture in Nineteenth-Century Paris* (Manchester: Manchester University Press, 2006).

3. Following scholarly convention, I am including Austrian Jews when I refer to German Jewish identity, as the terms "deutsche Juden" and "deutsch jüdisch" have traditionally encompassed both German and Austrian Jews. While there are significant differences between Austria and Germany in the interwar period, I believe one can make a strong argument for the contributions of Austrians such as Joseph Roth and Hugo Bettauer (who both had complicated national identities) to the discourses of German Jewish identity, the stranger, and modernity in the German context. Two important studies on the specificities of German-speaking Jews and their notions of identity are Scott Spector, *Prague Territories: National Conflict and Cultural Innovation in Franz Kafka's Fin de Siècle,* Weimar and Now (Berkeley: University of California Press, 2000), and Lisa Silverman, *Becoming Austrians: Jews and Culture Between the World Wars* (Oxford: Oxford University Press, 2012).

4. I agree with Hess that the term "acculturation" more accurately describes the relationship between German Jews and the dominant culture. I will, however, continue to use "assimilation" throughout the book, since it is this term that the writers I examine were struggling to define. See Jonathan M. Hess, *Germans, Jews and the Claims of Modernity* (New Haven, Conn.: Yale University Press, 2002), 9.

5. Ibid., 23.

6. In his overview of the term "modernity" in the German Jewish context, Hess demonstrates that the concept's significance and meaning were always contested and that this lack of consensus indicates the importance of exploring

modernity as an "object of study" rather than "a tool of analysis." Hess, *Germans, Jews and the Claims of Modernity,* 19–23.

7. David Myers, *Resisting History: Historicism and Its Discontents in German-Jewish Thought* (Princeton, N.J.: Princeton University Press, 2003), 164.

8. Ibid. There are similarities between Myers's approach toward antihistoricism and David Biale's toward Hasidism. See David Biale, "A Journey Between Worlds: East European Jewish Culture from the Partitions of Poland to the Holocaust," in *Culture of the Jews: A New History,* ed. David Biale (New York: Schocken, 2002).

Chapter 1

1. I have chosen to examine a few of Benjamin's key concepts and focus on a close reading of select passages of his works. In this endeavor I am indebted to a number of important works of Benjamin scholarship, particularly Michael Löwy, *Fire Alarm: Reading Walter Benjamin's "On the Concept of History,"* trans. Chris Turner (London: Verso, 2005); Graeme Gilloch, *Walter Benjamin: Critical Constellations,* Key Contemporary Thinkers (Malden, Mass.: Blackwell, 2002); Stéphane Mosès, *The Angel of History: Rosenzweig, Benjamin, Scholem,* trans. Barbara Harshav, Cultural Memory in the Present (Stanford: Stanford University Press, 2009).

2. Peter Nicholls provides a comparative overview of modernist literary movements using a similar definition of modernity as a condition that requires an aesthetics of distance. Peter Nicholls, *Modernisms: A Literary Guide,* 2nd ed. (New York: Palgrave Macmillan, 2009).

3. Walter Benjamin, *Illuminationen,* in *Ausgewählte Schriften 1,* ed. Siegfried Unseld (Frankfurt am Main: Suhrkamp, 1977), 204–5.

4. Walter Benjamin, *Illuminations,* ed. Hannah Arendt, trans. Harry Zohn (New York: Schocken Books, 1968), 172.

5. In the last two decades, the body of ideas and approaches known as the "spatial turn" has greatly influenced cultural studies. Space has been examined as a topic as well as an entry point that provides new insights into familiar subjects. And the subject of time, whether explicitly or implicitly, plays a critical role in these endeavors. Within the many projects that have undertaken discourses of space, there has often been a tension between a more universal understanding of space that allows one to draw connections across time and cultures, and a need to ground a particular kind of space in a specific time and historical context. The former is attractive because space as a topic and an approach can produce frameworks that ostensibly allow a multitude of times and spaces to coexist. These frameworks function by diminishing the importance of time and historical context. In other words, the times and spaces become abstractions so that they can coexist, thus losing their distinctive qualities and conflating into one abstract time and space. Mike Crang and Nigel Thrift point out in their anthology *Thinking Space* that we need to reexamine the role conceptions of time play in our understanding of space: "Though part of the reason for the turn to space has been a drive to move away from the tyrannies

of historicism and developmentalism, the fact remains that space without time is as improbable as time without space." Mike Crang and Nigel Thrift, eds., *Thinking Space* (New York: Routledge, 2000), 2. Two works that do undertake such a reconsideration in the German Jewish context are Spector, *Prague Territories,* and Todd Presner, *Mobile Modernity: Germans, Jews, Trains* (New York: Columbia University Press, 2007).

6. Benjamin, *Illuminationen,* 179.

7. Walter Benjamin, *Arcades Project,* ed. Rolf Tiedemann, trans. Howard Eiland and Kevin McLaughlin (Cambridge, Mass: The Belknap Press of Harvard University Press, 1999), 10.

8. Samuel Weber, *Benjamin's -abilities* (Cambridge, Mass.: Harvard University Press, 2008), 10.

9. Ibid., 9.

10. Ibid., 231.

11. Walter Benjamin, *Das Passagen-Werk,* ed. Rolf Tiedemann, vol. 5.1 of *Gesammelte Schriften* (Frankfurt am Main: Suhrkamp Verlag, 1982), 573.

12. Walter Benjamin, *Arcades Project,* 459.

13. Walter Benjamin, *Das Passagen-Werk,* 575.

14. Walter Benjamin, *Arcades Project,* 461.

15. In this interest in montage, there is not just a connection between the style and a disavowal of representation as a unified whole. There is also a relationship between an insistence on lack of intention and a privileging of a style of writing in which the writer is not obtrusive. We will explore these connections in more detail in the section on Alfred Döblin.

16. These are, of course, ideas that are also explored in Benjamin's *Über den Begriff der Geschichte* (*On the Concept of History*), particularly in relation to his concept of messianic arrest. Walter Benjamin and Gérard Raulet, *Über den Begriff der Geschichte,* vol. 19, *Werke und Nachlass* (Berlin: Suhrkamp, 2010).

17. For an insightful reading of Benjamin's flâneur in the context of sociology and the work of sociologists, an area I will not be focusing on, see David Frisby, "The *Flâneur* in Social Theory," in *The Flâneur,* ed. Keith Tester (New York: Routledge, 1994).

18. Simmel had a significant impact on the following generation of the interwar period and his works were viewed as relevant, both in topic and in approach, during this later time. His classes were popular, and his influence is evident in areas as diverse as film theory, economics, and the study of culture. Georg Lukács and Siegfried Kracauer were students and admirers. His influence can also be seen in the writings of Walter Benjamin and Helmuth Plessner.

19. Georg Simmel, *Fragmente und Aufsätze: Aus dem Nachlass und Veröffentlichungen der letzten Jahre,* ed. Gertrud Kantorowicz (Hildesheim: Georg Olms Verlagsbuchhandlung, 1967).

20. As quoted in David Frisby, *Georg Simmel,* ed. Peter Hamilton, Key Sociologists (Chichester: Ellis Horwood; London: Tavistock, 1984), 37.

21. Simmel does not try to piece together his observations about modernity to make a cohesive whole. According to Frisby, however, Simmel does not dismiss the possibility of a totality. Instead he attempts to access the totality

from the fragments; each fragment contains within it a totality, something that connects it to something beyond it. In his exploration of Simmel's work, Frisby places a strong emphasis on the role aesthetics play as a catalyst that allows one to see the totality in the fragments. I turn my attention to the historical contingency of the relationship between fragment and totality, thus shifting the focus from finding the eternal in the ephemeral to finding the ephemeral in the eternal. See Frisby, *Georg Simmel* and *Fragments of Modernity: Theories of Modernity in the Work of Simmel, Kracauer and Benjamin* (Cambridge, Mass.: MIT Press, 1986).

22. Arthur Salz, "A Note from a Student of Simmel's," in *Georg Simmel, 1858–1918: A Collection of Essays, with Translations and a Bibliography,* ed. Kurt H. Wolff (Columbus: Ohio State University Press, 1959), 235.

23. Frisby, *Georg Simmel,* 17.

24. Ibid.

25. Helmuth Plessner's treatise on community and society draws on a similar approach.

26. Ferdinand Tönnies, *Gemeinschaft und Gesellschaft: Grundbegriffe der reinen Soziologie,* 8th ed. (Darmstadt: Wissenschaftliche Buchgesellschaft, 1963).

27. Nicolai von Bubnoff, "Rezension von 'Grenzen der Gemeinschaft,'" ("Review of 'Limits of Society,'") in *Plessners "Grenzen der Gemeinschaft,"* ed. Wolfgang Eßbach, Joachim Fischer, and Helmut Lethen (Frankfurt am Main: Suhrkamp, 2002), 364. First published in *Archiv für Sozialwissenschaft und Sozialpolitik* (1925), 537–39.

28. Ferdinand Tönnies, "Rezension von 'Grenzen der Gemeinschaft,'" ("Review of 'Limits of Society,'"in Eßbach, Fischer, and Lethen, *Plessners "Grenzen der Gemeinschaft,"* 356. First published in *Kölner Vierteljahrshefte für Soziologie* (1926), 456–58.

29. Ibid.

30. Ibid.

31. Siegfried Kracauer, *Siegfried Kracauer: Aufsätze 1915–1926,* ed. Inka Mülder-Bach, vol. 5.1, *Siegfried Kracauer: Schriften* (Frankfurt am Main: Suhrkamp, 1990), 270. Originally published in *Frankfurter Zeitung,* October 30, 1924.

32. Helmut Lethen, *Verhaltenslehren der Kälte: Lebensversuche zwischen den Kriegen* (English title: *Cool Conduct: The Culture of Distance in Weimar Germany*) (Frankfurt am Main: Suhrkamp, 1994), 85.

33. Joachim Fischer, "Panzer oder Maske: 'Verhaltenslehre der Kälte' oder Sozialtheorie der 'Grenze,'" ("Armor or Mask: 'Cool Conduct' or the Social Theory of the 'Limit'") in Eßbach, Fischer, and Lethen, *Plessners "Grenzen der Gemeinschaft,"* 80–102.

34. Lethen, *Verhaltenslehren der Kälte,* 85.

35. Fischer, "Panzer oder Maske," 84.

36. Ibid., 85.

37. Plessner begins with the terms "Gemeinschaft" and "Gesellschaft" before referring to "Vertrautheitssphäre" and "Nichtvertrautheitssphäre" on page 55.

38. One way to understand the relationship between Sachgemeinschaft, Blutgemeinschaft, and Gesellschaft is to look at Plessner's conceptualization of the mind, body, and spirit. As Fischer points out, Sachgemeinschaft is the realm of reason, or the mind (Geist), Blutgemeinschaft is the realm of the body, and Gesellschaft is the spirit (Seele) that mediates between the other two. By mapping the realms on the body, one sees their interrelatedness and how the three together make up a whole; there is no question of separating them or of privileging one at the expense of the others. In this paradigm the mediating role of Gesellschaft/Seele is emphasized: when one focuses on the needs of the body, the mind is neglected, and the same is true in the other direction. In order to prevent a permanent state of discontent, the spirit allows for compromise and finds ways to accommodate conflicting needs.

Fischer further elaborates on how the three interact in his exploration of the connections between Plessner's 1923 work on the senses entitled *Die Einheit der Sinne: Grundlinien einer Ästhesiologie des Geistes* (*The Unity of the Senses: Principles of an Aesthesiology of the Mind*) and *Grenzen der Gemeinschaft.* In *Einheit der Sinne,* Plessner concentrates on the relationship between the senses as a way to understand the relationship between body and mind. He is primarily interested in the senses of sight and hearing. Sight is associated with distance and objectivity; the natural sciences are an example of its qualities and priorities. Hearing is about resonance, about immediacy, and music is its illustration. Music literally resonates sound waves that travel into our bodies through our ears and thus belongs to the body. Sight, with its distance between subject and object, belongs to the realm of reason. What mediates between them is, according to Plessner, language. Fischer draws a parallel between the Blutgemeinschaft/Sachgemeinschaft/Gesellschaft and sight/hearing/language paradigms in order to show that in both there is a need for a space of mediation—Gesellschaft and language serve similar functions. Furthermore, by drawing parallels between these two texts, Fischer elucidates the theoretical structures in which Plessner works and thus clarifies some of Plessner's more complex ideas and philosophies. Fischer, "Panzer oder Maske," 92–93.

39. One of Plessner's infrequent forays into gender differences is when he mentions that women have an easier time than men of maintaining a sense of Würde because they "nach dem Wort des Romantikers bei sich selbst bleibende Natur sind und nur das zu ambitionieren pflegen, was sie mit Hilfe der Männer zu erreichen sicher sind" (PG, 76) ["are, according to the romantics, permanently in tune with their nature and have ambition only for that which they can secure with the aid of men—that they find dignity and grace more easily" (PGE, 123)].

40. In describing everyday life Plessner uses the word "Verkehr" (traffic/interaction) more than once (PG, 80, 81).

41. The metaphor is continued on pages 82 and 83.

42. In this world, understanding and attention (*Verständnis* and *Achtung*) are one and the same.

43. Giorgio Agamben's conceptualization of community in *The Coming Community* (trans. Michael Hardt [University of Minnesota Press, 1993])

resonates with this definition of human nature. According to Agamben, community is never a finished product, and our understanding of it must allow for these constant fluctuations and shifts; community is always something that is coming into being but never just is. Agamben does not set up Gesellschaft as the alternative model, however, although he does reread notions of reification and the mechanization of the body as freeing us from former biological definitions and constraints. Instead, he proposes a radical acceptance of not belonging as a way of belonging: "Because if instead of continuing to search for a proper identity in the already improper and senseless form of individuality, humans were to succeed in belonging to this impropriety as such, in making of the proper being-thus not an identity and an individual property but a singularity without identity, a common and absolutely exposed singularity—if humans could, that is, not be-thus in this or that particular biography, but be only *the* thus, their singular exteriority and their face, then they would for the first time enter into a community without presuppositions and without subjects, into a communication with the incommunicable" (Agamben, *The Coming Community,* 64). In Agamben's model, aspects of Gesellschaft and Gemeinschaft as Plessner has outlined them conflate: we need the masks that are traditionally associated with Gesellschaft, but Agamben proposes becoming the masks. In Plessner's model, however, we are still more than our masks.

44. Referred to as both "Seele" (soul) and "seelenhafte Individualität" (soul-containing individuality) on page 63.

45. As will be seen shortly, even the immediacy animals experience is actually mediated as well.

46. See Caren Kaplan, *Questions of Travel: Postmodern Discourses of Displacement* (Durham, N.C.: Duke University Press, 1998).

47. Dagmar Barnouw, "Vielschichtige Oberflächen: Kracauer und die Modernität von Weimar," in *Denken durch die Dinge: Siegfried Kracauer im Kontext* ("Multilayered Surfaces: Kracauer and Weimar Modernity," in *Thinking Through the Things: Siegfried Kracauer in Context*), ed. Frank Grunert and Dorothee Kimmich (Munich: Wilhelm Fink, 2009), 16.

48. Ibid., 17.

49. Ibid.

50. Ibid., 23–24.

51. Gertrud Koch, *Kracauer zur Einführung* (English title: *Siegfried Kracauer: An Introduction*) (Hamburg: Junius Verlag, 1996), 153.

52. Ibid., 28.

53. The concepts of "natural" and "real" are not synonymous, but they do overlap and at times are also conflated in Kracauer's writings. I will go into more detail about the similarities and differences between the two in relation to Kracauer's text in my close readings.

54. For an informative study on the genres of crime stories and detective novels in Weimar Germany, and in particular a look at the significance of the fact that the former flourished in a way the latter did not in the German context, see Todd Herzog, *Crime Stories: Criminalistic Fantasy and the Culture of Crisis in Weimar Germany,* Monographs in German History (New York: Berghahn, 2009).

55. Georg Lukács, *Die Theorie des Romans* (*The Theory of the Novel*) (Munich: Deutscher Taschenbuch Verlag, 1994), 11.

56. Georg Lukács, *The Theory of the Novel,* trans. Anna Bostock (Cambridge: MIT Press, 1971), 17.

57. Siegfried Kracauer, "Die kleinen Ladenmädchen gehen ins Kino" ("The Little Shop Girls Go to the Movies"), in *Das Ornament der Masse* (*The Mass Ornament*) (Frankfurt am Main: Suhrkamp, 1977).

58. Siegfried Kracauer, "The Hotel Lobby," in *The Mass Ornament: Weimar Essays,* ed. and trans. Thomas Y. Levin (Cambridge: Harvard University Press, 1995), 172–85, 183.

59. As quoted in SK, 136.

60. Siegfried Kracauer, "The Hotel Lobby," 184.

Chapter 2

1. The lives of Roth and Döblin demonstrate just how complicated this concept of "West European assimiliated Jew" is, most prominently Roth's and Döblin's childhoods in border cities: Roth grew up in Brody, and Döblin was born and spent his early years in Stettin (now Szczecin).

2. Michel de Certeau, *The Practice of Everyday Life* (Berkeley: University of California Press, 1984), 99.

3. In my reading of travel texts, I will use the term "narrator" when it is not awkward in order to emphasize the constructed nature of the narrative and the distance between the historical figures and the literary figures who appear in the text. I use "Döblin" and "Roth" when referring to the narrators of the texts when necessary to mitigate confusion; the distance between narrator and historical figure remains implied.

4. See Claudia Sonino, *Exil, Diaspora, Gelobtes Land? Deutsche Juden blicken nach Osten* (*Exile, Diaspora, Promised Land? German Jews Look Toward the East*), trans. Ute Lipka (Berlin: Jüdische Verlagsanstalt Berlin, 2002), 117.

5. Ibid., 116–17.

6. Todd Presner's cultural geography of German Jewish modernity offers valuable insights into the particular importance of the railway system in the relationship between mobility, time, space, modernity, and German Jewish identity. Presner, *Mobile Modernity.*

7. Scott Spector explores questions of sexuality and gender in the related feminization of the Ostjude. Spector, *Prague Territories.*

8. Steven E. Aschheim, *Brothers and Strangers: The East European Jew in German and German Jewish Consciousness, 1800–1923* (Madison: University of Wisconsin Press, 1999), 127.

9. Paul Mendes-Flohr, *Divided Passions: Jewish Intellectuals and the Experience of Modernity* (Detroit: Wayne State University Press, 1991), 84–85.

10. Ibid., 97.

11. Ibid., 87.

12. It is also important to remember that Hasidism itself is not an ancient and timeless set of beliefs but is, rather, a movement in reaction to and in

dialogue with the Haskalah and other Jewish movements during the Enlightenment. That is to say, Hasidism is not antimodern, but part of Jewish modernity. See Biale, "A Journey Between Worlds."

13. Mendes-Flohr, *Divided Passions,* 143.

14. In the book's foreword, Buber thanks both Simon Dubnow and M. J. Berdyczewski for their contributions to his work. Although Buber, like Dubnow, emphasizes a sense of continuity and constancy with regard to Jewish culture and identity, there are also significant differences, which will be explored in a more detailed discussion about Dubnow.

15. I will address the concept of wandering in relation to Jewish identity, particularly in relation to the figure of the Wandering Jew, later in this chapter.

16. An example of a reading in this vein is that Döblin's text is read as being "Apollonian," whereas Roth's text is "Dionysian." In this reading Döblin's work is seen as having more artistic merit in form and presentation than Roth's. For more information on this topic, see Sonino, *Exil, Diaspora, Gelobtes Land?,* 140–41.

17. Joseph Roth, "Döblin im Osten," in Roth, *Werke,* vol. 2: *Das journalistische Werk 1924–1928,* ed. Klaus Westermann (Frankfurt am Main: Büchergilde Gutenberg, 1926), 535.

18. Assenka Oksiloff, *Picturing the Primitive: Visual Culture, Ethnography, and Early German Cinema* (New York: Palgrave, 2001). See also Fatimah Tobing Rony, *The Third Eye: Race, Cinema, and Ethnographic Spectacle* (Durham, N.C.: Duke University Press, 1998).

19. See Mary Louise Pratt, *Imperial Eyes: Travel Writing and Transculturation* (New York: Routledge, 2000).

20. For a look at the history of this conflation between rural and primitive spaces see ibid., 35.

21. The inclusion of these later remarks in this edition of the text are used to emphasize the text's relevance for a post-Holocaust audience. They simultaneously point out the unrest that can be seen as a precursor to events in the near future, and offer a glimpse of a world that no longer exists from a perspective that is now impossible.

22. Kabbalah and Hasidism are not synonymous, since kabbalah has a much longer tradition, but Hasidism bases many of its traditions and beliefs on kabbalah. It is also clear in these passages that Döblin is referring to the Hasidim because he mentions Baalschem Tov, the Hasidic leader; he also explicitly mentions the Hasidim once.

23. Although I am focusing on how Roth and Döblin portray East European Jews and the significance thereof, I find it is important to note that Hasidism is itself a modern phenomenon. I agree with David Biale that the "timelessness" of Hasidism is in reaction to and interacts with discourses of modernity, rather than having existed prior to these discourses.

24. The account begins with the following two sentences: "Aber wie ich am nächsten Vormittag auf einen Hof in Warschau gehe, zwischen Hütten, mit meinem Begleiter, lädt mich ein Chassid, ein Anhänger des Rebbe, ein, in seine Hütte zu treten. Wir sitzen in dem halbdunklen Raum" (AD, 109). ["But the

next morning, when my companion and I go to a courtyard in Warsaw and stroll amid huts, a Hasid, a follower of the rebbe, invites me into his hut. We sit in the semidark room" (ADE, 80)].

25. Even the book of the rabbi's teachings that Döblin uses to end this chapter must first be translated by someone else: "Das Büchelchen, das vorn das Bild des Gerer Rebbe trägt, lasse ich mir übersetzen" (AD, 110). ["I ask them to translate the booklet for me, the one with the portrait of the rebbe of Gura on its cover" (ADE, 81)].

26. The words in brackets are substitutions I made in the translation. It is not a question of correcting the translation, but rather of foregrounding those aspects of the text that are relevant to my reading.

27. Ibid.

28. Ibid.

29. The "Judenzählung" of 1916, a census of Jews serving in the German army during World War I, was only one of the manifestations of this sentiment. Initiated by antisemitic accusations that Jews were not doing their fair share of fighting, the census actually proved the opposite: that more Jews than were obligated to were serving in the army. These numbers, however, were not released to the general public.

30. I've substituted the translation of the word "Volk ("nation" in the original translation) with "people" in order to differentiate between Döblin's uses of "Volk" and "Nation."

31. For an in-depth look at the interactions between the Mitnagdim and the Hasidim in Eastern Europe see Biale, "A Journey Between Worlds."

32. Joseph Vogl, "Einleitung" (Introduction), in *Gemeinschaften: Positionen zu einer Philosophie des Politischen* (*Communities: Toward a Philosophy of the Political*), ed. Joseph Vogl (Frankfurt am Main: Suhrkamp, 1994), 13. His analysis of the terms is in the context of a reading of John Rawls.

33. Ibid., 14.

34. Vogl's reading of Jacques Derrida's deconstruction of the Declaration of Independence sums up this problematic: "Das Volk existiert nicht vor seinem stiftenden Akt, der selbst wiederum dieses Volk als autorisierende Instanz voraussetzt." Ibid., 20. [The people do not exist before the act that produces them, an act which in turn requires as a precondition this people as its legitimating authority.]

35. Simon Dubnow, *Die jüdische Geschichte: Ein geschichtsphilosophischer Versuch* (*The History of the Jews: A Historical-Philosophical Approach*), trans. Israel Friedländer, 2nd ed. (Frankfurt am Main: J. Kauffmann, 1921), 3.

36. See Myers, *Resisting History,* 123, for Leo Strauss's ambivalent critique of Dubnow's project.

37. Alfred Bodenheimer, *Wandernde Schatten: Ahasver, Moses und die Authentizität der jüdischen Moderne* (*Wandering Shadows: Ahasver, Moses and the Authenticity of Jewish Modernity*) (Göttingen: Wallstein, 2002), 8. In his essay "Ahasuerus, the Wandering Jew: Origin and Background," R. Edelmann writes about this chapbook: "Within a few decades after its first appearance in 1602, it had spread all over Europe, and everywhere the theme was taken up

and transformed in accordance with local conceptions and spiritual conditions. I want to draw your attention to the fact that, though the legend had been known in one version or the other during the Middle Ages, it did not have the character of a popular legend circulating among the illiterate common people, as became the case with the pamphlet from 1602." R. Edelmann, "Ahasuerus, the Wandering Jew: Origin and Background," in *The Wandering Jew: Essays in the Interpretation of a Christian Legend,* ed. Galit Hasan-Rokem and Alan Dundes (Bloomington: Indiana University Press, 1986), 8.

38. Edelmann, "Ahasuerus, the Wandering Jew," 4.

39. Bodenheimer, *Wandernde Schatten,* 8.

40. Edelmann, "Ahasuerus, the Wandering Jew," 6–7.

41. Bodenheimer, *Wandernde Schatten,* 8.

42. Ibid.

43. Ibid., 217.

44. Ibid., 19–20.

45. See Sander L. Gilman, *Jewish Self-Hatred: Anti-Semitism and the Hidden Language of the Jews* (Baltimore: Johns Hopkins University Press, 1986).

46. Reitter is specifically addressing the concept of "self-hatred," but his critique of Gilman (and Shulamit Volkov as well) can also be applied more generally to the relationship between German Jews and the dominant culture. See Paul Reitter, *On the Origins of Jewish Self-Hatred* (Princeton, N.J.: Princeton University Press, 2012), 35, 123–26.

47. Bodenheimer, *Wandernde Schatten,* 22.

48. Ibid.

49. Ibid., 21.

50. Ibid., 120.

51. Ibid., 125.

52. Lukács uses the word "Obdachlosigkeit" (literally, "without shelter") rather than "Heimatlosigkeit (without a home/homeland)." Lukács, *Die Theorie des Romans.*

53. I've substituted "captivated" for the original "enthralled" as a translation for "gefesselt."

Chapter 3

1. The following biographical information is based on Murray G. Hall, *Der Fall Bettauer* (Vienna: Löcker Verlag, 1978), 9–19.

2. The events that have contributed to Bettauer's "rediscovery" are primarily a 1977 television interview on the show *Teleobjektiv* with an unrepentant Otto Rothstock, Bettauer's murderer; Murray Hall's 1978 *Der Fall Bettauer;* the 1980 reprint of six of Bettauer's novels (including *Die Stadt ohne Juden*); and the discovery and restoration of the film *Die Stadt ohne Juden* in the 1990s.

3. I agree with Lisa Silverman that this absence should be read as an engagement with what Silverman terms "Jewish difference." See Silverman, *Becoming Austrians.*

4. As Murray G. Hall and others have pointed out, it is important to also see this novel as a product of its time. In his essay about the reception of the

novel and film, Hall cites the motivation Bettauer gives for writing the novel. According to an article Bettauer wrote for *Die Börse,* he was walking through Vienna when he saw the phrase "Hinaus mit den Juden!" written on a wall. This encounter was the inspiration for a novel about what Vienna would be like without Jews. The emphasis here is on the contemporary context rather than an attempt to see into the future. See Murray G. Hall, "'. . . alles arische Empfinden verhöhnt, verspottet und in den Kot gezerrt . . .': Zur Rezeption von *Die Stadt ohne Juden*" ("'. . . all Aryan sensibilities derided, mocked and dragged into the filth . . .': On the Reception of *Die Stadt ohne Juden*"), 105–46 in *Die Stadt ohne Juden,* ed. Guntram Geser and Armin Loacker (Vienna: Filmarchiv Austria, 2000), 106. Scott Spector's article "Modernism Without Jews" uses the same source to make his claims about the absurdity of the premise; he argues that Bettauer's novel was meant to be a light-hearted satire and that the notion of the novel's premise having any relationship to a historical reality or a possible future is ridiculous. Although both agree that the novel should not be seen as prophetic, they disagree about the novel's relationship to its historical context. Nevertheless, Hall and Spector work within the paradigm of accurate/inaccurate to support their interpretations of the novel and have a similar understanding of the notion of historical context, an understanding that I will challenge in my own reading of Bettauer and his work.

5. More than a third of the book is devoted to the *Er und Sie* scandal (a good portion of this coverage focuses on the antisemitism surrounding the attacks on the periodical and Bettauer), Bettauer's murder, and the subsequent trial of the murderer, Otto Rothstock, who was ultimately set free.

6. Hall, *Der Fall Bettauer,* 7.

7. Steven Beller, *Vienna and the Jews, 1867–1938: A Cultural History* (Cambridge: Cambridge University Press, 1989), 6.

8. Ibid.

9. Scott Spector, "Modernism Without Jews: A Counter-Historical Argument," *MODERNISM / modernity* 13, no. 4 (2006): 615–33.

10. "Das Land ohne Juden," *Die Wahrheit,* no. 29 (1924), as quoted in Hall, "'. . . alles arische Empfinden verhöhnt, verspottet und in den Kot gezerrt . . .,'" 108.

11. Alfred Rosenberg, "Der Fall Bettauer: Ein Musterbeispiel jüdischer Zersetzungstätigkeit" ["The Bettauer Case: A Paradigm of Disruptive Jewish Activities"], *Der Weltkampf: Halbmonatsschrift für die Judenfrage aller Länder* 2, no. 8 (1925): 339.

12. There is only one other brief mention of the book, and it relates to an article by Paul Stefan for the *Neue Badische Landeszeitung* in which he discusses Bettauer's success as an author by noting that *Die Stadt ohne Juden* had eighty printings. Rosenberg, "Der Fall Bettauer," 350. Rosenberg also spends a great deal of time criticizing the publication *Ich und Du,* which had nothing to do with Bettauer other than it was influenced by *Er und Sie.*

13. Spector, "Modernism Without Jews," 617.

14. Ibid., 626.

15. Ibid., 618.

16. Ibid., 620.

17. Silverman, *Becoming Austrians,* 21–25.

18. The contrast between one's beliefs and one's actions in the novel also presents an argument against the notion of an inevitable trajectory of antisemitism.

19. He does take on the role of the "True Christian" but only through flyers; I read this choice as an implicit argument that in his personal interactions such an insider role would provide him with no advantages.

20. A press release that appeared in Bettauer's *Er und Sie* describes the changes in the following manner: "Das Allzupolitische mußte aus ihm eliminiert, das humoristische verstärkt werden, und so wie der Film nun geworden ist, wird er unterhalten, fesseln, sensationell wirken, aber bei niemandem Anstoß erregen" (ES, 13.3.1924, 8). [The all too political had to be eliminated, the humorous elements had to be intensified, and as the film now stands it will entertain, fascinate, have a sensational effect, but will not offend anyone.]

21. Gerhard Vana, "Nie W-Wien: Anmerkungen zur Ausstattung von *Die Stadt ohne Juden*" ["Never W-Wien: Comments About Set Design in *The City Without Jews*"], in Geser and Loacker, *Die Stadt ohne Juden,* 241–72.

22. Fritz Rosenfeld, "Neue Filme: Die Stadt ohne Juden," *Arbeiter-Zeitung,* July 29, 1924.

23. It should be said that in this particular review, the critic Rosenfeld also finds the entire plot to be ridiculous, as all it seems to prove is that without Jews, the business of luxury goods would fail. This is a critique that could also apply to the novel, although Rosenfeld does not mention it. The rest of the criticism focuses on artistic choices that pertain only to the film.

24. Rosenfeld, "Neue Filme."

25. "*Die Stadt ohne Juden,*" *Licht-Bild-Bühne* 19, no. 172 (1926).

26. There was a right-wing response to this film in the form of stink bombs at showings and other disruptions, but Hall argues that these actions had more to do with the controversy surrounding Hugo Bettauer and his liberal attitudes toward sex and sexuality than with the film. See Hall, "'. . . alles arische Empfinden verhöhnt, verspottet und in den Kot gezerrt . . . ,'" 128–29. The *Licht-Bild-Bühne* review provides a counterargument: it draws a direct connection between the portrayals of Jews in the film and a violent response motivated by racial hatred.

27. Spelled "Carroni" in the film's opening titles.

28. It is primarily through allusions that the topic is addressed at all in the novel, and the focus is on recent Jewish immigrants from Eastern Europe—for example, when the concept of "undesirable" Jews is discussed, and when suggestions are made to allow Jews who came before World War I back into Austria without question and to use more stringent criteria to determine who among those who arrived later would be allowed to return. The word "Ostjude" does not, however, appear.

29. Beatrix Hoffmann-Holter, "'Ostjuden hinaus!': Jüdische Kriegsflüchtlinge in Wien 1914–1924" ["'Out with the East European Jews!': Jewish War Refugees in Vienna 1914–1924"], in Geser and Loacker, *Die Stadt ohne Juden,* 311–46: 311.

30. Ibid., 341.

31. Jens Budischowsky, "Politische Strömungen im Judentum der Ersten Republik" ["Political Currents in the Jewish Population of the First Republic"], in Geser and Loacker, *Die Stadt ohne Juden,* 347–83: 373.

32. As quoted in Michael Kitzberger, "Bild-Störung: Repräsentationen des Jüdischen in *Die Stadt ohne Juden*" ["Image Distortion: Representations of the Jewish in *The City Without Jews*"], in Geser and Loacker, *Die Stadt ohne Juden,* 415–44: 434.

33. Hall lists some of the historical figures that the depictions of these characters and others in the novel allude to; he also points out that the relationship between the characters and the historical figures is often a loose one. See Hall, *Der Fall Bettauer,* 26–27. Silverman explores the significance of the fact that only one character in the novel is referred to by her historical name—Ella Zwieback. See Silverman, *Becoming Austrians,* 66–102.

34. Ofer Ashkenazi's *Weimar Film and Modern Jewish Identity* makes it clear that in Weimar film the figure of the stranger was often used to explore notions of urban middle-class German Jewish identity, in films that span a wide range of genres and include those that are not overtly about Jewish topics. The book focuses on the following tropes: "the intricacies between identity and performance (and the tensions between these concepts and 'authenticity'); the metaphorical visualization of multilayered identity through the duality of private and public urban spheres; and the essential (yet concealable) difference between the protagonist and his social environment, which renders him an integral member of this society who simultaneously represents 'otherness' and contradictions." As Ashkenazi sees it, authenticity and performance are not diametrically opposed; in fact, in many of these films, performance makes an authentic identity possible. In this way, Ashkenazi's observations about Weimar film resonate with my readings of Plessner's masks and Simmel's notions of Geselligkeit, as well as my reading of Leo Strakosch as Simmel's stranger. Ofer Ashkenazi, *Weimar Film and Modern Jewish Identity* (New York: Palgrave Macmillan, 2012).

35. Although Simmel's essay does not directly equate "the stranger" with "the Jew," the association was automatic for anyone reading the essay. From the 1800s until the end of World War II, "the Jew" was "the stranger" in Germany. The connection is also made indirectly in the essay through historical references to Jews and also through discourses that resonate with contemporary debates about religion, assimilation, and nation in the German Jewish context.

36. Antonius Schneuzel in the novel.

37. In the novel Lotte is still named Lotte, but the Linders of the film are the Spineders in the novel.

38. A note about the intertitles in the reconstructed film: "Bei einer Analyse des Films sollten die Texte der Zwischentitel daher möglichst außer Betracht bleiben bzw. nur mit großen Einschränkungen berücksichtigt werden. Es kann jedoch davon ausgegangen werden, daß die Anzahl sowie die Positionen und Funktionen der Zwischentitel noch einigermaßen 'original' sind." Guntram Geser, "'Zeitfilm' versus historischer Großfilm: 'Die Massen' in *Die Stadt ohne*

Juden," in Geser and Loacker, *Die Stadt ohne Juden*, 273–303: 289. [An analysis of the film should refrain from considering the texts of the intertitles as much as possible, or at least only regard them with utmost restraint. Nevertheless it can be assumed that the number as well as the position and function of the intertitles is more or less "true to the original." "'Time Film' versus Historical Blockbuster: 'The Masses' in *The City Without Jews*."]

39. Based on the character of Wenzel Krötzl in the novel.

40. In the novel, he is not as understanding and resents what his father-in-law has done to him and his family.

41. This contrast also exists in the novel.

42. Lisa Silverman argues that Bettauer was transformed into a Jew by the *Er und Sie* trial and the trial around his murder: "Obviously, the fact that Bettauer had been born a Jew, and that Rothstock was an antisemite, played an important role in the murder. Nevertheless, it was the intense focus on Bettauer's Jewishness *after* the murder that reveals the degree to which he was more or less 'transformed' into a Jew by the context of the crime committed against him. In his case, sexual indecency and immorality were not deployed as superficial pretexts for killing a Jew; rather, these functioned as a way to buttress acceptance of the killer's crime and to make his act both explicable and politically 'useful.'" Silverman, *Becoming Austrians*, 55.

43. See Hall, *Der Fall Bettauer*, and Guntram Geser, "Hugo Bettauer: Journalist, Unterhaltungsliterat, und 'Film-Autor,'" in Geser and Loacker, *Die Stadt ohne Juden*, 37–54.

44. See Hall, *Der Fall Bettauer*, 65.

45. In this regard, Bettauer's novels share some similarities to crime novels of the time in that the criminals are symptomatic of a society's failings rather than aberrant misfits. See Herzog, *Crime Stories*.

46. Hall, *Der Fall Bettauer*, 27–35.

47. For a list of film adaptations of Bettauer's novels, see ibid., 187–92.

48. Geser, "Hugo Bettauer," 39.

49. Hall, *Der Fall Bettauer*, 80.

50. Peter Kaupp, *Das Heiratsinserat im sozialen Wandel: Ein Beitrag zu Soziologie der Partnerwahl* [*The Marriage Advertisement and Social Change: A Contribution to the Sociology of Partner Selection*] (Stuttgart: Ferdinand Enke Verlag, 1968), 9–10.

51. Ibid., 10, 102. For examples of early marriage advertisements as well as newspaper coverage on various other aspects of love and sexuality see Eberhard Buchner, *Liebe: Kulturhistorisch interessante Dokumente aus alten deutschen Zeitungen vom Ende des 17. bis zum Ende des 18. Jahrhunderts* [*Love: Culturally and Historically Interesting Documents from Old German Newspapers from the End of the 17th to the End of the 18th Centuries*] (Munich: Albert Langen, 1914).

52. Viola Riemann, *Kontaktanzeigen im Wandel der Zeit: Eine Inhaltsanalyse*, Studien zur Kommunikationswissenschaft [*Personal Ads in Changing Times: A Content Analysis*] (Opladen/Wiesbaden: Westdeutscher Verlag, 1999), 40.

53. Inke Deichmann, *"An Dr. Sommer und Co. . .": Illustrierte als medizinische Ratgeber* [*"To Dr. Sommer and Associates . . .": Illustrated Magazines as Medical Advisers*] (Münster: Waxmann Verlag, 1998), 27.

54. The assumption that marriage is the primary reason that one would place a personal ad does not prove to be the case if one looks at the ads in the subsequent issues of the paper. Although it is true that a good number of the ads are from people seeking a serious partner, a significant number of the advertisers clearly have a more casual relationship in mind. For example: "Akademiker, Mitte Zwanzig, Ehegegener, sucht Bekanntschaft temperamentvoller, reifer Dame voller Figur. 'Sportsmann 1115 an die Exp.' " (ES, 6.3.1924, 15). ["Academic, mid-twenties, against marriage, seeks acquaintance of a spirited mature lady with a full figure. 'Sportsman 1115 addressed to the dispatch.' "] I would argue that the exclusive mention of marriage is part of an attempt to legitimize the personal ad and remove some of its more sordid connotations, rather than a belief that this is the only use for them.

55. Although there is no author given for this article, it is most likely written by Bettauer, as it matches his style and he wrote a significant portion of the articles in the paper. At the very least Bettauer, as the editor of the paper, approved of the article.

56. Riemann, *Kontaktanzeigen im Wandel der Zeit,* 47.

57. There was a sixth issue ready to be printed, but according to Hall, the paper was discontinued after the fifth. Hall, *Der Fall Bettauer,* 51–56. The *Arbeiter-Zeitung* mentions that *Er und Sie* appeared six times, but I have been unable to find the sixth issue. "Der Prozeß wegen 'Er und Sie,' " *Arbeiter-Zeitung,* September 19, 1924.

58. The main focus of the trial was Bettauer, as Olden claimed to have played absolutely no role in the content of the paper and performed almost solely administrative duties. See *Neues Wiener Tagblatt,* September 19, 1924, and "Der Prozeß wegen 'Er und Sie.' "

59. The term used in German is "gewerbsmäßige Kuppelei."

60. "Hugo Bettauer legt die Herausgeberschaft von 'Er und Sie' nieder" ["Hugo Bettauer Steps Down as Editor of 'Er und Sie' "], *Neues Wiener Journal,* March 19, 1924. In addition to the reasons that Bettauer gives for his decision to step down, there were also the insurmountable financial losses caused by the frequent confiscations of the paper. See Hall, *Der Fall Bettauer,* 54–55.

61. Geser, "Hugo Bettauer," 39–40.

62. Although *Bettauers Wochenschrift* was continued by Bettauer's son Helmut Bettauer, the paper never achieved the readership and financial success it had had during his lifetime, and after two more years, it ended.

Conclusion

The concluding epigraphs are from Italo Calvino, *Invisible Cities,* trans. William Weaver (San Diego: Harcourt, 1974); the first quotation can be found on pages 10–11, and the second quotation is from page 44.

BIBLIOGRAPHY

Agamben, Giorgio. *The Coming Community.* Translated by Michael Hardt. Minneapolis: University of Minnesota Press, 1993.

Anderson, George K. *The Legend of the Wandering Jew.* Providence, R.I.: Brown University Press, 1965.

Aschheim, Steven E. *Brothers and Strangers: The East European Jew in German and German Jewish Consciousness, 1800–1923.* Madison: University of Wisconsin Press, 1999.

———. *Culture and Catastrophe: German and Jewish Confrontations with National Socialism and Other Crises.* New York: New York University Press, 1996.

Ashkenazi, Ofer. *Weimar Film and Modern Jewish Identity.* New York: Palgrave Macmillan, 2012.

Bauman, Zygmunt. *Modernity and Ambivalence.* Ithaca, N.Y.: Cornell University Press, 1991.

Beller, Steven. *Vienna and the Jews, 1867–1938: A Cultural History.* Cambridge: Cambridge University Press, 1989.

Benjamin, Andrew E. *Walter Benjamin and History.* Walter Benjamin Studies Series. London: Continuum, 2005.

Benjamin, Walter. *Gesammelte Schriften.* Edited by Rolf Tiedemann and Hermann Schweppenhäuser. 7 vols. Frankfurt am Main: Suhrkamp, 1972.

Benjamin, Walter, and Gérard Raulet. *Über den Begriff der Geschichte. Werke und Nachlass* 19. Berlin: Suhrkamp, 2010.

Bettauer, Hugo. *Gesammelte Werke.* 6 vols. Salzburg: Hannibal Verlag, 1980.

Bettauer, Hugo, and Rudolf Olden, eds. *Er und Sie: Wochenschrift für Lebenskultur und Erotik.* Vienna, 1924.

Biale, David, ed. *Cultures of the Jews: A New History.* New York: Schocken, 2002.

Bodenheimer, Alfred. *Wandernde Schatten: Ahasver, Moses und die Authentizität der jüdischen Moderne* [*Wandering Shadows: Ahasver, Moses and the Authenticity of Jewish Modernity*]. Göttingen: Wallstein Verlag, 2002.

Brenner, Michael, and Derek J. Penslar, eds. *In Search of Jewish Community: Jewish Identities in Germany and Austria, 1918–1933.* Bloomington: Indiana University Press, 1998.

Buchner, Eberhard. *Liebe: Kulturhistorisch interessante Dokumente aus alten deutschen Zeitungen vom Ende des 17. bis zum Ende des 18. Jahrhunderts* [*Love: Culturally and Historically Interesting Documents from Old German Newspapers from the End of the 17th to the End of the 18th Centuries*]. Munich: Albert Langen, 1914.

Buck-Morss, Susan. *The Dialectics of Seeing: Walter Benjamin and the Arcades Project*. Studies in Contemporary German Social Thought. Cambridge, Mass.: MIT Press, 1989.

Buse, Peter, Ken Hirschkop, Scott McCracken, and Bertrand Taithe. *Benjamin's Arcades: An Unguided Tour.* Encounters. Manchester: Manchester University Press, 2006.

Calvino, Italo. *Invisible Cities*. Translated by William Weaver. San Diego: Harcourt, 1974.

Crang, Mike, and Nigel Thrift, eds. *Thinking Space*. New York: Routledge, 2000.

"Das Land ohne Juden." *Die Wahrheit* no. 29 (1924).

de Certeau, Michel. *The Practice of Everyday Life*. Berkeley: University of California Press, 1984.

Deichmann, Inke. *"An Dr. Sommer und Co. . .": Illustrierte als medizinische Ratgeber* ["*To Dr. Sommer and Associates . . .": Illustrated Magazines as Medical Advisers*]. Münster: Waxmann Verlag, 1998.

"Der Prozeß wegen 'Er und Sie'." *Arbeiter-Zeitung*, September 19, 1924.

Deutscher, Isaac. *The Non-Jewish Jew and Other Essays*. Oxford: Oxford University Press, 1968.

"*Die Stadt ohne Juden.*" *Licht-Bild-Bühne* 19, no. 172 (1926).

D'Souza, Aruna, and Tom McDonough, eds. *The Invisible Flâneuse? Gender, Public Space, and Visual Culture in Nineteenth-Century Paris*. Manchester: Manchester University Press, 2006.

Dubnow, Simon. *Die jüdische Geschichte: Ein geschichtsphilosophischer Versuch* [*The History of the Jews: A Historical-Philosophical Approach*]. Translated by Israel Friedländer. 2nd ed. Frankfurt am Main: J. Kauffmann, 1921.

Eßbach, Wolfgang, Joachim Fischer, and Helmut Lethen, eds. *Plessners "Grenzen der Gemeinschaft."* Frankfurt am Main: Suhrkamp Taschenbuch Wissenschaft, 2002.

Ezrahi, Sidra DeKoven. *Booking Passage: Exile and Homecoming in the Modern Jewish Imagination*. Contraversions. Berkeley: University of California Press, 2000.

Frisby, David. *Fragments of Modernity: Theories of Modernity in the Work of Simmel, Kracauer and Benjamin*. Cambridge, Mass.: MIT Press, 1986.

———. *Georg Simmel*. Edited by Peter Hamilton. Key Sociologists. Chichester and London: Ellis Horwood and Tavistock, 1984.

Geller, Jay. *The Other Jewish Question: Identifying the Jew and Making Sense of Modernity*. New York: Fordham University Press, 2011.

Gemünden, Gerd, and Johannes von Moltke. *Culture in the Anteroom: The Legacies of Siegfried Kracauer*. Ann Arbor: University of Michigan Press, 2012.

Geschichte des ewigen Juden von ihm selbst geschrieben. Enthaltend einen kurzen und wahrhaften Abriß seiner bewundernswürdigen Reisen seit ungefähr achtzehn Hundert Jahren [*The Story of the Eternal Jew Written by the Man Himself. Containing a Short and True Summary of His Amazing*

Travels for About Eighteen Hundred Years]. Gotha: Ettingersche Buchhandlung, n.d.

Geser, Guntram, and Armin Loacker, eds. *Die Stadt ohne Juden*. Vienna: Filmarchiv Austria, 2000.

Gilloch, Graeme. *Walter Benjamin: Critical Constellations*. Key Contemporary Thinkers. Malden, Mass.: Blackwell, 2002.

Gilman, Sander L. *Jewish Self-Hatred: Anti-Semitism and the Hidden Language of the Jews*. Baltimore: Johns Hopkins University Press, 1986.

Gleber, Anke. *The Art of Taking a Walk: Flanerie, Literature, and Film in Weimar Culture*. Princeton, N.J.: Princeton University Press, 1999.

Goetschel, Willi. *Spinoza's Modernity: Mendelssohn, Lessing, and Heine*. Studies in German Jewish Cultural History and Literature Series. Madison: University of Wisconsin Press, 2004.

Grunert, Frank, and Dorothee Kimmich, eds. *Denken durch die Dinge: Siegfried Kracauer im Kontext* [*Thinking Through the Things: Siegfried Kracauer in Context*]. Munich: Wilhelm Fink, 2009.

Hall, Murray G. *Der Fall Bettauer* [*The Bettauer Case*]. Vienna: Löcker Verlag, 1978.

Hanssen, Beatrice. *Walter Benjamin's Other History: Of Stones, Animals, Human Beings, and Angels*. Weimar and Now. Berkeley: University of California Press, 1998.

Hasan-Rokem, Galit, and Alan Dundes, eds. *The Wandering Jew: Essays in the Interpretation of a Christian Legend*. Bloomington: Indiana University Press, 1986.

Heid, Ludger, and Julius H. Schoeps. *Juden in Deutschland: Von der Aufklärung bis zur Gegenwart* [*Jews in Germany: From the Enlightenment to the Present*]. Munich: Piper, 1994.

Herzog, Todd. *Crime Stories: Criminalistic Fantasy and the Culture of Crisis in Weimar Germany*. Monographs in German History. New York: Berghahn Books, 2009.

Hess, Jonathan M. *Germans, Jews and the Claims of Modernity*. New Haven, Conn.: Yale University Press, 2002.

"Hugo Bettauer legt die Herausgeberschaft von 'Er und Sie' nieder" ["Hugo Bettauer Steps Down as Editor of 'Er und Sie'"]. *Neues Wiener Journal*, March 19, 1924.

Idel, Moshe. *Old Worlds, New Mirrors: On Jewish Mysticism and Twentieth-Century Thought*. Jewish Culture and Contexts. Philadelphia: University of Pennsylvania Press, 2010.

Isenberg, Noah William. *Between Redemption and Doom: The Strains of German-Jewish Modernism*. Texts and Contexts. Lincoln: University of Nebraska Press, 1999.

Jelavich, Peter. *Berlin Alexanderplatz: Radio, Film and the Death of Weimar Culture*. Berkeley: University of California Press, 2006.

Kaes, Anton, Martin Jay, and Edward Dimenberg, eds. *The Weimar Republic Sourcebook*. Berkeley: University of California Press, 1994.

Kaplan, Caren. *Questions of Travel: Postmodern Discourses of Displacement.* Durham, N.C.: Duke University Press, 1998.

Kaupp, Peter. *Das Heiratsinserat im sozialen Wandel: Ein Beitrag zur Soziologie der Partnerwahl* [*The Marriage Advertisement and Social Change: A Contribution to the Sociology of Partner Selection*]. Stuttgart: Ferdinand Enke Verlag, 1968.

Koch, Gertrud. *Kracauer zur Einführung.* Hamburg: Junius Verlag, 1996.

———. *Siegfried Kracauer: An Introduction.* Translated by Jeremy Gaines. Princeton, N.J.: Princeton University Press, 2000.

Kracauer, Siegfried. *Werke.* 9 vols. Edited by Inka Mülder-Bach. Frankfurt am Main: Suhrkamp Verlag, 2004.

Lane, Richard J. *Reading Walter Benjamin: Writing Through the Catastrophe.* Manchester: Manchester University Press, 2005.

Lethen, Helmut. *Cool Conduct: The Culture of Distance in Weimar Germany,* Weimar and Now. Translated by Don Reneau. Berkeley: University of California Press, 2002.

———. *Verhaltenslehren der Kälte: Lebensversuche zwischen den Kriegen.* Frankfurt am Main: Suhrkamp Verlag, 1994.

Löwy, Michael. *Fire Alarm: Reading Walter Benjamin's "On the Concept of History."* Translated by Chris Turner. London: Verso, 2005.

Lukács, Georg. *Die Theorie des Romans.* Munich: Deutscher Taschenbuch Verlag, 1994.

———. *The Theory of the Novel.* Translated by Anna Bostock. Cambridge, Mass.: MIT Press, 1971.

Mattenklott, Gert. "Ostjudentum und Exotismus." In *Die andere Welt: Studien zum Exotismus* [*The Other World: Studies of Exoticism*], edited by Thomas Koebner and Gerhart Pickerodt, 291–306. Berlin: Philo, 2000.

Mendes-Flohr, Paul. *Divided Passions: Jewish Intellectuals and the Experience of Modernity.* Detroit: Wayne State University Press, 1991.

Mosès, Stéphane. *The Angel of History: Rosenzweig, Benjamin, Scholem.* Translated by Barbara Harshav. Cultural Memory in the Present. Stanford: Stanford University Press, 2009.

Myers, David. *Resisting History: Historicism and Its Discontents in German-Jewish Thought.* Princeton, N.J.: Princeton University Press, 2003.

Neues Wiener Tagblatt, September 19, 1924.

Nicholls, Peter. *Modernisms: A Literary Guide.* 2nd ed. New York: Palgrave Macmillan, 2009.

Oksiloff, Assenka. *Picturing the Primitive: Visual Culture, Ethnography, and Early German Cinema.* New York: Palgrave, 2001.

Parsons, Deborah L. *Streetwalking the Metropolis: Women, the City, and Modernity.* Oxford: Oxford University Press, 2000.

Plessner, Helmuth. *Gesammelte Schriften.* Edited by Günter Dux, Odo Marquard, and Elisabeth Ströker. Frankfurt am Main: Suhrkamp Taschenbuch Wissenschaft, 2003.

Pratt, Mary Louise. *Imperial Eyes: Travel Writing and Transculturation.* New York: Routledge, 2000.

Presner, Todd. *Mobile Modernity: Germans, Jews, Trains.* New York: Columbia University Press, 2007.

Rabinbach, Anson. *In the Shadow of Catastrophe: German Intellectuals Between Apocalypse and Enlightenment.* Weimar and Now. Berkeley: University of California Press, 1997.

Reitter, Paul. *On the Origins of Jewish Self-Hatred.* Princeton, N.J.: Princeton University Press, 2012.

Riemann, Viola. *Kontaktanzeigen im Wandel der Zeit: Eine Inhaltsanalyse [Personal Ads in Changing Times: A Content Analysis].* Studien zur Kommunikationswissenschaft. Opladen/Wiesbaden: Westdeutscher Verlag, 1999.

Robertson, Ritchie, ed. *The German-Jewish Dialogue: An Anthology of Literary Texts 1749–1993.* Oxford: Oxford University Press, 1999.

———. *The "Jewish Question" in German Literature 1749–1939: Emancipation and Its Discontents.* Oxford: Oxford University Press, 1999.

Rony, Fatimah Tobing. *The Third Eye: Race, Cinema, and Ethnographic Spectacle.* Durham, N.C.: Duke University Press, 1998.

Rosenberg, Alfred. "Der Fall Bettauer: Ein Musterbeispiel jüdischer Zersetzungstätigkeit" ["The Bettauer Case: A Paradigm of Destructive Jewish Activities"]. *Der Weltkampf: Halbmonatsschrift für die Judenfrage aller Länder* 2, no. 8 (1925): 337–51.

Rosenfeld, Fritz. "Neue Filme: Die Stadt ohne Juden." *Arbeiter-Zeitung,* July 29, 1924, 10.

Roth, Joseph. *Werke.* Edited by Klaus Westermann and Fritz Hackert. 6 vols. Cologne: Kiepenheuer & Witsch, 1989.

Schoeps, Julius H., Karl E. Grözinger, Willi Jasper, and Gert Mattenklott, eds. *Deutsch-jüdischer Parnaß: Rekonstruktion einer Debatte. [German-Jewish Parnassus: Reconstruction of a Debate.]* Vol. 13. Menora: Jahrbuch für deutsch-jüdische Geschichte, 2002; Berlin: Philo, 2002.

Silverman, Lisa. *Becoming Austrians: Jews and Culture Between the World Wars.* Oxford: Oxford University Press, 2012.

Simmel, Georg. *Gesamtausgabe.* Edited by Otthein Rammstedt. Frankfurt am Main: Suhrkamp, 1989.

Sonino, Claudia. *Exil, Diaspora, Gelobtes Land? Deutsche Juden blicken nach Osten [Exile, Diaspora, Promised Land? German Jews Look Toward the East].* Translated by Ute Lipka. Berlin: Jüdische Verlagsanstalt Berlin, 2002.

Sorkin, David. *The Transformation of German Jewry, 1780–1840.* Oxford: Oxford University Press, 1987.

Spector, Scott. "Modernism Without Jews: A Counter-Historical Argument." *MODERNISM / modernity* 13, no. 4 (2006): 615–33.

———. *Prague Territories: National Conflict and Cultural Innovation in Franz Kafka's Fin de Siècle.* Weimar and Now. Berkeley: University of California Press, 2000.

Spencer, John Malcolm. *In the Shadow of Empire: Austrian Experiences of Modernity in the Writings of Musil, Roth, and Bachmann.* Studies in German Literature, Linguistics, and Culture. Rochester, N.Y.: Camden House, 2008.

Steinberg, Michael P. *Judaism Musical and Unmusical.* Chicago: University of Chicago Press, 2007.

Sternburg, Wilhelm von. *Joseph Roth: Eine Biographie.* Cologne: Kiepenheuer & Witsch, 2009.

Tester, Keith, ed. *The Flâneur.* New York: Routledge, 1994.

Tönnies, Ferdinand. *Gemeinschaft und Gesellschaft: Grundbegriffe der reinen Soziologie* [*Community and Society: Key Terms of a Pure Sociology*]. 8th ed. Darmstadt: Wissenschaftliche Buchgesellschaft, 1963.

Vogl, Joseph, ed. *Gemeinschaften: Positionen zu einer Philosophie des Politischen* [*Communities: Positions on a Philosophy of the Political*]. Frankfurt am Main: Suhrkamp Verlag, 1994.

Volkov, Shulamit. *Germans, Jews, and Antisemites: Trials in Emancipation.* Cambridge: Cambridge University Press, 2006.

Weber, Samuel. *Benjamin's -abilities.* Cambridge, Mass.: Harvard University Press, 2008.

Windholz, J. L. *Ahasver. Einsiedler. Zwei Erzählungen* [*Ahasver. Hermit. Two Stories*]. Vienna: Lumen, 1909.

Wolff, Janet. *Feminine Sentences: Essays on Women and Culture.* Berkeley: University of California Press, 1990.

Wolff, Kurt H., ed. *Georg Simmel, 1858–1918: A Collection of Essays, with Translations and a Bibliography.* Columbus: Ohio State University Press, 1959.

Yerushalmi, Yosef Hayim. *Freud's Moses: Judaism Terminable and Interminable.* New Haven, Conn.: Yale University Press, 1991.

Zweig, Arnold. *Das ostjüdische Antlitz* [*The Face of East European Jewry*]. Berlin: Welt-Verlag, 1920.

INDEX